CHARLES COLSON

CHARLES COLSON

A STORY OF POWER, CORRUPTION, AND REDEMPTION

JOHN PERRY

BROADMAN
&HOLMAN
PUBLISHERS

NASHVILLE, TENNESSEE

0–8054–2512–8

Published by Broadman & Holman Publishers,
Nashville, Tennessee

Dewey Decimal Classification: B
Subject Heading: COLSON, CHARLES \ PRESIDENTS—UNITED
STATES—STAFF—BIOGRAPHY \ PRISONERS—BIOGRAPHY

Mere Christianity by C. S. Lewis copyright © C. S. Lewis Pte. Ltd. 1942,
1943, 1944, 1952. Extract reprinted by permission.

1 2 3 4 5 6 7 8 9 10 08 07 06 05 04 03

Dedication

This book is dedicated with respect and admiration to Mrs. Patty Colson.

Though she has not shared in her husband's celebrity, she has shouldered a partner's share of his work. A private person by nature, she has lived her life gracefully and selflessly in the public eye in the support of his ministry, and in obedience to the will of God.

Who can find a virtuous wife?
For her worth is far above rubies.
Her children rise up and call her blessed;
Her husband also, and he praises her.
                    (Proverbs 31: 10, 28 NKJV)

Contents

Preface

I asked Chuck Colson when he first knew about the secret White House taping system revealed during the Watergate hearings.

"When I saw it on television," he answered.

And so Chuck Colson and I learned about the secret tapes that would bring down an American presidency at the same moment. He was recently retired as a special counselor to President Richard Nixon, and I was an Army private who happened to be walking past the TV in the company dayroom when former White House staffer Alexander Butterfield spilled the beans.

Watergate remains one of the most confusing and mysterious episodes in American history. Thirty years after the fact, various accounts are still mutually exclusive, and a writer keen on telling the truth has no choice but to use triangulation and take his best shot. In addition to Colson's own account, one of the best analyses comes from Fred Emery, a BBC producer who brings the whole matter some unaccustomed perspective (see bibliography).

The minute details about Watergate aren't essential to the story of Charles Colson. What's important, and what most people don't realize, is that Colson was a key link in the chain of events that produced both the Pentagon Papers case and Watergate, but that he didn't know it at the time. Everybody from covert operations planner Gordon Liddy to presidential chief of staff Bob Haldeman to the people on the White House tapes themselves reveal that Colson was not only unaware of the Watergate plan, he was categorically excluded from subsequent meetings when the cover-up was devised.

Colson was a facilitator: he made things happen. That was why Nixon liked him so much. But there were times when, as an experienced and successful lawyer, Colson knew that the less he knew, the better. Yet, as careful as he was, he didn't know until too late that the president he served so faithfully had betrayed him, first by keeping the cover-up from him even as he defended the president in public, then by secretly taping his conversations (which actually vindicated Colson rather than otherwise), and finally by denying him a presidential pardon even though Nixon himself received one from his successor, Gerald Ford.

To the extent that it activated or accelerated his search for Christ, Watergate was the fulcrum that Charles Colson's life turned upon. Before it he was one man, and after it, another. He was innocent of all the charges leveled against him by the government; but he pleaded guilty to a crime neither his lawyer nor the judge had ever heard of because he felt called as a Christian to do so. This is another surprise to many people: Colson didn't become a Christian because he went to prison; he went to prison because he became a Christian.

Out of the national horror and personal tragedy of Watergate, Charles Colson built a prison ministry that has touched the lives of millions. As he is the first to admit, only God could make a prisoner who hated the sights and stench and brutality of prison return as a visitor within a week of his release. Only God could turn Chuck Colson, prisoner, into Chuck Colson, prison evangelist.

Since Colson's release from prison in January 1975, he has chronicled his own path in dozens of books and thousands of speeches, interviews, and radio broadcasts. The aim of this book is not to repackage those eloquent and heartfelt expressions. Therefore most of the story here is of the pre-Watergate Colson, the story that hasn't been told in full before. Because the more we can understand the man Charles Colson was, the more we can appreciate the man he is.

Soli deo gloria
John Perry
Thanksgiving Day, 2002
Nashville, Tennessee

Acknowledgments

I wish that writing a book like this had been my brainstorm to begin with. But that distinction goes to my friends at Broadman & Holman for suggesting the idea of writing about living American public figures whose names were well known, but whose faith journeys weren't. They have labored cheerfully alongside me these many months; here's hoping this book is the template for others that will follow. Thanks in particular to publisher David Shepherd, editorial director Leonard Goss, project editor John Landers, and copy editor Amanda Sauer.

My research at Wheaton College was made vastly easier thanks to Wayne Weber at the Billy Graham Archive, and vastly more comfortable thanks to my great friend Rick Jones, who cosseted me in unaccustomed splendor at the Union League Club during my time there. And once more, my colleague Wes Driver helped me sort, organize, and keep up with all the bits and pieces of paper collected at Wheaton and in Washington.

Though this is not an "authorized" biography, Chuck Colson has been gracious and encouraging to me and generous with his time, even to the point of granting an interview in the middle of his summer vacation so that I could meet my writing deadline. Thanks also to Prison Fellowship chief of staff John Dawson for his many kindnesses; to Danny Johnson in the PF photo archives; to Nancy Niemeyer, my first point of contact with PF; and especially to Val Merrill, my most frequent phone correspondent and indefatigable guide to the inner workings of the PF organization.

I owe an unpayable debt to Doug Coe at The Cedars for his time and hospitality. I still don't know how many senators or ambassadors he kept waiting one busy Tuesday in order to give a stranger from Nashville some unhurried insights into Chuck Colson's Christian walk. My hope is that he will see his investment of time repaid in an accuracy and completeness within these pages that would have been impossible otherwise. I'm also grateful to Wendell Barnett, the Hon. Bob McEwen, Luis Palau, David Laux, Anne Bennett, Jeff Edwards, and others who so readily extended a hand of Christian friendship. Thanks as well to Jon Milburn for his Virginia bed and board.

And as always, I'm blessed by the unwavering encouragement of my wife, Susan Ann, and children, Charles and Olivia, forgiving as they do the bizarre schedule and weird behavior of a husband/daddy during the process of birthing a book. Those three are this writer's greatest gift.

"The line between good and evil passes not between principalities and powers, but through every human heart, and it oscillates back and forth."

—Aleksandr Solzhenitsyn

"Colson's troubles are not likely to sadden his former White House colleagues. He was probably more disliked, as well as feared, than any other White House aide . . . If Colson actually performed half the various acts of which he has been accused, he was easily the least principled of all Nixon's associates."

—*Time* magazine, September 24, 1973

"I can work for the Lord in prison, or out of prison, and that's what I intend to do."

—Charles Colson
moments after sentencing, June 21, 1974

"Therefore if any man be in Christ, he is a new creature: old things are passed away; behold, all things are become new."

—2 Corinthians 5:17

Two of a Kind

CHAPTER 1

Senator Leverett Saltonstall was in a bind, and Chuck Colson's job was to get him out of it.

Against all odds, the senator had risen through the political ranks to become, by the fall of 1960, Massachusetts' revered elder statesman. When he defeated Boston mayor James M. Curley in the governor's race back in 1938, Saltonstall was the first Republican governor in a generation, ending forty years of what the newspapers called "Beacon Hill machine" Democratic Party rule. He spent three terms in the statehouse before winning the U.S. Senate seat that Henry Cabot Lodge gave up in 1944 to serve as an Army officer in Italy.

Senator Saltonstall was reelected in 1948 and again in 1954 despite the stark differences separating him on the surface from many of his Bay State constituents: Democratic, working class, Catholic voters represented by a patrician, Harvard-educated, Chestnut Hill Republican millionaire, a Unitarian whose ancestors' roots in Boston reached back to 1630. Quiet, self-effacing, and modest, Saltonstall was passed over more than once as Senate Republican leader because the party thought he lacked the energy and bluster the job required. Yet that same attitude of unaffected humility helped him remain popular across a broad demographic range for decades. He handily survived the statewide Democratic sweep that helped carry Truman to the White House in '48.

But 1960 was another story, and Chuck Colson had seen a tough and treacherous campaign trail ahead ever since Massachusetts' junior senator, John F. Kennedy, won the Democratic presidential nomination. Kennedy was a war hero who'd served in the House, come to the Senate in 1952 (defeating Saltonstall's old friend and Republican colleague Senator Lodge by nearly 69,000 votes), and had been reelected in 1958. The photogenic young presidential candidate had reenergized the state Democratic party, and, the way Chuck saw it, all the excitement and inertia of a national Kennedy campaign posed a real threat to Saltonstall's prospects for a fourth Senate term.

Though scarcely three weeks past his twenty-ninth birthday, Chuck Colson was already a seasoned political operative. When he joined the senator as an administrative assistant four years before, he had been the youngest administrative assistant on Capitol Hill. He was smart, he was tireless, and he had the ability to analyze a situation and get at the heart of it in a way that set him apart from the hundreds of other eager young underlings on the Hill, streaming like ants up and down the marble staircases and through the mahogany doorways of Washington in their white shirts, dark suits, and close-cropped hair. His skill, energy, and success in getting things done captured Saltonstall's attention, and now had landed him the job of campaign manager. If anybody in the office resented Chuck's elevation to the top spot for the 1960 race over older, more experienced staff members, they kept it to themselves—or Chuck kept them too busy to complain.

Standing together at a campaign event, Colson and Saltonstall were visual opposites to an almost comical degree. The senator was sixty-eight, tall and lanky, with a long craggy face, square chin, horn-rimmed glasses, and a thick shock of gray hair turning to white. The young campaign chief stood six-feet-one and just under two hundred pounds, trim and muscular, with brown hair and piercing eyes—still very much the image of the Marine Corps officer he had been not many years before. His plump, almost babyish face could give a first impression of inexperience and naiveté. But it was an impression that never lasted long.

Colson's first task for 1960 was to do all he could to make sure his boss had the weakest opponent possible. In the beginning the front runner was Governor Foster Furcolo, who had also been Saltonstall's unsuccessful challenger in 1954. Though Furcolo was associated with indictments charging misdeeds and financial mismanagement in the state highway department during his administration, he was still a two-term Democratic heavyweight with plenty of friends, solid support, and a capable campaign staff. He would make a formidable candidate.

Looking methodically and tirelessly for an alternative, Colson found one in the ambitious but little-known mayor of Springfield, thirty-five-year-old Thomas J. O'Connor. Colson fed the rumors about Furcolo's questionable highway deals, and stirred up latent feelings against him in the Kennedy camp that were left over from the days when both men were congressmen. At the same time, he encouraged positive press about Mayor O'Connor.

When O'Connor won the Democratic primary, Colson was delighted. Now instead of a sitting governor and former member of Congress, Saltonstall would weather the Kennedy whirlwind opposed by a relative unknown with no big favors to bestow and no standing army of supporters across the state to pitch in and help him with the campaign.

What Colson didn't anticipate was how serious a threat O'Connor's candidacy could be. Immediately following his primary upset, the mayor organized a statewide blitz, shaking hands at factory gates and work benches, making speeches and giving interviews, and publicizing his positions for the hundreds of thousands of voters who hadn't cast ballots in the primaries. The Saltonstall strategists emphasized their man's experience on Capitol Hill, reminding constituents of the senator's position as the second ranking Republican on the powerful House Appropriations Committee. Even so, O'Connor's position in the polls as election day approached showed that Saltonstall was vulnerable. Some reports had the two running neck and neck.

Colson's team went looking for an issue that would break O'Connor's stride, and they found it. Property taxes had recently gone up in Springfield. Keeping his plan a secret from Saltonstall—fearing the senator might not approve—Colson clandestinely whipped up a citizen's protest on the steps of city hall. Scarcely three weeks before the election, a crowd of 4,500 angry residents stormed the building to rally against the increase. The media gave the "taxpayer revolt" wide coverage and grilled Mayor O'Connor about what happened. Lost in the shuffle was a key fact: O'Connor had actually lowered property tax rates during his term; the higher bills were on account of property reevaluations recently completed by an outside firm.

With O'Connor on the defensive, Colson turned his attention to the bigger picture. The nationwide presidential race, with Senator Kennedy opposing Vice President Richard Nixon, was too close to call, though three major polls gave Kennedy a razor-thin edge. As a Democrat and a Catholic, however, the junior senator was a clear favorite in Massachusetts, projected to carry the state by 500,000 votes.

How could Chuck Colson harness some of this awesome Kennedy energy that threatened his laconic, easygoing candidate's chances and use it to improve them instead? It was like the martial arts training he'd had in the Marine Corps: use the enemy's own strength and inertia against him.

Colson resolved to do whatever it took to grab on tight to Kennedy's coattails, and soon developed a two-pronged strategy: one prong aboveboard, and the other, deceptive and duplicitous, hidden not only from the public but from Saltonstall as well. As with the Springfield tax protest, the old gentleman would never approve of such shenanigans; better just to keep him out of the loop.

Aboveboard, Colson emphasized the professional friendship between Kennedy and Saltonstall and their collaboration in Washington for the benefit of Massachusetts voters. In their eight years as Senate colleagues, the two often worked together and had in fact developed a true friendship. With covert help from Kennedy staffers, Colson produced "The Saltonstall Story," a half hour documentary film that included several newsreel shots of Kennedy and Saltonstall together, with a narration that pointed out numerous examples of agreement between the two on legislation and issues. The campaign slogan, "Massachusetts Needs Saltonstall," omitted any reference to party identity, though Saltonstall dutifully endorsed Nixon in his speeches.

On October 30, a headline in the *New York Times* reported, "Kennedy's Magic Aids Saltonstall: G.O.P. Senator Is Depicted in Film as Working with His Junior Colleague," and went on to note that Saltonstall "is using the Kennedy name in his own bid for reelection. The two have been personal friends and legislative collaborators for years."

Although the Kennedy/Saltonstall connection was clearly made in the media, Colson's hidden campaign to cement it even more effectively flew into overdrive as election day approached. Polls taken a week ahead of the vote showed that Irish Catholics were the key swing voters in the state. Colson secretly persuaded six prominent Irish Catholic Democrats to sign a letter endorsing Kennedy and Saltonstall. Then he rented rooms in a fleabag Boston hotel, filled them with young volunteers at long folding tables, and put them to work addressing envelopes to everyone in the city telephone book with an Irish-sounding name—more than 300,000 in all. Saltonstall, unawares, kept endorsing Nixon during his campaign appearances.

Colson convinced a sympathetic postmaster to process the letters the weekend before the election. The only scare came when one of the volunteers, a college coed whose father was a strong Nixon supporter, threatened to tell Republican party headquarters about the mailing. Exhausted, pressed for time, and sequestered in his dingy hotel workroom, Chuck faced a sudden crisis. If the voters learned that Republicans had set up the whole operation, solicited the endorsements, and paid for sending the letters, the Democratic support would be exposed as bogus; Saltonstall would be branded as a turncoat and his credibility destroyed. But if the plan remained a secret, Mayor O'Connor would face the embarrassment of having his own party endorse his opponent—without time for a rebuttal, or even time to trace the source.

Thinking fast, Chuck handed a hundred dollars in cash to a trusted male campaign worker. "Take this girl out and get her loaded . . . whatever you have to do until Election Day," he ordered. The mailing remained a secret, the letters arrived in 300,000 mailboxes the following Monday, and Tuesday, November 8, Leverett Saltonstall won a fourth Senate term.

Nixon's Massachusetts campaign organization was livid. How could Saltonstall align himself with the enemy like that? How could he allow his name to be used in a way that surely cost Nixon precious votes in an election he ended up losing by fewer than 113,000 votes out of 68 million?

They had a point. But as plenty of people could attest, when given the chance, the vice president had no qualms about using questionable tactics of his own.

In 1950, when Chuck Colson was a college sophomore in Rhode Island, Richard Nixon was a two-term California congressman with his eye on the Senate. He had already gained national recognition as a member of the House Un-American Activities Committee (HUAC), which investigated Communist infiltration of American college campuses, unions, the entertainment industry, and other organizations. After World War II, Communism was seen by many government officials and opinion leaders as a grave menace to the freedom so recently defended at so great a cost. Popular opinion branded Communists as traitors and a threat to security, and acquiesced to new levels of investigation and intrusion in order to root them out.

Nixon had campaigned for his House seat as a virulent anti-Communist, a reputation that was reinforced during the HUAC investigation of Alger Hiss, president of the Carnegie Endowment for International Peace, who had also been the founding secretary-general of the United Nations. In the summer of 1948, Hiss was accused by Whittaker Chambers, an editor at *Time* magazine, of leaking State Department secrets to the Communists during the 1930s. Following a sensational, nationally publicized inquiry—including such cloak-and-dagger episodes as hiding rolls of microfilm in hollowed-out pumpkins—Hiss was branded as an enemy sympathizer. He was eventually convicted of perjury in federal court for denying his involvement in pro-Soviet espionage, and sentenced to five years in prison.

The Hiss case earned Nixon a nationwide reputation as a foe of Communism, and his opponent in the 1950 Senate race could scarcely have been a more perfect target for his Red-baiting rhetoric. Helen Gahagan Douglas was a fellow member of the California House delegation, a refined, elegant, well-connected liberal Democrat and one of the first women in America to win election to Congress. She was a New Dealer, believing the people of America had the right to expect their government to fund a variety of social programs to provide a more secure lifestyle and greater opportunity.

Her politics were diametrically opposed to Nixon's conservative views, but what Nixon quickly pounced on as the centerpiece of his campaign was that Mrs. Douglas was a Hollywood insider. According to the HUAC, Hollywood was one of the most fertile breeding grounds for Communist sympathizers—"pinkos," "fellow-travelers," "Reds," or "Commies," as Nixon called them in his speeches. He had become a national political figure as a foe of Communism, and soon marshaled all his energies and resources in attack after attack against Douglas and her supposedly pinko leanings.

Helen Gahagan had a short but highly successful career as a Broadway star before marrying her leading man in *Tonight or Never*, Melvyn Douglas. In 1931 they moved to Hollywood so that Douglas could play opposite Gloria Swanson in the film version of *Tonight or Never*. Helen gradually retreated from professional acting after her marriage, but remained very much a part of the film star social scene as her husband's career advanced over the next decade, including his 1939 starring role opposite Greta Garbo in *Ninotchka*.

Melvyn Douglas enlisted in the Army as a private in 1942; by the time the war was over he had been promoted to major. Meanwhile, Helen stayed busy with bond drives and various other Hollywood fund-raising efforts in support of the war. Eager to "make a difference" and to ensure all Californians had a share in postwar prosperity, Helen ran for—and won—a seat in the House of Representatives, though she had no previous political experience. Her heartfelt concern for others resonated with California voters; as a result of her acting experience, her speaking style was warm, relaxed, and confident. She dressed, looked, and spoke like the Broadway star she had been—and could easily be again, except that she felt her husband and children were more important. As a member of Congress she could make the world a better place for them.

Her years in the House revealed her to be a thoughtful, serious, hardworking representative, and she felt she could do even more for her state as a member of the U.S. Senate. She thought her record, her honesty and forthrightness, and her easy confidence in public would be enough to win. But Nixon immediately put her on the defensive, declaring almost a year before the election that the choice between Mrs. Douglas and himself was "simply the choice between freedom and state socialism."

He hammered away at her Hollywood connections, implying time and again that if there were Communists in the movie business and her husband was a Hollywood star, then she must be at the very least a Commie sympathizer or hiding Commie secrets. (The fact was that Melvyn Douglas had been involved in pro-Communist activities early in his film career.) While Douglas had not a single seasoned political strategist on her campaign team, Nixon was surrounded with advisors poised to dig up whatever dirt there was on his opposition.

One of Nixon's associates was Murray Chotiner, a brilliant but ruthless Los Angeles lawyer who had finished law school at age twenty and spent most of his time defending bookies before signing on with Nixon in 1946. Press advisor and publicist Herb Klein was a former reporter for the *San Diego Union* and had also been with Nixon since '46, writing promotional campaign literature and lending a hard edge to his public statements. Two young UCLA graduates, John Erlichman and Bob Haldeman, were also key lieutenants who scouted for information. Haldeman's father, Harry, was an advertising executive and major Nixon contributor.

While Douglas tried to highlight her record on domestic programs, Nixon harped endlessly on the Communist threat and how no one could be sure anyone married to a liberal Hollywood actor could be trusted. Moreover, Melvyn Douglas's real name was Melvyn Hesselberg, and he was a Jew—all the more reason, according to Nixon, to be concerned. One Nixon staffer's full-time job was "systematically scouring every statement or association Douglas had ever made." On the campaign payroll she was listed as "researcher."

Surprised, flustered, and completely unfamiliar with down-and-dirty personal politics, Douglas was transformed from an erudite, capable campaigner into a cautious, even timid candidate who allowed herself to be drawn away from her strengths into a ceaseless debate, controlled by Nixon, about whether she was a loyal American or not. She never had a chance to speak about her record or her programs; rather, she spent all her time trying to convince the public that she wasn't the Commie sympathizer Nixon insisted she was.

Douglas thought that eventually the public would tire of all of Nixon's anti-Communist posturing and demand debate on the real issues. But as week after week went by, the accusations and innuendoes grew bigger, and everything else faded away almost to nothing. Nixon also played up the difference between his family and hers. He portrayed her as a rich Beverly Hills society hostess, while he lived in his modest starter home on Honeysuckle Lane in Whittier with his wife, Pat, and their two daughters, four-year-old Tricia and her little sister, Julie.

Douglas's problems were further complicated by a shortage of funds. It was true that many of her friends and supporters were very wealthy, and almost any other time she could have raised a fortune with a few campaign dinners. But Hollywood was running in mortal fear of the HUAC. Being branded as a Communist, whether true or not, could cost a director, writer, actor, or producer his career. Making a contribution to a Senate candidate with even a whiff of suspicion about her loyalty would be artistic and financial suicide. The contributions could be anonymous, but everyone was afraid Nixon would find out somehow.

Congressman Nixon, meanwhile, not only had plenty of money from California conservatives and business interests, but he had also convinced the head of the Republican Senate Campaign, Owen Brewster of Maine, to borrow $5,000 personally and secretly transfer it to the Nixon operation.

As election day drew closer, Mrs. Douglas hung on to one bright ray of hope: a promise from President Harry Truman that he would come to California and endorse her. Truman had won the 1948 presidential race by a very narrow margin, but he had swept a host of Democrats into office across the country. He was popular, outspoken, and in agreement with many of Douglas's positions on the issues. Though the president had hedged and delayed, she still expected him to travel west and use his appeal and personal charisma to refocus the Senate race on the issues, her record, and her potential.

Waiting for word from Truman, Mrs. Douglas gamely kept up her campaign speeches and appearances. Numerous prominent Democrats endorsed her, including Speaker of the House Sam Rayburn. But Nixon's tactics—relentlessly slipping in references to "pro-Communist" votes, allusions to the fact that she was a woman, and calling her "Mrs. Hesselberg"—were taking their toll, particularly a flyer that kept cropping up that the press and the public had started calling "The Pink Sheet."

"The Pink Sheet" was Murray Chotiner's idea. It was a legal-size flyer that compared Mrs. Douglas's voting record in the House with that of Vito Marcantonio of New York, acknowledged as one of the most liberal members in Congress and supporter of left-wing causes the anti-Communists targeted for criticism. Titled "Douglas-Marcantonio Voting Record," it pointed out how many times the two had voted alike, especially on "un-American activities and internal security" and "national defense."

The most cursory examination of the facts would have revealed that many of the votes were on mundane procedural matters. Many others displayed Douglas's social liberalism, which was far from radical, and which she shared with numerous other members of Congress. There was no vote that overtly supported Communism. Yet the implication was that because Douglas and Marcantonio had similar voting records and Marcantonio was associated with pro-Communist causes, Douglas was a Communist too.

And just in case anybody didn't get it, the flyer was printed on pink paper. One source later quoted Chotiner as saying they used pink "because it was all the printer had on hand."

The media plastered these latest accusations across front pages all over the state. "The Pink Lady," some called her, "pink right down to her underwear." William Randolph Hearst held fast to his earlier assertion that her political views were "softly suffused with pink, like the sky at morning, when tenderly touched by the rosy fingers of dawn." To Douglas, the implication the flyer made was the most egregious lie yet from the opponent she had started referring to as "Tricky Dick." When she first saw the Pink Sheet distributed at a rally in August, she laughed at it. Who would put any stock in such childish tactics? Nevertheless, it was one of the things that put her on the defensive early in the campaign, and she never regained control.

The Truman trip failed to materialize. Hidden behind his excuses and apologies to Helen was the fact that if he came to California on her behalf, the president would also have to endorse James Roosevelt, FDR's son, the

Democratic candidate for governor. Truman despised the younger Roosevelt and, in the end, could not bring himself to support his friend Mrs. Douglas in person at the expense of assisting a sworn political enemy.

She had been confident of her victory in the beginning, heralded by national Democratic figures and endorsed by Edward G. Robinson, Ronald Reagan, and a few other brave show business personalities who refused to be cowered by the Red-baiting tactics of her opponents. But by the time the campaign was over, Helen Gagahan Douglas was exhausted and shaken. Nixon operatives attended her appearances and asked embarrassing or misleading questions from the floor; her poise and confidence in front of an audience vanished.

Somehow the contest had become a public referendum on her loyalty as an American. As if Nixon needed any encouragement, Murray Chotiner kept telling him to be a fighter because the people like a fighter. And fight he did, even if he had to make up the enemies himself: Communism, Beverly Hills elitism, the very idea of a woman in Congress, questioning Mrs. Douglas's judgment about having a career when most American women were homemakers and polls showed 80 percent of them were happy about it.

Douglas was trounced in the election, retired from politics, and returned to raise her children and support her husband's career (which eventually garnered him a Tony, an Emmy, and two Oscars). Many years later in her autobiography, *A Full Life*, she summed up her race against Richard Nixon in a single sentence: "There's not much to say about the 1950 campaign except that a man ran for Senate who wanted to get there, and didn't care how."

John F. Kennedy, reelected to the House from Massachusetts for a third term on the same day Douglas was defeated, was more straightforward in his assessment. He personally preferred Nixon, a fellow military veteran and anti-Communist, over Douglas, a fellow Democrat. But looking back years later, he described his choice as "the biggest da—nfool mistake I ever made."

A Very Fortunate
Young Man

═══════════════ **CHAPTER 2** ═══════════════

It was graduation day at Northeastern Law School. The crowded auditorium was hot and moist inside, jammed full of proud parents, beaming young wives, and a generous scattering of relatives and friends, all ignoring the closeness, intent on watching the slow-motion parade of graduates gliding one at a time across the stage in caps and gowns to receive their diplomas.

Among the crowd, Chuck Colson seemed perhaps a little out of place. Though he was as excited and wrapped up in the ceremony as anybody that spring afternoon, there were scarcely any other people his age in sight. A name was called: "Wendell Ball Colson." Chuck craned his neck for a better view. Above the row of heads in front of him he could see a black mortarboard with a tassel hanging down begin to move. He looked between the heads, zigzagging back and forth for a better view, and smiled broadly at the familiar figure that strode across to collect the rolled piece of paper awaiting him at center stage.

Chuck felt like clapping right then. But nobody else was doing it and he wasn't sure it would be okay. After all, he was only eight.

His father had been going to school since before Chuck was born, first in accounting then in law—twelve years all together. Young Colson knew the story well: His father's father, Joseph Colson, was born to newly-arrived immigrants from Stockholm who both died when he was still a boy. Raised in an orphanage, he learned to play the cornet and eventually became a soloist with the Boston Symphony.

Joseph married into an old Colonial family, the Balls, but died tragically during the 1919 influenza epidemic, leaving Wendell, his sister, and mother to make their way in America alone. Barely twenty, Wendell shelved any thoughts of college to go to work. He married Inez Ducrow, the daughter of English immigrants of Hugenot descent who remained lifelong British citizens. Hoping to continue his education eventually, he took a job as a bookkeeper in a meat-packing plant for thirty-two dollars a week.

The Colsons' only child, Charles Wendell, was born in a Boston hospital on October 16, 1931. His parents took him home to Winthrop, a working-class but comfortable collection of solid homes and solid families gathered on a peninsula four miles northeast of downtown. Nestled incongruously on the harbor side were several exclusive yacht clubs.

Chuck and his parents lived in a walk-up apartment in an old Victorian house. The first few years of his life were the worst years of the Great Depression. Some of his earliest memories were of riding his tricycle, sitting with his dad on the back porch, and seeing food lines in the streets: a sad, static parade of men, some dressed in expensive suits, stretching around the block waiting patiently for a free meal. Because his dad had a secure and steady job, the family was better off than many. But part of their evident prosperity was because Inez Colson, with an eye for the finer things, regularly managed to spend more than Wendell brought home.

As Chuck recalled many years later, "Moderately comfortable, we were also moderately in debt. When bills mounted too high, Mother would hold sales of our furniture and other possessions. I remember the shock of coming home from school one day, seeing perfect strangers carrying chairs out of our living room." She tended to be the one in the family who called the shots.

Chuck's father was forty when he got his law degree, and he admonished his son to work hard and study hard. "Nothing comes easy in this life," he advised. "There are no shortcuts." Then he invariably added, "Tell the truth always. Lies destroy you." As he grew older, Chuck saw his father more clearly as a friend and trusted advisor.

The Colsons moved several times during Chuck's early years, first to Melrose, Massachusetts, then to nearby Newton. Not long after his dad finished law school he became a staff attorney for General Foods, which had acquired the meat packing plant where he had worked for so long, and was transferred to the corporate headquarters in Scarsdale, New York. In 1942, as his parents settled into a new house on Drake Road, Chuck was enrolled at Browne and Nichols, a prep school in Cambridge. Having suffered so much because his own education was first interrupted then delayed, Wendell Colson was determined to make sure Chuck had a better chance to get ahead.

When World War II began, Chuck felt a surge of patriotic pride and a strong sense that he should do something tangible for the war effort. But what could an eleven-or twelve-year-old boy do that would make any difference? By word and deed his father had drilled into him the value of hard work and doing every job, even the most menial one, to the absolute best of his ability. He decided that everybody could do something to help, so he wrote an essay titled, "How Americans Should Do Their Part to Win the War." He sent it to a Boston newspaper, and it became Chuck Colson's first published work.

Chuck also contributed money to Uncle Sam. He built and sold model airplanes, then donated the money toward the cost of a jeep. Before long the Boston paper carried the story of how young Mr. Colson donated a jeep to the U.S. Army, along with a picture of a round-faced boy posed beside it with a smiling officer.

In 1944, when the Colsons moved to Westport, Connecticut, Chuck transferred from Browne and Nichols to the Riverdale School in Riverdale, New York. Two years later the family moved back to Massachusetts, and Chuck returned gratefully to Browne and Nichols. But to his disappointment, it looked for a while as though he might end up retracing his father's long and difficult path to higher education after all.

After a promising start at General Foods, Wendell Colson was forced by poor health to resign his position. The same move back to Massachusetts that marked Chuck's return to Browne and Nichols also marked the end of the Colson family's brief period of prosperity. Counselor Colson opened a law practice of his own and carried on as well as he could, but making ends meet was a struggle, especially as he looked ahead to putting Chuck through school.

Chuck worked hard and studied hard, and by the time he graduated from Browne and Nichols in the spring of 1949 he could claim a long list of successes. He was captain of the debating team, editor of the school newspaper, president of the student government, voted most likely to succeed by his classmates, a member of the football, basketball, and baseball teams, and class valedictorian. His valedictory address was about pride— the pride they all should have in their country, their school, their class, and themselves.

Chuck had worked summers since he was eleven to help pay his tuition. College would cost twice what prep school had, and he knew that, as hard as his father worked, the two of them together would never be able to afford it. The summer after graduation, he took the highest paying job he could find as a messenger for a Boston brokerage firm, applied for scholarships at Harvard and Brown, and waited impatiently to see what would happen next.

Brown's answer came first. Though founded during Colonial times and a member of the Ivy League, Brown University, in Providence, Rhode Island, was considered second-rate by Boston's Harvard-educated elite. Even so, Chuck was elated to hear he had been awarded a full naval ROTC scholarship, plus fifty dollars a month spending money. His college expenses would be paid by the government's Reserve Officers Training Corps in exchange for a few years' military service after graduation.

Weeks later a letter arrived from the office of the dean of admissions at Harvard inviting Chuck to come in for an interview. Harvard was almost as old as the city of Boston itself, and widely acclaimed as the most prestigious college in America. Arriving at the appointed time, Chuck entered a bright, spacious corner office in the main administration building that radiated a sense of elegance, permanence, superiority, and old money.

Amongst the clutter of rare books and fine antiques stood the dean, looking every inch the part, in British tweeds, with close-cropped gray hair and an air of absolute assurance. Dressed in the blue double-breasted suit he'd bought for graduation from Browne and Nichols, Chuck apprehensively took a seat. He was nervous and at the same time mad at himself for being nervous. Harvard men were no better than he was; they just thought they were.

After a few introductory pleasantries, the dean told Chuck he was "a very fortunate young man" in that he'd been awarded a full scholarship to Harvard University by the Board of Overseers. Then he paused, relaxing back in his chair to wait for Colson's grateful and elated acceptance.

Methodically the dean filled his pipe and lit it. Taking a generous puff, he looked at Chuck with a knowing smile. "Well, I assume you have a lot of questions—the house you will live in and of course your academic schedule."

After a moment Chuck finally spoke. "But I haven't really decided, Dean, whether I will be coming to Harvard."

Even such impeccable breeding as the dean had could not completely hide his surprise. "I cannot imagine anyone turning down a scholarship to Harvard," he said, carefully enunciating the unfamiliar words. The smile was gone.

Prestigious though it was, as well as a ticket to Boston's best-paying jobs and highest social circles, Chuck actually resented the idea of a Harvard education. Harvard men—snooty, aloof, conceited, and petty—ruled the city's institutions and had done so forever. Winthrop, his home-town, was named after a Harvard man. All the top politicians were Harvard men: the House member from the eleventh Massachusetts district, John F. Kennedy, and both senators, Leverett Saltonstall and Henry Cabot Lodge. (Lodge's grandfather and namesake had earned Harvard's first Ph.D. in political science.)

Furthermore, Chuck had been convinced for years that the reason his father fared so poorly with his law practice was that, as a night-school graduate from immigrant stock, he was shut out of the Harvard-dominated circle of law firms, clients, and referrals. He wasn't Harvard material. He didn't measure up.

The day he graduated from Browne and Nichols, Chuck had looked across the way at the buildings of the Harvard Yard half a mile distant. Half of his fellow seniors were on their way there. Stepping to the rostrum for his valedictory address that day, he had talked about pride.

Pride was what prompted him to apply to Harvard in the hope he would have the indescribable pleasure of turning them down. And turn them down he did.

In the fall of 1949 Chuck Colson enrolled at Brown, and enlisted as a midshipman in the Naval Reserve in fulfillment of his scholarship contract. Founded by Baptists before the American Revolution, Brown University had discarded the last vestiges of its religious affiliation by the time freshman Colson stepped off the train in Providence with a suitcase and twenty dollars in the pocket of his new blue suit.

It was an exciting time. Millions of servicemen returning from World War II were enrolling in college at government expense on the GI Bill, raising standards and expectations, and causing overcrowding in classrooms and dormitories nationwide. Colson settled in and, true to form, launched into his studies determined to be the best, remembering his father's admonition: "Study hard and work hard."

Chuck's undergraduate years were busy and productive. He did well in his studies, and earned high marks in ROTC drill. He liked the fact that in the military a man's heritage or the size of his bank account didn't matter: every soldier succeeded or failed on his own merit. His interest in military matters was heightened the summer before his sophomore year. On June 25, 1950, Communist North Korea invaded U.S.-supported South Korea, bringing war to a region where conflict between pro- and anti-Soviet forces had simmered since the end of World War II.

That fall, Chuck joined the Beta Theta Pi fraternity and became friends with a senior fraternity brother named Bill Maloney. Bill was also a Navy ROTC member and decided to take his officer's commission in the Marine Corps. Bill talked up the Corps at the Theta house, and from his description Chuck got the idea that of all the armed services the Marines had the highest standards. Marines were the best.

Feeling his pride working inside him—the pride he'd talked about at graduation, the pride that led him to turn down a Harvard scholarship—Colson decided that when the time came, he'd join the Marine Corps too. He only hoped the Korean War would still be around when he finished college and accepted his commission.

June of 1953 was a busy month for Charles Colson. He received his bachelor's degree, "with distinction," from Brown, and, that same afternoon, got married to a beautiful native Bostonian named Nancy Billings. Nancy and Chuck were the same age, both born and raised in and around the city. But while Chuck was the grandson of immigrants going to college on a government scholarship, Nancy came from a well-to-do and socially prominent family. Their elegant wedding in the suburb of Acton was proof to the world that Chuck Colson had arrived. By himself, he could never enjoy the deep-rooted social status successful Bostonians always seemed to have. But he could marry into it. Certainly he loved Nancy deeply, but the newfound family connections would definitely be a plus.

Also in June, Chuck left Providence for Marine Corps training at Quantico, Virginia, though not without a surprising encounter with a crusty recruiting officer named Lieutenant Cosgrove. While he was still in school, Colson had gone to the lieutenant and told him he wanted to join the Marine Corps.

Cosgrove gave the young reserve midshipman a steely look. "You're a bit premature, Colson. First we'll have to see whether you're good enough for the Marine Corps."

Good enough? Chuck Colson not good enough? The challenge fanned his pride to a white heat. If he had liked the weekly campus ROTC drill before, he poured even more into it now. He spit-shined his uniform shoes, polished his brass to a mirror sheen, and even adopted Lieutenant Cosgrove's rigid posture and strict military bearing. Out of the corner of his eye he could see Cosgrove watching him during drill.

One day Colson was summoned to the lieutenant's office. He stood at attention while the recruiting officer swiveled back and forth in his creaky wooden chair, eyes down, fiddling with a pencil. After what seemed an eternity Cosgrove looked up. "Colson, we think you're good enough."

And so before the month of June was out, newlywed college graduate and newly commissioned Marine lieutenant Chuck Colson found himself in the Virginia coastal swamp south of Washington, D.C. in Marine Corps basic training. A truce was signed in Korea the following month, denying him the battlefield experience he had so eagerly awaited. Still, there was plenty to challenge him, and Chuck reveled in the Marine Corps life, learning time and again that what he considered his best could often be better.

In January 1954, Lieutenant Colson finished his training at Quantico and reported to his new duty station at Camp Lejeune, North Carolina. Soon he was commanding a platoon in a division led by legendary General Chesty Puller. Salty and fearless, General Puller was the only man in history to earn five Navy Crosses, the Navy and Marine Corps' highest award, given for extraordinary heroism against an armed enemy.

A short time later, orders came for Lieutenant Colson to report to camp with his seabag for emergency duty. Within hours he and his platoon were aboard the *USS Mellette* with the rest of their battalion bound for Central America. The World War II-era transport vessel had seen better days; hard use followed by years of inactivity gave it a worn-out look.

Slicing through the Atlantic after nightfall, the ship became part of a convoy that set a course for Guatemala. Officially, the Marines were headed to this poor tropical country to protect American lives during a time of civil unrest. The country's largest landowner, American-owned United Fruit Company, had had thousands of acres of banana plantations nationalized and confiscated by the local government. But the real reason for the mission was to assist the Central Intelligence Agency in an operation to overthrow the pro-Communist president, Jacobo Arbenz Guzmán.

Working with the U.S. State Department, the CIA had trained and equipped Guatemalan exiles in neighboring Honduras to depose Guzmán and establish a pro-U.S, pro-democracy government. But as the invasion drew closer, American authorities were unsure how capable the invaders would be or how much resistance the Guatemalan army would mount against them to defend their elected leader. The Marines were coming to stand by in case the invasion force needed help.

Lieutenant Colson, who had a top secret security clearance as a Marine officer, attended a shipboard briefing on landing plans with other platoon leaders. Troops were issued live ammunition, and tons of reserve ammo and other supplies were readied for offloading. As the ship came to a stop, Colson could stand on deck and see the jagged outline of the Santa de las

Minas Mountains on the horizon, and closer, the sand along the shoreline glowing eerily in the tropical night by the light of a brilliant moon and countless thousands of stars.

Protected from Caribbean currents by a peninsula called Punto Barrios, the sea around the *Mellette* was as calm as a lake, smooth and quiet. Looking at the beach, breathing in the still, muggy air, Colson found himself wondering about what was going to happen. How would he handle himself? He was about to find out whether that leathery recruiting lieutenant was right when he said, "Colson, we think you're good enough." Was he?

And what about his men? It wasn't just his life that was on the line. His decisions could spell life or death for the forty-five men of his platoon who trusted him to keep them safe, who would obey his orders without question because that's what they were trained to do. Colson knew General Puller had given orders that doomed men to die. The orders were his job; dying was theirs. Everybody knew Chesty could make the tough decisions, and they loved him for it. But what would Lieutenant Charles Colson do?

Until that night, Colson could never remember feeling any interest in religion. But gazing up from the rail of a military transport, with the stars above him and the red and green running lights of other ships in the convoy anchored around him, he felt an undeniable certainty that God was out there somewhere. He was an insignificant pinpoint in the universe, one man on one ship, in one ocean, on one planet, in one solar system of millions of stars and galaxies. He wondered to himself, "Where does it all end?"

Somehow in that moment, the young Marine Corps officer felt an unfamiliar yet comforting assurance that God was in control, ruling over all creation, keeping everything in perfect order according to some divine plan that he couldn't understand or even imagine. It was a miracle. And there, alone in the dark, floating in a tropical sea thousands of miles from home, he prayed.

He had been to the Episcopal church and Sunday school once in a while as a boy, but nothing much had ever registered with him on any spiritual or emotional level. But now, without thinking about it ahead of time or really thinking about it at all, Charles Colson prayed, knowing God was there. The only uncertainty was about whether He had time to listen with everything else He had to do.

Before daybreak the word came from Washington: The invasion was a success. The president was out, the CIA-backed invaders were in, and the Marines could stand down. Spared the dangers of combat, the troops stayed off the coast of Guatemala six weeks to make sure the transition of power was completed smoothly. And though for a while Lieutenant Colson vividly remembered how real and powerful God had been to him that night on deck in the starlight, the memory and the feeling gradually faded away, replaced by newer, more urgent matters.

Early in the summer Lieutenant Colson and his men shipped out from Camp Lejeune to Vieques, a craggy island off the east coast of Puerto Rico and the site of a big U.S. military training camp.

Landing on the beach, Colson and his men were ordered to reach a point up toward the mountainous center of the island. There were two ways to get there: the first was a long, winding and relatively flat path; the second, straight up a sheer rock face sixty feet high. The platoon was ordered up the cliff.

Years later Colson recalled what happened next. "For a few moments I couldn't believe it. It was only a training exercise and as I stared at the menacing volcanic ash, I thought it was not only foolhardy but impossible. Someone, maybe me, would get killed. 'But Marines can do anything,' I reminded myself, and then led my forty-five men up and over the cliff, clawing every inch of our way with picks, ropes, and bare hands.

"When we got to the top I looked back at the beach below, the sea beyond, and in that instant realized that Puller was right: when a man throws everything into it, he can do the impossible."

Within a year, Colson was promoted to first lieutenant (and later to captain in the reserves). He had met every challenge military service and command could throw at him. He had proven he was good enough, and felt ready to move on to other challenges. Besides, Nancy had given birth to their first child, Wendell Ball Colson II, in 1954, and it was time to think about settling down and moving ahead.

He was interested in law school, in part to honor his father by showing all those insufferable Harvard types in Boston that no Colson needed a Harvard degree to be successful. Politics attracted him, too, and he had been intrigued by the political process ever since he worked as a volunteer for Governor Robert Bradford's reelection campaign in 1948. It was a rough-and-tumble world that rewarded hard work, taking chances, and doing whatever it took to get things done. It was no place for kibitzers or theorists who were afraid to get their hands dirty, afraid to lay it all on the line.

In September 1955 Lieutenant Colson resigned his regular commission and joined the reserves. He had applied to law schools at Duke, Georgetown, and George Washington. All three accepted him, and on the advice of a fellow Marine Corps officer he chose George Washington, in the District of Columbia.

The next step was to find a job near the campus. He heard about a junior management assistant program in Washington run by the Navy Department. He took a qualifying test by mail, passed it, and was invited to come for an interview. Poised and confident, Colson passed the interview and was hired immediately. He moved his young family to a new home in Arlington, Virginia, just across the Potomac from the capital, and enrolled in night classes at George Washington University law school.

Chuck was at the point of quitting the management program because he thought it was boring, when he received an appointment as assistant to assistant secretary of the Navy for Materiél Raymond H. Folger. It was a prime perch for observing how government really worked. The people in charge were confident, proud of who they were and what they did. Chuck was proud too, eager to move on to bigger challenges and more responsibility. He'd been a star in prep school, a distinguished graduate in college, and a leader in the Marine Corps. Now he was ready for the next test, whatever it was.

Big Ambitions

CHAPTER 3

The Navy Department that Chuck Colson joined in the fall of 1955 was in the middle of a historic transformation. Battleships—World War II vessels whose marine pedigree traced back to nineteenth-century British dreadnoughts—were still commissioned ships of the line. But those relics of the past served alongside a herald of the future: the *USS Nautilus*, the world's first atomic-powered submarine and the first man-made object in history propelled by nuclear energy. Top secret plans were already in the works to fit these atomic subs with atomic offensive weapons.

Having been in the Marine Corps, which was under administrative control of the Navy, Colson now saw military service from the other side, at the point where policies were established and the most important decisions were made. There were good people in the department, but there were also the petty and small-minded who hid behind a title. The dynamics were fascinating. It was pretty heady stuff for an eager, impressionable man just turned twenty-five.

The pace of activity and the sense that something important was happening captivated Chuck. It was almost like Washington was where he'd always belonged but never realized it. He was in his element. Even more than at Browne and Nichols, even more than in the Marine Corps, Colson felt at home.

Though he'd had a secret security clearance in the military, he received a higher level one as an assistant in a cabinet-level department. The threat of Soviet espionage was an ongoing concern in government, and policy required a thorough FBI background investigation of new hires. The Red-baiting era of Senator Joseph McCarthy was over, yet there was an underlying residue of caution from those years that was still strong. Russia had the atomic bomb and continued to flex her muscles threateningly in Eastern Europe. The House Committee on Un-American Activities and the Algier Hiss case, spearheaded by Vice President Richard Nixon, seemed to prove that spies could function undetected deep inside the country's borders.

Chuck had worked in the Navy Department only about a year when F. Bradford Morse, the senior administrative assistant to Senator Leverett Saltonstall from Colson's home state of Massachusetts, offered him a job as the number two man in Saltonstall's office. Chuck accepted a post as executive secretary. Colson had been one of the youngest company officers in the Marine Corps. Now he was the youngest senior congressional staff member on Capitol Hill. Morse later described his associate as "an extraordinary fellow, talented, with a keen intellect."

In 1956 President Dwight Eisenhower and Vice President Nixon were running for reelection. The president was popular, economic prosperity was at a historic high, and his prospects for four more years in office were likely. Not so for the vice president. He had been a controversial figure since the 1952 campaign, when a secret personal fund established for him by friends during his Senate career came to light. Some Republican leaders thought Nixon, tainted by the appearance of impropriety, should step aside for another running mate.

Instead, Nixon went on national television to defend his integrity and asked viewers to contact the Republican National Committee with their opinion whether he should withdraw from the race or not. Later enshrined as the "Checkers Speech," after the family dog mentioned in the remarks, the broadcast presented Nixon as an earnest and honest man. Party headquarters were flooded with calls demanding Nixon remain on the ticket.

After four years as the vice president, it seemed Nixon had more enemies and not fewer in Washington. His brusqueness and his obsession with public opinion annoyed many voters as well, especially independents and Democrats who had voted for Eisenhower in '52. According to some observers, Eisenhower's poor health leading up to the '56 campaign convinced party leaders to recommend staying with Nixon. In September of 1955 while on vacation in Colorado, Eisenhower suffered a heart attack. The next summer he underwent intestinal surgery. Some strategists insisted Nixon be dropped, because if Eisenhower died in office he would lead the party to defeat in 1960. Others argued that ousting Nixon would be a clear signal Eisenhower's health was failing, and that a sick president would never be reelected. Better to keep him on board as a sign all was well.

Though he had only been in his new position a few months, Colson was tapped to help write a speech for Governor Christian A. Herter of Massachusetts nominating Nixon for another term as vice president. Later during the campaign, Colson met Nixon for the first time when he delivered a draft of the speech to the vice president's office. There were several people in the room, and Nixon continued talking with them while he read the speech and made "just a few changes." When he handed the pages back to Colson, the young staffer saw that the speech had been completely rewritten on the spot, all while carrying on a conversation about something else.

To Colson it was a remarkable display of mental agility, and gave him a first impression of the vice president as a sharp, dedicated public servant who was quick to assimilate the facts. Chuck also saw something of himself in Nixon's life and career: humble beginnings, success through dogged and relentless determination, a military career (he was a naval officer in New Caledonia during World War II), and a devotion to getting things done no matter what it took. Later he also took note of Nixon's legal credentials. Nixon earned his LL.B. from Duke, which had been on his own short list of law schools. Law, it seemed, helped clear the path to success in Washington, and it was in Chuck Colson's blood.

In 1958 Bradford Morse left his position with Saltonstall to run for Congress from the Massachusetts fifth district. In recommending his own replacement, Morse took note of Colson's tenacity and dedication in pursuing a law degree at night despite the pace of activity on Capitol Hill. He was also impressed by what he later called Colson's "devotion to the highest standards of honesty and integrity" demonstrated "on a daily basis," and went on to describe him as "one of the most thoughtful, conscientious, responsible, dependable, and reliable men I have ever known."

One incident in particular impressed Morse. With Morse's approval, Colson did something he thought later might lead to embarrassment for the senator. Believing he had made a serious error in judgment, Colson insisted, over Morse's objection, upon telling Saltonstall what happened and offering his resignation. Saltonstall had only praise for Colson and turned down his resignation offer. Clearly Colson had a strong and reliable conscience that would steer him right in any situation, even to the point of admitting to crimes that otherwise would go unnoticed.

While he gained more experience and responsibility in Senator Saltonstall's office, Colson's responsibilities at home also grew. In 1956 two-year-old Wendell welcomed a new brother, Christian, to the house. A couple of years later, daughter Emily joined the family. By that time the Colsons had moved from Arlington to a bigger house in Alexandria. Nancy stayed home with the children—all three of them under six years old—in the traditional role of wife and mother.

As a senator's chief assistant by day and law school student by night, Colson had little extra time for his family. He was immersed in the challenges of education and career. While he loved his wife and children, there was a sense of excitement and importance to his work that he found irresistible: the give-and-take on legislation; the adrenaline rush of late-night strategy sessions; and meetings of the Senate Appropriations and Armed Services committees, of which Saltonstall was the ranking Republican member, in the lofty paneled conference rooms of the Senate Office Building or the Capitol. Chuck also went through three more FBI security clearances, including a Special Agency clearance in 1957.

As he had in prep school and at Brown, Colson excelled in his studies at George Washington and was elected to the Order of the Coif, a national honorary legal society. He graduated in 1959 and became a member of the American Bar Association the same year.

He knew his law degree represented a tremendous opportunity for the future in the form of more money and more career options. For now though, his main focus was on getting Senator Saltonstall reelected in

November of 1960, when it seemed certain his young, popular, photogenic colleague, Senator John Kennedy, would lead the presidential ticket for the Democrats. Still, as the campaign surged forward in the summer of the year, Colson made inquiries and considered offers from several Boston law firms. Another option was to stay put in the senator's office—a secure, prestigious, well-paying job for another six years.

After the election, Chuck Colson was widely recognized as the architect of a masterful and successful campaign. The Greater Boston Chamber of Commerce selected him as one of ten Outstanding Young Men of 1960. Even professional campaign consultants went to school on the Saltonstall strategy. Campaign USA, which offered a self-described "equalizer service" compiling polling data, candidate voting and attendance records, verbatim quotations, and other information for independent or underdog clients, admired Colson's campaign. One newspaper described Campaign USA as "'Hatchet Men' for the Outs."

His success, however, was no indication that Colson was universally admired. On the contrary, success seemed inevitably to mean stepping on a few toes. A fellow member of Senator Saltonstall's staff later recalled: "I didn't particularly like him but I respected him. He was skillful and hard-nosed but seemingly sweet . . . a smooth operator with big ambitions. When he decided he wanted something and put about getting it, butter wouldn't melt in his mouth. His prime concern was getting things done for constituents; he was concerned with influence and political matters. Others of us dealt with the legislative side."

Getting things done: that was the hallmark of a Colson-led project.

Scarcely three weeks after the election, on November 26, 1960, the *New Bedford Standard-Times* reported that Charles Colson would open a Washington, D.C. office on January 1, 1961, as a trade representative of the New England Council. Senator Saltonstall supported him in the career change, saying it would "be a great boost to New England as a whole and will help the region achieve a strong and effective voice in the nation's capital."

Had Bradford Morse not been elected to the House in 1960, he and Colson planned to go into practice together. In the end, Colson decided to form a law partnership with Charles Morin, whom he first met on the Washington political circuit and who soon became his best friend. With five thousand dollars he had saved plus what money Morin could contribute, the two opened a two-office practice, with Colson in Washington and Morin in Boston. Though Morin was one of those Harvard men, he was not cut from the typical Ivy League cloth. He was a Catholic, with Canadian and Irish roots—his family hadn't come over on the *Mayflower* and he was proud of it.

Early on, Colson's chief responsibility in Washington was representing the interests of the New England Council, a trade group comprised of the state governments of Maine, Vermont, New Hampshire, Massachusetts, Rhode Island, and Connecticut. As an incisive and observant member of Senator Saltonstall's staff for more than four years, Colson had learned a lot about what New England business interests needed and how to lobby for it in Congress.

From his small office suite in the VFW Building, Colson began working old contacts and establishing new ones with typical energy and enthusiasm. He was in business less than a year when Maine Senator Margaret Chase Smith accused him publicly of a conflict of interest—a sure sign, in his estimation, that he was getting attention and making a difference for his small but growing list of clients.

As Senator Saltonstall's chief aide, Colson had served as secretary of the New England Senators' Conference. He continued in the position even after he began representing the New England Council, a private business group. Senator Smith saw Colson's participation as a conflict of interest, a lawyer employed by big business in a too-influential position with the region's senators. Colson explained the council was a "quasi-public organization," and that it made sense for him to continue working with the senators he had known for four and a half years.

Senator Smith disagreed, and boycotted the meetings of the conference until Colson severed all ties with it.

On January 25, 1963, two days after resigning from the New England Senators' Conference, Colson accompanied Senator Saltonstall, Senator Ted Kennedy, Speaker of the House and Boston Congressman John

McCormick, and a client from the Harrington and Richardson Arms Company to the office of Secretary of Defense Robert McNamara. Their mission was to keep the government from discontinuing a contract to produce M-14 rifles for the military. Though a *Washington Post* story at the time described the meeting as "sympathetic," Knight Newspapers Syndicate later filed reports of a heated exchange "ending in a near fistfight between Colson and McNamara." The facts were that the men had a cordial meeting, exchanged their views, and went their separate ways. The source of the fight rumor was never discovered, though it would be repeated time and again in years to come. It was, Chuck concluded, drawn entirely from "the overheated imagination of journalists."

Before his five thousand dollars in savings ran out, he and Charlie Morin had attracted enough business to make the small firm self-sustaining. In fact, only a few months after hanging out their shingle, the two men needed another lawyer on staff. Their friend Elliot Richardson, fellow Bostonian, military veteran, and Harvard graduate then serving as U.S. attorney, recommended a promising young attorney named Joe Mitchell.

Any other law graduate with Mitchell's credentials would have been snapped up at a far more generous salary than Colson & Morin could pay. But Joe Mitchell couldn't get a job because he was black. Without hesitating, the firm hired him in spite of warnings from well-meaning colleagues that he would cost them business. On the contrary, Mitchell proved to be an excellent hire, and within two months other firms were trying to entice the Boston bar's first black attorney to come to work for them.

Colson was a gifted and persuasive speaker even in his student days. Watching Washington politicians in action and attending law school further honed his skills, so it wasn't long after he set up shop that he began appearing at luncheons to talk about issues of interest to the New England Council. His position invariably was that New Englanders faced particular challenges in the present day, and deserved help from the government and others in dealing with them: rail passenger service, which was declining as airplanes got safer and faster; the textile industry, a traditional mainstay of the regional economy facing serious offshore competition for the first time; the cost of coal and fuel oil, which the Northeast relied on more heavily than any other area; and the minimum wage, important both to countless small businesses and the millions of blue collar wage earners searching for a workable compromise.

Colson also laced his speeches with observations and pronouncements on political trends of the moment, particularly as they affected his clients. He had been a strong anti-Communist at least since his Marine Corps days, and he never missed an opportunity to compare a free society with a totalitarian one.

His speech at the Rotary Club luncheon in Washington on Pearl Harbor Day, December 7, 1962, was typical of the period, covering a wide range of topics, filled with incisive analysis, and stumping persuasively for New England interests.

Colson stood at the lectern in the conservative dark suit, white shirt, and narrow tie that were the unofficial uniform of Washington. Tall and muscular, he kept his sandy brown hair cut short on the sides, a little longer on top. A pair of piercing blue eyes—his Scandinavian ancestry showing through—shone out from his soft, round face.

He had a big smile that seemed to animate his entire body; it made him engaging and personable. His voice was a strong baritone that carried well even without a microphone, made all the more interesting by his Boston Bay accent. His was a confident voice that commanded attention.

He started off with his favorite icebreaker, something to build a rapport with an unfamiliar audience. It was a story about Al Smith, legendary governor of New York and 1928 Democratic nominee for president. During a reelection campaign, Governor Smith happened to drive by Sing Sing Prison. He told his driver to go in and assemble the inmates so he could give a speech. When the inmates were gathered in the dining hall, Smith stood up in front of them and began as he began all of his campaign speeches: "Fellow Democrats!"

Quickly he realized that wasn't very smart politics, so he recovered and tried again: "Fellow Citizens!"

That wasn't good either, because some of the convicts would have lost their citizenship rights. So he gamely tried a third time: "It's good to see so many of you here!"

"And so," Chuck would say to the crowd at that point, "it's good to see so many of you here."

With the audience thus at ease, he went on to speak about the worldwide struggle between "communistic slavery" and "our democratic way of life." He had just returned from India, his first trip outside the country since his military assignment in Guatemala. He talked about the awesome contrast between wealth and poverty in that struggling nation, between intelligence and ignorance, ambition and diffidence. "India is the most populous democracy in the world," he said, "but it has no basic ideological connection to the West. Its one desperate objective is to remain free." Until there was a stable democracy there, the Indian government had no resources to spare for anything else.

Coming closer to home, Colson turned to the responsibility of the men in his audience to their communities, states, and nation. It was their job to unlock the potential in the people and circumstances around them by "asserting responsibilities for leadership."

He explained how the lack of leadership hobbled New England. The biggest problem there, he said, was "mismanagement or lack of management in political affairs."

"Corruption in politics has become a way of life in many of our communities," he continued, going into detail about misdeeds in highway programs and sweetheart deals in public works projects.

On the other hand, when people work together diligently and honestly, any problem could be overcome. The Northeast had been decimated by the loss of jobs in the textile industry, an essential force in the economy for two hundred years. But energetic and resourceful community leaders and elected officials pulled together to build an electronics industry, to court manufacturers, and go out of their way to attract new capital. The result: for every textile job lost, two had been created in electronics at twice the pay scale.

In summary, cooperation and flexibility led to success and prosperity; corruption and the failure of leadership led to disaster.

Colson & Morin grew rapidly. Within a year both the Boston and Washington offices had expanded dramatically and their payroll was twenty thousand dollars a month. The problem was that as fast as the firm grew, its debt grew even faster. Just before Christmas 1962 the two partners spent a long night in the Boston office discussing their financial prospects and how to improve them. If they stayed on the current track they'd be out of business by spring.

Flying back to Washington the next morning, Chuck found himself looking out through the curtained window imagining that the scene below him was not the snow-covered New England countryside, but the sandy beach of Vieques. It was his responsibility to lead a company of Marines straight up a cliff. It was an impossible job and yet he did it anyway.

His thoughts flitted to the Saltonstall campaign, waged against the Democratic forces inspired by a young, handsome Irish Catholic on behalf of a gaunt, craggy-faced Boston blue blood whose hobby was raising chickens. Whether at the height of a military training assault or the closing minutes of election night, the adrenaline rush was the same. And now he felt it again: the surge of energy, the fire that the challenge of long odds set raging inside him.

Using his briefcase as a desk, he started a letter to Charlie outlining a plan to go after new clients. He had friends at Grumman Aircraft, and there were several companies in California he could call on. As the propellers droned outside and the farms and towns rolled by below, he went on page after page with a plan of attack. It was time to take his own advice and exhibit some "responsible leadership."

In time, every company Chuck wrote down that day became a client of Colson & Morin.

Each year Charles Colson was a featured speaker at the annual meeting of the New England Council. While he always had information and encouragement about policies important to the region—such as price supports for sugar beets—he shared his insider perspective on the latest social and economic trends. In his 1963 annual speech he noted how the federal government was making more of an impact on the daily lives of citizens.

For the most part he saw this as a positive step. Meaningful civil rights legislation was working its way through Congress and transforming the social landscape of America. The Job Corps and the Peace Corps were started, and discussion in the House and Senate about Medicare and a federal Office of Economic Opportunity intensified. President Kennedy challenged America to put a man on the moon and return him safely by the end of the decade. These were confident, prosperous times, and both Colson and his firm were riding high.

In contrast to his professional success, however, Colson's personal life was crumbling. By the time of their tenth anniversary in June 1963 Chuck and Nancy had already been separated for some time. She had little interest in the world of politics her husband found so irresistible. She preferred staying home with their children—nine-year-old Wendell, seven-year-old Christian, and little Emily, five—and moving in her own social realm.

When they were first married, Chuck found a sense of assurance and social acceptance in Nancy's family connections and deep Boston roots. Now things were different. He was self-confident and successful, making a name for himself in important Washington power circles. The excitement and challenges he craved weren't at home, but at the office, in the meeting room, the strategy sessions, at the negotiating table.

Eventually it became clear that the chasm between them would never be bridged. Beginning soon after he and Charlie opened for business, Chuck confided to his friend and former boss, Congressman Bradford Morse, that he and Nancy were estranged, and looked to him for understanding and counsel. Husband and wife maintained a deep respect for each other through a gray and troubling period that ran on for years; Colson committed himself to fulfilling his responsibilities to his children as well as circumstances would permit. Just after Christmas 1963 they finally decided that divorce was their only remaining option. To avoid the long and potentially embarrassing legal process in Washington he flew to Juarez, Mexico, where their divorce decree was issued on January 24, 1964.

Less than three months later, Chuck married a cheerful and attractive Capitol Hill staffer from Springfield, Vermont, named Patricia Hughes. Patty had come to work in 1958 in Senator Saltonstall's office, where she soon earned a reputation as one of the most efficient and hardest-working members of the administrative team. Patty was outgoing and vivacious, a former Cherry Blossom Queen with what Chuck described as a "radiant smile." And she was as captivated by politics as he was.

In 1960 Colson left Capitol Hill to open his law office, and Patty left the Senate for a position on the House side. But they kept in touch, and in time their friendship grew into love. They began seeing each other during the last years of Colson's marriage, after his separation from Nancy; when the divorce was final, Chuck and Patty were free to wed. They were both disappointed to learn they would not be able to have a church wedding. Patty was a Catholic, and her church did not recognize Chuck's divorce.

Instead, they held a simple civil ceremony at the Army chapel near Arlington Cemetery, then took a honeymoon trip to Bermuda. Later, Chuck looked into Catholic teaching in hopes of resolving matters and clearing the way for a church celebration. He engaged the problem with the same zeal he fought for his clients' viewpoints in Washington. But the tenets of Patty's religion were even more of an obstacle than the cliffs of Vieques. "For a while I studied Catholicism," he wrote years later, "but my divorce appeared an insurmountable barrier to the blessing of her church and in time I dropped it."

Since starting his own firm, Chuck had moved from one residence to another in Washington every year. Now he and Patty settled into comfortable quarters on Fourth Street S.E.: a new marriage, a new home, a new start.

And there was new excitement on the political front as the 1964 presidential election drew near. Though he wasn't directly involved in any candidate's campaign this round, he had the opportunity to consult with his old acquaintance Richard Nixon. After his narrow loss to Kennedy in 1960, the former vice president returned to California, hoping to solidify a constituent base by running for governor. But Nixon was humiliated, losing to Democrat Pat Brown by more than 300,000 votes—over twice the margin of his presidential defeat. The morning after the election, Nixon famously told the members of the press covering the California campaign, "You won't have Nixon to kick around any more, because, gentlemen, this is my last press conference."

Nixon had moved to New York and joined a law firm where his annual compensation was as much as he had earned in eight years as vice president. In his office in lower Manhattan's financial district, Colson met with Nixon during the spring of 1964 and discussed the future of the beleaguered Republican Party. Colson saw Nixon as "a man of uncommon intellect and capacity, with visions for his country and party which I enthusiastically shared," and was convinced that, though he had sworn off politics, Nixon was the man who could restore the party after the disaster they agreed was inevitable in November.

Nixon was a prideful man, and that was a force Colson well understood. Nothing would please Nixon more than to overcome the politicians and opinion leaders who saw the former vice president as a broken political has-been. And the stage was being set as the Republicans moved toward the nomination of Senator Barry Goldwater of Arizona, a conservative firebrand who openly suggested a preemptive nuclear strike against the Soviets and disdained the massive federal social programs that were just beginning to take hold on a national scale.

Nixon was the perfect rallying point for the Republican faithful once the storm had passed, and Colson encouraged him to begin rebuilding the bridges to party operatives, donors, the press, and others that had collapsed so publicly two years before. The need became even more apparent after Goldwater won the Republican nomination on the first ballot that summer, declaring in words some listeners found ominous that "extremism in the defense of liberty is no vice and moderation in the pursuit of justice is no virtue." Colson endorsed Goldwater, but knew he was too conservative to win the presidency.

Chuck had many friendships and connections with labor unions and other traditionally Democratic groups by virtue of his years representing the New England Council. Considering his loyalty more to the ideal, the candidate, and his clients than to the party, he organized a $50-a-plate fund-raising dinner for Maine's Senator Edmund Muskie, a popular moderate Democrat and former governor running for reelection to a second term.

Goldwater was trounced at the polls by Lyndon Johnson, the incumbent who had succeeded to the presidency after Kennedy's assassination. There was really no national figure around which the shattered Republicans could rebuild. But Colson and Nixon both saw a pathway that led to a new golden age for the Republicans with Nixon at their head. "For Richard Nixon and me," Colson later recalled, "the dream remained vividly alive."

The Job of a Lifetime

CHAPTER 4

With President Johnson elected to a full term and the Republicans licking their wounds, Charles Colson turned his attention to building up the Washington business of his law firm. His rising star in the capital and increasing presence and clout in government caught the attention of senior Washington insiders. One of the most seasoned men to join Colson & Morin was Edward N. Gadsby, chairman of the Securities and Exchange Commission during Eisenhower's second term. Though Colson was a founder and managing partner of the Washington office, he treated Ned Gadsby with the courtesy and deference due a respected senior member of the Republican establishment.

It was what Colson referred to as "general corporate practice": besides the New England Council, the company was a registered lobbyist for U.S. Rubber, Grumman Aircraft, and several mutual fund managers. In the words of another partner, the firm specialized in "corporate clients which have problems with the federal government": tax legislation, regulations, and federal procurement policies.

Colson's firm went through a series of name changes as various career attorneys and Washington figures came and went, eventually becoming known as Gadsby & Hannah after Ned Gadsby and Paul Hannah, a senior partner who had previously been general counsel for Raytheon, a huge Massachusetts electronics company that held important government contracts. The firm prospered, and in time Colson's total annual compensation climbed to over $100,000, the salary of a powerful and important man at a time when $200 a week supported a middle-class lifestyle.

At some point around 1966, Charles Colson met a man who at the moment seemed like just another client, but who would one day play an essential role in his life. When Paul Hannah joined Colson's firm he brought Raytheon's business with him into the Boston office. Pleased with the service, Raytheon decided to expand Gadsby & Hannah's responsibilities to include representing them in Washington. That job naturally fell to Chuck Colson. Raytheon's president, Thomas L. Phillips, soon recognized his new Washington counsel as "energetic and imaginative, a man who got the job done, and a great asset to the company." Phillips himself was a hard-charging and successful executive who, as the company president, headed the largest employer in Massachusetts. He knew an effective advocate when he saw one.

As the midterm elections of 1966 approached, Colson predicted that the new Congress would change the political landscape profoundly. The voters were restless. After campaigning against increased involvement in Vietnam, President Johnson had reversed course and sent 180,000 American soldiers to the region. Since February 1965 American planes had been bombing targets in communist North Vietnam, and by 1966 more than 350,000 Americans were engaged in the war. Some citizens vehemently opposed both the war and the military draft that supplied its fighting force. Protests grew larger and more violent.

At the same time, racial tensions reached a fever pitch. Black activist Malcolm X (born Malcolm Little), an ex-convict who founded the Organization of Afro-American Unity, was assassinated in Harlem in 1965. Later that year, Baptist minister and Nobel Peace Prize winner Martin Luther King, Jr., led 25,000 people on a march between Selma and Montgomery, Alabama, protesting segregation and the brutal racism of the police.

As so often is the case, the party in power was blamed disproportionally for the troubles of the time. The 1964 Congress had 295 Democrats and 140 Republicans; in 1966 the balance changed to 248 and 187, including 90 Southern Democrats, 60 of whom usually voted with the Republicans. Assisted by the war and race issues, the Republicans were slowly recovering from the Goldwater debacle and finding a new base of power in the American electorate. Colson predicted big battles in the coming years over appropriations and fiscal policy. The nation's political mind-set would determine how it spent its money: future funding of the war and the Great Society would set the stage for a budget battle royal.

In his speeches before trade groups and civic organizations, Colson bemoaned the "lack of control, the loss of leadership, the lack of sense of national purpose and national commitment." World War II gave everybody a common enemy and a common goal, and the momentum thus created lasted almost twenty years. By the mid-1960s the force was spent and the common bonds unbundled. Looking for a new sense of purpose, the country found itself mired in an unpopular and seemingly unwinnable war in Southeast Asia, rocked by racial discord, and adrift compared to the confidence and sense of direction of the previous postwar years.

"These are deeply troubled times," Colson told his audience. "National problems are universal—trade, taxes, foreign investment, civil disorder, the war, the budget, monetary crises, and inflation. In a very significant way, how the nation copes with those issues will chart the course for not only ours but many generations to come."

Always a patriot, Colson felt his American pride well up more than ever. His nation needed direction, strong leadership, and honest, capable, dedicated public servants whose hands could securely hold the public trust. More and more he felt Richard Nixon was the man who could get the nation back on the right track and guide it into the future with purpose and confidence: Nixon the foe of Communism, Nixon the visionary leader, Nixon the seasoned Washington insider who knew how to get things done. Moreover, Colson felt that Nixon was one of those rare politicians who was involved in public service for the good of the country and not for personal gain.

Even as the political world was crashing around the Republican Party in the fall of 1964, Nixon wondered aloud in a conversation with Colson how many delegates he could count on if he were in the running. Chuck felt Nixon was on his way back to the top, and was determined to do what he could to help the ex-vice president claim a position of leadership in the public arena. The goal was the presidency. And the closer the 1968 campaign got, the more possible it appeared that Nixon had a shot at winning, and that Colson would be serving him in some capacity after he did.

On the personal side, Chuck and Patty were enjoying their new home on Fourth Street in Washington. After the tension and uneasiness in the last years of his previous marriage, Chuck reveled anew in the joys of married life. The two seemed the perfect match, and the Colsons were popular guests on the Washington social circuit. Chuck's business connections with clients on one hand and government contacts on the other garnered him and Patty frequent invitations.

One of the few things missing from their family life was children. Chuck kept in close contact with his and Nancy's three children, and dutifully continued his role as a father even at a distance. But Chuck and Patty wanted children of their own. In time they decided to adopt, and filed an application with a local adoption agency. When the time came for the Colsons' assessment interview, Chuck was confident they'd sail through with flying colors. He was wealthy, successful, well-connected, and lived in an upscale part of town.

But as the interview went on, he felt things weren't going too well. To him it seemed that the interviewer thought he was too dedicated to his work to have time for children, and that his ignoring home in favor of the office had been bad for Wendell, Christian, and Emily—and had been a major factor in the breakup of his first marriage.

As Colson later recalled the interview, the adoption agency representative finally laid it on the line: "You're very clear about what you want, aren't you? I suppose you don't think you have ever failed in anything in your life."

"That's right, I haven't," Colson answered coolly.

She shot back, "Don't you think your divorce was a failure?"

Remembering his reaction years afterward, Colson wrote, "The questions stung. Deep down I knew I had failed but I couldn't admit it to myself or anyone else. The turndown by the agency could have been a valuable checkpoint for me: a chance to take a hard look at the person I was becoming. But it wasn't. I blamed it on the baby shortage, the pill, and liberalized abortions. The tough exterior coating that I had layered over myself during all the years of driving and succeeding was impenetrable."

Tough as he was, Charles Colson had a sense of compassion, as he proved when he was appointed by a local court to defend a poor teenager arrested for burglary. It was the young man's fourth offense, and he seemed like a textbook example of the kind of small-time hood who could expect to spend the rest of his life in and out of jail. Too often, when a busy law partner gets assigned a pro bono case he either hands it off to a junior associate, or, after a quick review of the facts, enters a guilty plea.

But because the case was assigned to him personally, Colson considered it his personal responsibility. He managed the case himself, questioning the boy to get the facts, and challenging the prosecution in court to produce proof of the defendant's guilt. The proof was insufficient and the case was dismissed. Though he could have stopped there, Chuck took the time to talk with the boy and his father about the importance of obeying the law and the high place of justice in American society. The boy stayed out of trouble from then on.

As the 1968 campaign flew into high gear, Colson became steadily more involved in planning and policy for the Nixon team. After sewing up the Republican nomination that summer, Nixon invited Colson to join his inner circle of advisors. For a Republican candidate, Colson's easy access to blue-collar voters, labor leaders, and other traditional Democratic constituencies was a rare advantage. Colson decided to take a four-month leave of absence from Gadsby & Hannah beginning in August to advise Nixon full-time.

Colson was installed as counsel to the "key issues committee," a group operating separately from the candidate's official organization and separate from the Republican Party. Formed in April, the committee was mostly congressmen, senators, and governors. Chuck was an unusual addition in that he was not an elected official. And it wasn't long before his work brought him more attention than either he or Nixon wanted.

In September a confidential letter, signed by Richard Nixon, was sent to a select list of 3,000 leaders and decision makers in the securities industry, chiefly to mutual fund brokers on Wall Street. The letter criticized the Johnson administration's "heavy-handed, bureaucratic regulatory schemes" and policy proposals that would give the federal government "wide, sweeping new regulatory powers over the mutual fund industry, which powers would be tantamount to price fixing."

Depending on a reader's interpretation, the letter could have been an expression of Nixon's views on regulating mutual funds or a veiled promise that if he were elected in November, he would see to it that these widely despised proposals were never made law, and that Nixon's election would put a friend and admirer of Wall Street in the White House.

On October 2, one of the recipients leaked the letter to the press, and it wasn't long before charges of conflict of interest—the ghost of Senator Smith's charges in 1961—were being raised both in the media and on the Senate floor, along with a host of other charges, some of which would ring eerily familiar in years to come.

Writing for the *Washington Post*, reporters Rowland Evans and Robert Novak revealed a number of curious connections in an article published October 20, 1968:

- Investors Diversified Services (IDS), a giant mutual fund holding company, was one of the largest of many that stood to gain from a reversal of Johnson administration policy such as Nixon was recommending;
- Until early 1968, Richard Nixon was a member of the IDS board of directors;
- Gadsby & Hannah, Chuck Colson's law firm, was the registered lobbyist for IDS;
- Yet both Nixon and Colson denied producing the Wall Street letter.

On the Senate floor, Thomas McIntyre of New Hampshire spoke for many Democrats when he accused Nixon flat out of buying votes. There were, he said, "secret promises which the Republican nominee for

President [has] made to certain campaign contributors on Wall Street that, if elected, he would see to it that the securities laws which were enacted for the protection of small investors would not be enforced."

Though the letter bore Nixon's signature, Nixon campaign headquarters denied the candidate's advisors had been involved once the controversy began to swirl. They explained it had been produced by a key issues committee operating independently. It was the *Wall Street Journal* that first broke the story, saying Colson had written the letter. Colson insisted, "I am not the author."

Senator McIntyre considered these tactics par for the course from Colson. "I have high regard for his legal abilities," he admitted. But he went on to recall meetings with Colson as a mutual fund lobbyist who "was often in my office with all sorts of ingenious proposals on behalf of his clients to legitimize the undue extraction of money from widows, orphans, and others who are sometimes the beneficiaries of hastily considered estate-planning relying upon mutual fund shares. Fortunately for the public, all of these proposals were rejected by the committee [Senate Committee on Banking and Currency]."

Warming to his subject, Senator McIntyre spoke for many in Congress who were suspicious of Nixon's motives and methods—and this with Johnson still in the White House, Vice President Hubert Humphrey on the stump for the Democrats, and the '68 election a month in the future:

> And so the pattern continues. Mr. Nixon wrote a secret
> letter. When the secret letter was made public, Mr. Nixon
> denied that he had written the letter. He said it was written
> by a committee. The committee had a secret counsel. When
> the secret counsel was made public, the counsel denied that
> he had written the letter. And so it goes.
>
> Once again, the Nixon camp is busily engaged in the
> denials, coverups, and other signs of guilt over getting
> caught with a hand in the cookie jar. The Nixon-Wall Street
> affair is just one more reason why Mr. Nixon should work
> up his courage and agree to meet his opponent in open,
> public debate . . . [T]he last time that Mr. Nixon engaged in

> open, public debate with his opponent and permitted the
> American people to learn what his position on the issues
> was, he lost. The lesson of the past is clear to me. Perhaps it
> is all too clear to Mr. Nixon's staff as well.

Accustomed as he was to political scrapping, Colson was startled to see the controversy go public and read his name in the *Washington Post* and *Wall Street Journal*. He had no interest in personal notoriety, and much preferred working behind the scenes. Before long the flap died down and the media turned to other aspects of the election. In the end, a nation weary of the conflict in Vietnam and optimistic about Nixon's evident stability and sense of purpose chose him over Vice President Humphrey.

Chuck and Patty spent election eve in the ballroom of the Waldorf Astoria Hotel in New York, where hundreds of Nixon's friends, campaign operatives, and contributors assembled to watch the returns. Excitement built through the night as the popular vote went first one way and then the other. In the Electoral College, however, Nixon began pulling away, and when the night was over he had won with 301 electoral votes and a popular plurality of half a million.

The elegant Waldorf ballroom rang with music, applause, and shouts of excitement and triumph as a Nixon victory became probable, and then inevitable. When the victorious candidate appeared, the sound became a roar—eight years of frustration at being on the outside looking in relieved with joyful abandon.

After the election Colson returned to Gadsby & Hannah. On one hand, the future had never been brighter. The whole time he'd been in Washington there had been a Democrat in the White House. As effective as Colson was in the past, he could surely do even more for his clients in the future when the president would be not only a Republican but a man Colson had known personally for more than a decade.

But on the other hand, practicing law seemed pretty tame after serving as a member of the president-elect's inner circle. That's where the real power was going to be, and Colson well knew it.

It wasn't long before Chuck Colson's Massachusetts friends came calling with job offers in the new administration. Former Massachusetts

Governor John Volpe was named secretary of transportation and tendered an offer to work in his department. Elliot Richardson, Nixon's new undersecretary of state, wanted to make his friend Colson assistant secretary of state for congressional relations.

Still uncertain about what he wanted, Chuck indicated an interest in the State Department position. Though he then began undergoing the security checks that would clear him for jobs at the highest level of government, he delayed his formal acceptance of the assistant secretary offer because he was waiting for what he characterized as "the one call, the one telling me that the *president* needed *me*."

He continued working informally with the Nixon staff through the first half of 1969, when presidential counselor Bryce Harlow would call him in occasionally for specific consultations. At last, near the end of the administration's first year, the summons Colson had been hoping for came through.

Prompted in part by Harlow's recommendation, Nixon offered Chuck Colson the job of a lifetime: one of four special counsels to the president. The other three were Clark Mollehoff, a former investigative reporter; Harry Dent, former aide to Senator Strom Thurmond of South Carolina; and Nixon's old campaign strategist from his days as a California congressman, Murray Chotiner. Mollenhoff's job was to ferret out wrongdoing in the federal bureaucracy; Chotiner and Dent were the president's political advisors; and Colson's area of responsibility was to be the presidential liaison between outside interest groups—conservationists, citizens organizations, labor unions, and so forth—and inside policy makers.

Colson's only hesitation about taking the job was the dramatic pay cut it would require. His income from the law firm was now approaching $200,000 per year. The White House position paid $36,000. Though he could supplement his income with an annuity, he would have to put his investments in a blind trust.

In the end, the opportunity was simply too exciting and too much an honor to decline. To no one's surprise at Gadsby & Hannah, Colson announced his decision to leave the firm and join the White House staff. On November 1, 1969, the partners sent out engraved cards to their clients announcing, "Charles Wendell Colson has withdrawn from the firm to serve as special counsel to the President."

And on November 3, 1969, a few days ahead of his official appointment, Charles Colson reported for his first day of work in the sun-splashed Oval Office of the president of the United States.

Into the Deep End

CHAPTER 5

By the time of his first official day of work on November 6, a Thursday, Colson was already deeply immersed in White House operations. He actually moved in to his office on Monday; had his preemployment physical on Tuesday; and at 10 A.M. Wednesday he attended his first White House staff meeting in the Roosevelt Room of the West Wing.

During a news conference on November 6, President Nixon's press secretary, Ron Ziegler, was asked exactly what Colson would do. "He will be providing legal counsel and so forth . . . Beyond that, I believe that, consistent with the way I have observed the way Bob [Haldeman] works with his staff, he will be, I am sure, assigning special projects beyond legal matters to Mr. Colson."

Another question was whether Colson, clearly one of the most well-connected lobbyists in Washington, was a lobbyist: "Had Colson engaged in any lobbying activities in the past?"

"I'm not aware that he did engage in lobbying activities," the press secretary replied.

Like the other men with the title Special Counsel to the President—Murray Chotiner, Harry Dent, and Clark Mollenhoff—Charles Colson reported to the president's chief of staff, Harry R. "Bob" Haldeman. Haldeman was a former California advertising executive with the J. Walter Thompson firm, and his father, also in the advertising business, had been a contributor to Nixon during his congressional days. It was Haldeman who got assignments for the special counsels from the president, then passed them along to the right man based on the nature of the project.

Chotiner, who by this time had worked twenty-three years off and on for Nixon, handled political matters involving states in the far west, midwest, and northeast. (His appointment actually came after the other three, on January 13. Despite his long history with Nixon, Chotiner had stayed out of the spotlight ever since questions of influence peddling had been raised by a Senate investigation in 1956.) Dent took care of political projects in nineteen southern and southeastern states. Mollenhoff was in charge of digging up information on past, present, or prospective opponents of the administration. And Colson described his job as "the president's liaison with the outside world," a broker between outside interest groups and lobbyists and inside administration policy makers.

After a whirlwind first week, Colson spent Saturday, November 8 in his office doing background reading and getting organized. His legal training prompted him to gain command of the politics and personalities of his new assignment as soon as possible. He also wrote letters to key government figures who had been instrumental in garnering him the job offer at the Department of State: Rogers C. B. Morton, chairman of the Republican National Committee; Pennsylvania Senator Hugh Scott, minority leader; and House Minority Leader Gerald Ford of Michigan. In closing his letter to Ford, Colson said, "I hope that whether it is here or elsewhere that I will continue to enjoy your confidence and friendship over the years."

Two Saturdays later, Colson sat down at his desk, picked up a yellow legal pad, and wrote at the top of the page, "Random notes about the 1st three weeks." These were historic times for a night school graduate of the George Washington College of Law, and he wanted to capture them while the memories were still fresh. On the eight pages that followed, the special counsel to the president outlined his assessment of the situation, identified goals that best served the administration, and sketched out plans for achieving them. His keen intellect, powers of observation, and understanding of human nature led him to a clear plan of action after only three weeks on the job. The rest of Nixon's team was still, for the most part, alarmingly unfocused after ten months.

The big problem in Colson's eyes was that the Nixon White House didn't know how to get things done; they had plenty of ideas but not enough people who knew how to command the apparatus of government to put them into action. The staff, Chuck observed, was "very bright, very young [he himself had just turned thirty-eight], and very efficient," but they had "practically no knowledge as to how to apply the broader powers of the government, i.e. how to get things done . . . " They were so focused on the executive branch that anything beyond the White House circle was "foreign" territory. There was, in other words, "practically no understanding of how to use the resources of government."

Presidential Liaison Bryce Harlow and Special Counselor Harry Dent were, Chuck thought, "the only two professionals on the staff in this regard." In other words, they knew how the Washington political system worked, while the rest were outsiders.

Colson saw how this lack of political savvy could jeopardize Nixon administration policies during a meeting in the Roosevelt Room between members of White House staff and a group of cabinet officials over a bill pending in Congress that would increase size and weight limitations of trucks. The cabinet representatives "attempted to box the White House into taking a position in support" of the legislation, though it was at odds with the president's policy.

The room was surprised when Colson "outlined the only acceptable compromise and instructed D.O.T. to go back, rewrite the bill, and bring it back to us." This quickly became Colson's pattern, and a successful one: listen to all sides, insist that the legislation conform with Nixon's position, and engineer a compromise reasonably consistent with the administration line. In these first three weeks he had already brokered compromises in meetings with the National Association of Women's Clubs and the American Automobile Association.

Chuck had also met several times to discuss strategy for bolstering public support of the administration's position on Vietnam. In a series of confidential meetings and phone calls, Colson and others on the White House team labored to get veterans groups fired up and vocal in their endorsement. But at the same time they had to keep the White House connection secret; if the media knew the impetus for the support came from the administration and not the veterans themselves, the impact would be blunted and Nixon's political enemies would have one more thing to hold against him.

Furthermore, Colson was at the heart of clandestine discussions with Texas billionaire H. Ross Perot, who had offered the Republican Party ten million dollars that could be funneled into administration coffers through a patriotic organization to be known as United We Stand—Tell It To Hanoi. Colson feared that so much money would give Perot too much power; Perot, in Colson's estimation, was looking for "fame, respectability, and access to [Nixon]."

The lawyer in Colson made him instantly wary of Perot's offer. The administration had noble goals, and while confidential deals were a fixture of politics, this one smelled fishy and Colson wanted nothing to do with it. Branding it as a "slush fund," Colson vetoed Perot's contribution.

(Perot, whom Colson would later characterize as one of the most colorful figures he met during his White House tenure, eventually convinced the president and his advisor Alexander Butterfield that he could get American prisoners of war home from Vietnam. He offered to donate thirty million dollars to support pro-Nixon interest groups. Bob Haldeman assigned Colson to help set it up. Chuck made all the arrangements, but Perot kept stalling on the money, though for a private citizen he enjoyed a rare level of access to the president while the plans were being completed. Finally Colson had enough. Perot appeared unexpectedly outside his office one afternoon while he was changing for a white tie dinner at the White House. Colson invited Perot in and, standing in his underwear, told him to put up the money or forget about the whole thing. Perot left, and Colson never saw him again.)

Continuing with the notes about his first impressions on the job, Colson recorded his thoughts on Nixon. He had admired him ever since their first meeting during the 1956 campaign season, and he admired him even more after his reemergence from defeat and humiliation following the 1962 California disaster, gradually returning to power and, finally, hauling the Republican Party out of the ashes of their 1964 defeat to victory and into the Oval Office four years later. Nixon as president was confident, assured, a man in charge of his destiny who took "obvious pleasure with what he is doing."

Taking stock of his own position, Colson found it remarkable that there was so much high level work going on that he was so deeply involved in. There was no trial period or supervised training. He had jumped into the deep end of national affairs and loved every minute of it. He was "very impressed by the way in which the White House staff have very quickly looked to me as a source of power because of my relationship with outside groups and my relationship with H. R. H[aldeman] and therefore my access to the president. Other things to be noted relate to . . . the great way in which everyone has accepted my knowledge of government. Also interesting, . . . I survived any adverse publicity regarding my background as a so-called lobbyist and also my involvement in the Securities letter."

Somehow in all the whirlwind of activity, Chuck carved out a few minutes to write an important note to his father. Wendell Colson was seventy that year, and his son thought such a birthday milestone merited more than a card. Chuck was proud of his father, and felt sure he would never have made it to the White House without his father's example to inspire him. His handwritten message lifted the curtain to reveal, however briefly, something of the new presidential counsel's innermost feelings at so important a turning point in his own life:

"I am not sure what measures a man's success—certainly not money or any other material things. I think I will feel I am a success if I can provide the same opportunity and good example for my sons as you have provided me.

"The common sense, determination and Christian ethic that has been so much of your life, I hope will guide me. I am sure had you not fought your way through to obtain an education, I would not have had either the opportunity or will to do so. And I am sure I wouldn't be sitting here today . . . "

Sitting here today—the grandson of immigrants advising the president of the United States.

Continuing to take the measure of his new situation, Colson made a quick but thorough study of the president's relationships with outside groups and how best to improve them. Within a few days, he had prepared a memo for Haldeman outlining the types of organizations he thought the White House should cultivate relationships with:

(1) Conservationist groups
    National Resources Council
    Audubon Society
    National Wildlife Federation
    Conservation groups—good PR
(2) Rural affairs groups
    National Cattlemen's Association & etc.
(3) Trade groups
(4) Vietnam activities
    support of the silent majority endorsement of administration policies
(5) Latin American Council
(6) Trucking legislation
    heavier trucks, billboards, etc.

Colson's position was a new one on the White House staff, and the details of his responsibilities and the working chain of command were developed on the fly. Up until Colson was hired, presidential administrations had always kept up with outside interest groups informally, assigning several members of the staff to deal with a handful of groups each in addition to their regular duties. As reporter Dom Bonafede wrote in the *National Journal,* "President Nixon, recognizing the impact which the private sector can have on public policy, has formalized the liaison office."

Another benefit Chuck and the other special counselors brought to the White House was political experience and intuition. One executive branch official observed that before the special counselors were added to the president's staff, "too many things were falling between the cracks. We needed some good tough political handymen to help the advertising crowd who came in with the president, and now we have them."

As an Ivy League graduate and lifelong New Englander, Colson was certainly not cut from the same cloth as Nixon's California team, a number of whom made their connection to the White House through the network of West Coast advertising professionals that led through Bob Haldeman. They were California conservatives who looked upon Colson's Eastern Establishment pedigree with suspicion.

Colson also locked horns early on with John Mitchell, manager of Nixon's 1968 campaign and newly appointed attorney general. Mitchell and Nixon had been working together since their New York law firms merged in 1967. Nixon admired Mitchell's strategic and political prowess, but Colson questioned his judgment and had what he characterized as a "run-in" with him during the '68 campaign.

Comfortable with Nixon's advantage over Humphrey in the closing months of the campaign, Mitchell had insisted that the Nixon team lay low, not make any mistakes, and ride out their lead. Colson watched with alarm, and argued with Mitchell in vain as the lead steadily shrank over the summer and fall until it was statistically insignificant. Colson was convinced that Mitchell's poor judgment had almost cost the Republicans the White House.

During an interview with the *Boston Globe* soon after joining the Nixon White House, Colson was asked by a reporter what he thought about Mitchell's strategy for nominating Supreme Court justices.

Colson was too politically astute to say what he really thought.

The Supreme Court drama had been front-page news during the fall. Justice Abe Fortas had retired under pressure after it was revealed he had accepted a retainer from a foundation whose chief benefactor was under federal indictment. Though this happened before Colson's formal appointment, he was advising Nixon on the nomination of Fortas's successor. Attorney General Mitchell insisted to Nixon that his nominee to fill the vacancy should be from the South, and so Nixon chose Clement F. Haynsworth of South Carolina.

Mitchell was convinced that Haynsworth was a shoo-in, though Bryce Harlow and others argued Nixon should withdraw the nomination because Haynsworth would never be confirmed; he was too conservative.

But Mitchell insisted on his man, and Haynsworth went down in a very public defeat.

Furious, Nixon nominated G. Harrold Carswell of Florida; Carswell was rejected as well. Finally Nixon had to abandon his Southern strategy and tapped Harry A. Blackmun of Minnesota, who was swiftly confirmed.

Colson thought it was clear that Mitchell's advice had been bad for the president even as Chuck had been working behind the scenes arguing that the president had constitutional authority to "appoint" Supreme Court justices, and that it wasn't the Senate's place to block such an appointment.

In reply to the reporter's question, Colson said he had "no comment" on Mitchell's Supreme Court strategy. When Chuck saw his interview in the paper the next morning with the headline, "Mitchell No Hero: Colson," he expected to be fired on the spot. No one crossed the attorney general in private, much less in the *Boston Globe*, and survived; one word to the president and the offender was out the door. But, as Colson later speculated, "Perhaps Mitchell was so taken aback by my brashness, which he didn't know was unintentional, that he failed to call Nixon to have me unceremoniously dumped out onto Pennsylvania Avenue."

A larger crisis early in the Nixon presidency revealed Chuck Colson's intellect and operating methods on several levels.

In the closing days of the Johnson administration, a presidential commission recommended that the Post Office Department, in existence since 1789, be abolished. The plan was to replace it with a semiautonomous agency that would be more efficient, more cost-effective, and less susceptible to political patronage.

As the proposal for a new United States Postal Service was being considered, parties with the biggest stake in the outcome jockeyed for position: the labor unions representing post office workers, the postmaster general, and the office of the president, which faced a huge political liability should either the general public or the unions be unhappy with the outcome.

On top of all the proposed changes and the natural animosity between management and labor, the situation was further complicated by the fact that the president of the largest union, the National Association of Letter Carriers, James H. Rademacher, and Postmaster General Winton M. Blount despised each other.

Colson thought Rademacher was bending over backwards to help the administration, even to the point of alienating the union's executive council. Blount, on the other hand, seemed rude, inflexible, and argumentative in Colson's view, an impediment to a harmonious partnership.

Colson well knew the political fallout the president would face if postal reform was abandoned, or if implementation of it was a disaster. By December 1969, postal reform appeared all but dead. The postmaster general had never even invited the union president to his office to discuss the matter. Determined to break the impasse, Colson asked Postmaster General Blount for permission to contact Rademacher directly. After several conversations that ultimately included John Erlichman, Bryce Harlow, and the president himself, Colson got the permission he wanted and went to work.

Colson's union experience, legal knowledge, persuasive powers, confident manner, and courtesy toward Rademacher soon won him over. He invited the union leader for lunch at the White House to persuade him to agree to the administration's position on employee benefits and a host of other issues under the new Postal Service. On December 17, he arranged for Rademacher to meet with Nixon personally in the Oval Office.

By early 1970, the postal union had agreed to the reorganization of the Post Office in exchange for a pay raise and a new employee benefits package. Then, with negotiations at a critical point, Blount backed away from his earlier promise on employee benefits. It was Colson who kept Rademacher from abandoning the talks, and Colson who gathered Erlichman, Harlow, and others to convince Blount he had to honor his previous commitment.

As a result of Colson's tireless mediation efforts, Blount and Rademacher spent most of the week together leading up to the House committee vote on legislation authorizing the new postal system. A vote the previous October deadlocked 13–13. This time the vote was 17–6 in favor. "The only difference," Colson observed, "was Rademacher's support"—support that was a result of Chuck Colson's political savvy and negotiating skill. After the vote, President Nixon called to thank Rademacher for his cooperation. There was no word from Blount.

Then in a surprise move, the full Congress failed to act on the legislation. Confused and suspicious of all the changes the new organization would mean, postal workers staged a strike. Rademacher called Colson and told him the administration had to meet with union representatives to forestall a disaster at the Post Office Department. But Blount had already told Colson he would not talk with the union until all the strikers were back at work. Rademacher tried to call Blount directly, but the postmaster general refused to take his calls.

Rademacher then contacted Colson to say the executive council had voted to call a national strike. The union chief convened a press conference in Washington to announce the strike, but minutes before it began, Secretary of Labor George Shultz called him and promised the government would pass the legislation. At his press conference then, instead of announcing a strike, Rademacher asked the workers who had already walked out to return to work. In the days immediately following, Colson stayed close to Rademacher, thanking him for his pro-administration stand and reinforcing his decision.

The nation's postal workers went out on strike March 18, 1970, but returned to their jobs a week later with the promise of a six percent pay increase.

In an interview released by the Knight Newspapers Syndicate, Rademacher explained the outcome from his perspective: "Colson was responsible for breaking the stalemate. He went over Postmaster General Blount's head to do it. He is probably the most effective member of the President's staff."

The postmaster general blamed Colson and his cozy relationship with Rademacher for the strike, denying he had given approval for Colson to negotiate directly with the union. The union president was loyal to Nixon to the point of losing control of his executive council; even so, Nixon saw him after the House committee vote as a liability. Once the strike was settled, President Nixon ordered Haldeman to sever all ties between the administration and Rademacher.

Haldeman assigned the task to Colson, who not only thought Blount was looking for a scapegoat—Colson himself—to blame for the strike, but who couldn't understand why someone who had served the administration so selflessly and at such personal cost as Rademacher had done should now be cast adrift.

Colson wrote a four-page memo in longhand outlining his position and reviewing the facts. Because of the sensitive egos, mercurial temperaments, and politically sensitive information involved, he decided he couldn't even risk dictating a letter to his secretary. He made it clear that he suspected Blount was out to get him. He also delicately questioned the decision to turn against Rademacher after he had risked so much to defend the White House position. But in the end, reverting to cold political calculation, he agreed:

"I only want to do what is best for the President. If it's important to the President, I'll cut Rademacher off completely, and, by the way, I agree that at this point, I have to. It's the right strategy."

And elsewhere in the memo: "I was a captain in the Marine Corps once and I still know how to say 'Yes Sir' once a decision is reached."

It was with more than a touch of irony that Colson described his role in the postal crisis to an interviewer from the *National Journal*: "It is a perfect illustration of what this office is all about."

The Levers of Power

CHAPTER 6

Chuck Colson was fast acquiring the reputation as the guy close to the president who could get things done. This reputation was enhanced by an extraordinary effort that began with a very ordinary Oval Office visit he had arranged. On June 22, 1970, the *New York Times* ran a story that included Colson's recollection of "a meeting between the President and a group of Catholic educators who had trouble seeing him. Mr. Nixon became so interested in their recital of the difficulties of parochial schools, Mr. Colson said, 'that he hauled out a piece of paper, named a commission to study the problem, and decided to double the amount of funding for library assistance.'"

But that was only the tip of the iceberg. The whole story revealed how adroit Colson had become at achieving results in the executive branch after only a short time on staff; and it showed how much Nixon longed for a close ally he could depend on to produce results, not excuses.

On a Friday morning, a group of Catholic school teachers and administrators met with President Nixon to remind him of his campaign promise to form a commission to help support parochial education. In fact, Nixon hadn't forgotten the promise, and had asked for an executive order months before. But Attorney General Mitchell questioned the constitutionality of a government commission set up to help a religious organization. Teachers' unions would be dead set against it. Various presidential aides had dragged their feet and shuffled the request back and forth among them without taking any action.

At five o'clock that afternoon, the president summoned Colson to the Oval Office. "Chuck, I want a commission appointed *now*," Colson remembered him saying. "I've been thinking about what those men said this morning. I ordered it a year ago and no one pays any attention. You do it. Break all the _____ china in this building but have an order for me to sign on my desk Monday morning."

With his entire staff consisting of exactly one secretary, Joan Hall, and less than six months on the job, Colson set out with Marine Corps determination to give his commander in chief what he ordered. There was a strict and inviolable protocol that everything involving domestic policy had to run through John Erlichman's office, but Erlichman was out of town for the weekend. Bob Finch, the Secretary of Health, Education, and Welfare, was on vacation; his assistant found the file on forming the commission buried in a stack of paperwork.

Using old orders as a pattern, Colson drafted and dictated the new one to Joan, then began working the telephone. He reached Secretary Finch and got approval for the commission; he tracked down the budget director on the golf course and got the funding approved. Neither Erlichman nor his assistant returned Colson's calls, but he had what he needed. And on Monday morning, the president had what he wanted: an authorized and fully funded presidential commission on Catholic schools.

Both Mitchell and Erlichman were livid that Colson had done an end run around them, but Nixon was delighted. At last he had found somebody who wasn't afraid to "break all the _____ china" to accomplish what he wanted without questions or excuses.

Chuck Colson's stock rose rapidly in the White House. By the end of the summer his staff had grown from one secretary to four, plus two assistants, George Bell and Henry Cashen, and a part-time aide, Daniel Hofgren, who divided his time between Colson's office and negotiations on the Panama Canal treaty then under consideration.

There were other perks of power as well. Colson's office in the Executive Office Building on the White House grounds, 184 EOB, was immediately adjacent to the president's private working office—a telling assessment of his importance in a city where access to the president is the ultimate status symbol. He also enjoyed another benefit of the highest reaches of the Washington power structure: a shiny black government limousine to chauffeur him from his house to the White House every day, and anywhere else he wanted to go.

Describing his broadening role on the Nixon team, Colson said, "The President believes that the government doesn't use the resources of the private sector enough. Our office tries to make sure we have an input from the outside and sees that the President is not cloistered by the government apparatus. I get terribly peeved when I read that the President is isolated. I'm one of the people who sees he is not isolated."

There was hardly any such thing as a typical day for Charles Colson because his day revolved around the president's. But most days began with the arrival of a White House limousine at his front door about 7:20 A.M. Easing into the back seat, he picked up the daily White House briefing books waiting on the cushion beside him. In the half hour it took to go from the Virginia suburbs to Pennsylvania Avenue, he read through them in preparation for whatever meetings or events were scheduled that day. There was also a copy of the *Washington Post* for him to scan.

The car eased through the White House gates a little before 8 A.M., and Chuck walked straight to the Roosevelt Room, in the West Wing of the White House near the Oval Office. At 8 o'clock the daily senior staff meeting began, and ten or twelve of the president's most senior advisors began the process of coordinating the activities of the day. Over the next hour they ran down the president's schedule, discussed domestic and foreign news and politial affairs, and laid out their own responsibilties.

As soon as that meeting was over, Colson hurried next door to the Executive Office Building to chair a 9:15 meeting with his own team. (He would eventually have a staff of twelve, plus secretarial support.) He handed out assignments, listened to reports, and fine-tuned his schedule of appointments.

The rest of the day was a flurry of visitors, paperwork, decision-making, and a steady stream of special assignments from the president. Nixon would call Colson into his EOB private office, hand him something, and say "I want this handled." Everything else would then be shifted around to give Chuck time to take care of the president's personal request.

By the summer of 1970 Nixon was regularly giving Colson direct assignments, bypassing White House protocol and, in particular, cutting Bob Haldeman out of the loop. Though he denied it happened often, and denied it bothered him, Haldeman was furious at Colson's direct access. The president never intended it as an indictment against his chief of staff; it was just that when he wanted results fast, no questions asked, Colson was the man for the job.

A twelve-hour day was the norm; weekend days could be even longer. He and Patty had no private life to speak of. Chuck came home at night, the two of them had a cocktail, then dinner, then went to bed. Even on rare occasions when they went out, Colson carried a White House pager that kept him electronically tethered to the president, and the president frequently called him.

When a White House operator paged him, he was supposed to find a telephone and call in. This made for interesting situations, such as the time he and Patty were in a movie theater and the pager went off. Colson went to the manager's office and explained he needed the phone to call the White House. The manager thought he had a kook on his hands until Colson signaled the White House operator to call the manager. When the phone rang and the operator said, "This is the White House calling for Charles Colson," the manager not only turned over the phone, he stood guard in the hallway to make sure the call wasn't interrupted.

Chuck described those days as "grueling hard work, dizzying rounds of meetings, and mounds of opinion papers detailing the conflicting views of government agencies in policy questions . . . Each paper demanded an opinion, a careful recommendation, but some days there was scarcely time to do more than react. Pressures were unrelenting, days vanishing into night, passing by like wisps of smoke. I never once doubted that I could get the job done, whatever it was. It was just straight ahead, pushing and driving, the simple formula I had followed all my life."

Part of Colson's strategy in dealing with interest groups was convincing them that they had more at stake than whatever narrow issue had brought them to him in the first place. He encouraged them to look at other legislation and administration policies that helped them indirectly—proof that the Nixon administration had their best interests at heart even if he couldn't grant a specific request.

"The President has never refused to see a group which I've recommended," Colson boasted to the press. "Almost invariably he runs over the allotted time. He always asks a lot of questions and is a good listener . . . He enjoys it enormously."

After Nixon announced plans to establish the Environmental Protection Agency on July 9, 1970, Colson fielded requests for briefings from 150 different groups. By explaining the goals of the agency to them early in the process and asking for their opinions, he got their approval. He was the lightning rod for public reaction to administration policy, and devised ways to turn that reaction into political support.

When the National Association of Home Builders expressed concern about the shortage of mortgage money, Colson made sure they were heard, and explained what the administration was doing to help.

When 100,000 construction workers and longshoremen marched through New York City in support of Nixon's Vietnam policy, Colson recognized a signal opportunity. Antiwar protests were in the news almost every day, yet here was a huge number of blue-collar workers signaling their approval of the president's stance on the war. Despite opposition from the White House senior staff, Nixon allowed Colson to invite Peter Brennan, the president of the National Building & Construction Trades Council, and some union members to the White House. Two days later, a parade of hard-hatted workers marched into the Oval Office for a meeting that, in Colson's words, "signaled an unprecedented political alliance between a Republican President and organized labor."

Chuck also enjoyed keeping up with his old colleagues at Gadsby & Hannah. From their penthouse offices a block from the White House they represented many of the groups seeking presidential access through their former partner. In less than a year, Charles Colson had become one of the most powerful men in Washington.

For all his success, there were still times when Colson had his hand slapped. One day Chuck accepted a lunch invitation from Joseph Kraft, a syndicated columnist with liberal leanings and a big following in the press. Another White House staffer, a far-right conservative named Lyn Nofziger, saw them at the table together, and came over to criticize Colson for hobnobbing with such a "flaming liberal."

Colson thought Nofziger was putting on an act for Kraft's sake until he got back to the office and was ordered to Bob Haldeman's office. "If you want to stay around here, stay away from that _____!" Haldeman growled. Surprised but ever loyal, Colson agreed.

There were far more serious matters to deal with in the summer of 1970 than who was lunching with whom: the continuing agony of Vietnam, signs of a thaw in the long cold war with China, the power politics of midterm elections, and a growing hostility between the administration and the press. And Chuck Colson was in the middle of it all, one hand on the telephone and the other on the antacid dispenser that was always within reach atop the elegant polished desk in office 184 EOB.

The Vietnam War had cost President Lyndon Johnson his political legacy. During five years in office Johnson tripled the number of American soldiers on active duty in Southeast Asia and authorized the training and equipping of a half million native South Vietnamese soldiers by U.S. troops. Nixon was determined to avoid his predecessor's mistake, not only on account of the political cost but the human cost as well.

In a speech broadcast worldwide on November 3, 1969, Colson's first unofficial day at the White House, the president had said, "This week I will have to sign eighty-three letters to mothers, fathers, wives, and loved ones of men who have given their lives for America in Vietnam. It is very little satisfaction to me that this is only one-third as many letters as I signed the first week in office. There is nothing I want more than to see the day come when I do not have to write any of those letters."

Earlier in the same speech, he reassured his audience that they could rely on him to tell them the truth; that knowing the truth could help heal the violent fracture in American society the war had caused: "I believe that one of the reasons for the deep division about Vietnam is that many Americans have lost confidence in what their Government has told them about our policy. The American people cannot and should not be asked to support a policy which involves the overriding issues of war and peace unless they know the truth about that policy."

He knew, he said, that there was a "silent majority" of Americans who supported his administration in general and the war effort in particular. The "Silent Majority" quickly became both a household phrase and a topic of public debate over exactly who and how numerous it was.

By the spring of 1970, American B-52 bombers were attacking Communist enclaves and supply bases in Cambodia, and the president authorized a ground invasion with South Vietnamese soldiers trained and equipped by U.S. military advisors. Three days later American troops made up a second invasion wave.

Key officials in the State Department and the Pentagon opposed the action, which the *Boston Globe* later characterized as "primarily a Nixon-Kissinger affair." Nixon kept the early raids a secret even from the Senate, with military brass at the Pentagon submitting false reports. Nixon also claimed the leader of Cambodia, Prince Norodom Sihanouk, agreed to the incursion, a statement the prince hotly disputed.

When the story of the Cambodian raids broke, college campuses across the country erupted in protest. The evening of May 4, 1970, Colson had been working late and took a dinner break in the White House staff mess—a small oak-paneled dining room for senior staffers known, as all White House dining facilities were, by the traditional military term for any food service, from field chow to white-tie banquet.

There was a television on in the corner. Before Colson's food came to the table, the first reports flashed on of a confrontation between National Guard troops and protesters at Kent State University in northeastern Ohio. Students demonstrating against the Cambodian incursion had apparently been shot by inexperienced guardsmen, who panicked and opened fire on campus. Chuck stared in shock and disbelief at the images of soldiers in battle dress, clouds of tear gas, and students on the ground bleeding.

No one in the staff mess took a bite, said a word, or moved. Even the red-jacketed dining stewards stood rooted in place. All eyes were on the television as the grisly details came to light: four students dead, killed by unidentified National Guard riflemen; eleven wounded. The father of a dead co-ed, his face contorted with outrage and sorrow, shouted, "The president is to blame!"

Colson's first reaction was to defend the president in his own mind. Then suddenly he asked himself what he would think if it had been his daughter, Emily, who was killed. Chuck thought to himself that if the man's reaction was even partly fair, then he was responsible too. He had helped Nixon make the Cambodia decision. "For one awful instant," Colson later revealed, he felt the grieving father "was right in that room, that his tear-filled eyes were looking straight into mine, and I felt unclean. I skipped dinner."

While the Kent State tragedy touched Colson as a father and a man of some compassion, it taught him that he couldn't afford to invest emotionally in decisions affecting people's lives. It was stark proof that his advice to the president was literally a matter of life or death. It was easy to consider decisions in the abstract, but far different to live with the consequences that were all too real and immediate. When he heard of prisoners captured in Vietnam, he had visions of men in bamboo cages infested with rats and spiders. They were, he said, "daytime nightmares, real as life." The only solution was to put emotion and the personal costs aside and deal strictly with the numbers.

Kent State threw the country into turmoil. More campus protests followed nationwide, including some by faculty members. Two black students at Jackson State in Mississippi were shot dead by state police. Cabinet secretaries leaked stories to the press saying they didn't agree with Nixon's decision; Walter Hickel, Secretary of the Interior, published a letter critical of the president (for which Nixon praised him in public and vowed to have him fired in private). The stock market tumbled. Four senators introduced legislation to cut off all funding for the war. There were even murmurs in the halls of the Capitol that this was an impeachable offense.

On his way to another weekend at the office on Saturday, May 9, Colson found his limousine stopped by police in riot gear at Nineteenth and E Streets. One hundred and fifty thousand students had gathered in Washington to stage a protest and were swarming around the Capitol and the White House. Hundreds of Washington D.C. buses were parked end to end encircling the White House in a protective blockade. Colson's big Cadillac picked up a police escort and proceeded through the cordon of buses onto the White House grounds.

In the basement of the Executive Office Building was a battalion of 82nd Airborne troops in battle fatigues prepared to fend off the crowd if ordered. To Colson it was a reminder of what he had seen "twice before in Central American countries: uniformed troops guarding the palace against its enemies." Looking out an upstairs window at an ocean of students and their supporters, Colson concluded, "Whatever was right or wrong in our foreign policy was irrelevant if moral leadership could not be regained."

Later in the afternoon the protesters moved forward. Police waded into the crowd with clubs flying. Colson heard the thunk of tear gas canisters being fired, then soon felt the tingle on his skin and burning in his eyes that even a whiff of the chemical agent CN (alpha-chloroacetophenone) produced as it seeped into the building. The students quickly dispersed and the military troops sitting on the marble floor of the EOB basement were never mobilized.

Colson wasted no time shoring up the president's battered image. True, Nixon had deceived the country with the Cambodian incursion, but it was also true that the bombing and ground action destroyed vast reserves of Communist supplies. In the midst of the crisis, Colson had decided the right foreign policy decision was worthless without a moral foundation. But once the heat was off, he reverted to the increasingly common mindset among Nixon's inner circle that the ends justify the means.

Working his contacts, Colson helped organize a massive show of support for Nixon's war policy. At his suggestion, civic organizations, interest groups, and influential Republicans showered the White House with letters and telegrams hailing the commander in chief as a great patriot and a visionary leader. The president's public support took a strong swing upward.

Chuck paid special attention to the media. Public relations had been a problem for Nixon almost as long as he had been in the public eye. Nixon and the press profoundly disliked each other, as history had recorded—among other times—in the aftermath of the 1962 California governor's race, when the defeated candidate promised reporters they wouldn't have Nixon to kick around anymore. It was part of Colson's job to keep the lines of communication open and present the president in a positive light.

The Vietnam protests in May 1970 had a long-term effect on Colson's role as media peacekeeper that remained in the background for a time, almost subliminal. It was a significant milestone on the way to what Colson saw as an "us against them" mentality. Nixon despised the media, and the feeling was mutual. The president made Vice President Spiro Agnew his agent for criticizing what he felt was biased, anti-administration reporting. While conservatives and Republicans loved Agnew's public assault, it made reporters and editors hammer all the harder on Nixon and his policies. This news offensive made the administration still more evasive and adversarial, further escalating the us-versus-them tension.

As in other areas of the administration, Colson thought the biggest challenge in foreign policy was that the staff didn't know how to take full advantage of the tools and the power they had available. After a meeting with Henry Kissinger covering Strategic Arms Limitation Talks (SALT), Russian disarmament, and a host of other issues, Colson wrote in his notes, "Accomplishments have been unspectacular pragmatic systematic analysis. Never an effort to create a moral victory . . . Biggest problem, the bureaucracy . . . weakness . . . lack of loyalists."

In spite of his growing clout in the Nixon White House, Chuck Colson remained very much behind the scenes until a shakeup in the administration staff ahead of the 1970 midterm elections. Several senior aides resigned in protest over the secret Cambodia bombing. Others were shuffled around to answer the charge that Nixon's closest advisors were too isolated from political reality and too much alike.

Special Counsel to the President Clark Mollenhoff resigned and went back to the newspaper business. Two cabinet secretaries moved into White House jobs: Robert Finch from Health, Education and Welfare, and George Shultz from Labor. An article in the *New York Times* for June 22, 1970, described Colson as the "most obscure" of the president's three remaining special counsels, who as a group were characterized by an unnamed White House source as "the original backroom boys, the operators and the brokers, the guys who fix things when they break down and do the dirty work when it's necessary."

Colson, the *Times* reported, "came to a staff that was suffering badly from political inexperience, and he was promptly ordered to begin manipulating the levers of political power." Colson was the mediator and broker. His role was in contrast to longtime Nixon confidante Murray Chotiner who, according to the reporter, "friends describe as 'the perfect political technician' and enemies condemn as 'the complete political hatchetman.'"

But Chuck Colson had a hard edge of his own, even if it was hidden from public view for the most part. On August 25, a front page headline in the *Washington Post* announced, "Nixon Aide Hits Curbs On Textiles." The administration had recently agreed to import quotas on textiles and affirmed support for existing quotas on imported oil. In a San Francisco speech, Hendrik Houthakker, a member of the Council of Economic Advisors and identified as one of the president's "top economic advisors," revealed that the endorsement of a textile quota was made reluctantly in the hopes of negotiating voluntary curbs on textiles with manufacturers in the Far East.

Said Houthakker in his speech, "The quota provisions inserted into the president's trade bill are essentially a know-nothing approach to the delicate problems of international domestic relations. They would sell the American consumer, the American farmer, and the American export manufacturer down the river."

The *Post* observed, "It was not clear what impact the CEA member's all-out attack on import quotas will have within the administration or on Capitol Hill."

The impact on the president's personal and political image was certainly clear to Colson, and he made his position plain in a confidential memorandum to Bob Haldeman the same day headed *EYES ONLY*:

> Not only does this reflect gross insubordination as far as
> the President is concerned but it is politically devastating.
> I would think that we could easily write off a couple of

Senate seats if the President's commitments with respect to
textiles and oil are undercut this way. What is really bad is
that it makes the President appear to be insincere.

I don't know how long we are going to allow guys like
this to run off and pitch their own line with complete disregard for the President's decision and welfare. It seems to me
that Houthakker should be fired summarily . . . One of
these days if we make an example of someone we may be
able to put an end to this kind of independent frolic.

This was the sort of hard-hitting analysis and direct action Bob
Haldeman knew the White House organization needed. More and more,
Colson's ability to cut to the heart of an issue and devise a clear plan of
action impressed the president's chief of staff, even though Colson's special access to Nixon continued to annoy him. The last week in September,
1970, Haldeman decided Colson was the man to take on a special new
assignment.

For over a month, Haldeman had been trying to collect quotations
from Democratic hopefuls likely to oppose Nixon in 1972, in order to use
their own words against them if they changed position on an issue or made
a statement that could be couched as inflammatory or controversial. The
former ad executive saw the PR power of tripping up would-be candidates
without having to attack them head-on.

Republican political operatives identified Senators Hubert Humphrey
(running to regain his seat in Minnesota after his 1968 presidential defeat),
Edmund Muskie (Maine), Ted Kennedy (Massachusetts), George
McGovern (South Dakota), and Walter Mondale (Minnesota) as the short
list of presidential prospects for the opposition. Haldeman had his game
plan ready to go, but he couldn't get anybody to carry it through.

In a confidential White House memo to Colson, Haldeman vented his
frustration:

So far, this effort has labored mightily and hasn't even
given birth to a mouse yet. We have pages and pages of
trivia—nothing organized—stuff coming from all different

sources, nobody sorting it out, nobody determining what is useable and what isn't, nobody looking with a cold, clear eye at evaluating the stuff . . .

Having failed at this venture otherwise, I am now asking you to take overall control of it and get it done . . .
[I hope] that you can force the [Republican] National Committee and our other sources to get off their tails and get going on this thing so that we can, for once, do something effective and in time.

Our need is not for reports, it is for results . . . I am sorry to pile this on top of all the other things you're supposed to be tending to this week, but it is vitally important that it get done and, so far, it hasn't been.

As the election of 1970 entered its final stages, Colson's star continued its rise. Still a year shy of 40, the special counsel was not only in charge of executing a crucial component of the campaign; he was already plotting how best to position Nixon for a reelection victory more than two years in the future by hammering his prospective opponents now. Cambodia was behind them, secret disarmament talks with the Russians were promising, American troop strength in Vietnam was decreasing, and the economy at home was strong. Richard Nixon was in a solid position, and Chuck Colson was determined to keep him there.

Lightning Rod

CHAPTER 7

Colson lost no time getting to work on the campaign ads Haldeman considered so important. Valuable weeks had already been wasted by well-meaning but ineffective bureaucrats. In a process that had become his standard procedure, Colson assembled the available information, developed a strategy, and had the project rolling along within a week.

Less than three weeks after Haldeman handed off the assignment, Chuck Colson had supervised preparation of layouts, body copy, a compilation of quotes and other information to use in preparing the final text, and a media plan along with minimum budget recommendations.

"Each one in each state has to be different, both as to format and text," Colson explained in a memo to Haldeman on October 12, 1970. "They will be tailored to the amount of peacenik, left wing money that has gone into the state (and been reported) as well as the kinds of statements that the individual has made. Where neither situation is useful, we'll try to hang them with statements of other extremists."

The resulting ads didn't cost any prospective presidential contenders their midterm victories, but they did raise plenty of eyebrows, especially in the media. Though there was a front organization—official sponsors of the ads, tying the senators in with radicals and extremists—the ads were widely recognized as a Nixon operation. Reporters and seething Democrats pointed both at Colson and Chotiner; both strenuously denied any involvement. The objections became so strident that two of the three organizations that signed the ads disavowed their connections with them.

Colson had more success in torpedoing the reelection of Senator Joseph Tydings of Massachusetts. Colson supplied a *Life* magazine reporter with information implicating the senator in a plan to use his influence to get a federal contract for a company he held stock in. After the election, the government released a statement that the allegation was untrue. Pressed for a reaction, Colson's only words to the media were, "No comment."

Colson continued to insist that publicity made his job harder; he liked manipulating the limelight but took no pleasure standing in it. He was happy to be the presidential counselor the *Boston Globe* characterized as a "shadowy figure who shuns publicity."

That made matters all the easier when projects didn't turn out the way he wanted. The previous spring during the president's run-in with Congress on the Carswell nomination to the Supreme Court, Colson provided the president with notes for a letter to Republican Senator William Saxbe (Ohio). Again the issue was the president's frustration with implementing his programs, policies, and preferences; again Chuck Colson was the one who articulated the president's position and pulled together the counteroffensive:

"What is centrally at issue in this nomination is the constitutional responsibility of the President to appoint members of the Court—and whether this responsibility can be frustrated by those who wish to substitute their own philosophy or their own subjective judgment for that of the one person entrusted by the Constitution with the power of appointment."

James Reston, the influential columnist for the *New York Times,* declared the letter was "full of bad history and bad law." The Carswell nomination was resoundingly defeated, and Colson's position was widely disparaged—though never by Nixon.

In his hard-hitting special counsel, Nixon had a fiercely loyal ally who could break operational logjams everybody else just sat and stared at. He could get the president's policies enacted. He could make Republicans toe the line and put Democrats on the defensive. He was fearless when it came to breaking china if that's what it took to carry out the president's directives. Colson's "instinct for the political jugular and his ability to get things done," Nixon later wrote, "made him a lightning rod for my own frustration at the timidity of most Republicans in responding to attacks from Democrats and the media. When I complained to Colson I felt confident that something would be done, and I was rarely disappointed."

The results of the 1970 elections were not particularly encouraging for a president already jockeying for position in his own race two years down the road. The Republicans had a net loss of nine seats in the House, gained one in the Senate, and gave up eleven governorships. Chuck Colson had worked hard to persuade pollster Lou Harris to time the release of his opinion polls to the Republicans' advantage, and even convinced him to revise the way results were stated in order to make Nixon appear more popular. Still he reported to Haldeman that Harris was "an arrogant egoist of the first order" and that he would never "show us as favorably as Gallup."

Colson consoled the president by insisting his support had kept the Republican losses from being even more severe. "The results, had you not campaigned, would have been far worse," he said in a memo just after election day. Even so, Chuck knew President Nixon's public image needed burnishing. His campaign tactics had come off as harsh and unfair—and this only a few months after the uproar over Cambodia. To head off Senator Muskie or any of the other likely '72 presidential opponents, the public Nixon persona had to be improved.

As soon as he could after the election, President Nixon held a confidential summit meeting of his closest advisors at his home in Key Biscayne, Florida. Colson was there, along with Haldeman, Erlichman, and Mitchell, plus Donald Rumsfeld, Bryce Harlow, and Robert Finch. Between election day and Christmas, Colson produced remarkably complete analyses and recommendations on a variety of issues Nixon would have to deal with to win reelection:

- Some of the Republican Party's biggest and most enthusiastic financial backers were seriously displeased with the way their money was spent, and felt they had been solicited too often by too many people. Colson suggested the president host an intimate dinner for a half dozen or so of the top contributors, let them in on campaign planning for '72, and set up a system where one senior party member cleared all requests for money.

- The media characterized Nixon's tactics in support of the midterm elections as negative and even unethical. Nixon had to concentrate on acting presidential, establishing "a certain aloofness (without isolation) along with the mystique and grandeur of the Office." He had to keep attacking the Democrats, but keep the connection between the messages and the White House as well-hidden as possible.

- Foreign policy was Nixon's strong suit, and the administration had to be more effective in showcasing his accomplishments— withdrawing troops from Vietnam, disarmament talks with the Soviet Union, thawing relations with Communist China.

- On the domestic front, the president had to distill his objectives into a few clear goals that would have broad popular appeal. According to Colson's political radar, "vast environmental programs, new schemes to help the poor, or expanded aid to the cities gets us absolutely nothing politically . . . Revenue sharing and value added tax have real political appeal because they combine reform in government with tax benefits to the constituency which we must reach."

- Colson spent a lot of time on plans for influencing the media. Not only was the president receiving his customary grilling in the press, but Colson himself was too important and too close to the president to stay out of the news any longer. Vera Glaser wrote a column for the Knight Newspaper chain reporting the fund-raiser Colson had arranged for Senator Edmund Muskie in 1964. The fact was that throughout the 1960s, when he was a lobbyist representing New England interests in Washington, Colson attended literally hundreds of events by and for senior office holders of both parties. He admitted he might have attended the event, though he claimed he "probably" didn't buy a ticket and, as he told Glaser in a phone call, "damn well" didn't organize it. And while he was at it, he took issue with her repeating the old Washington tale about his supposed row with Robert McNamara: "I didn't come anywhere close to having a fist fight with Mr. McNamara."

On a wider media front, Colson recommended to Nixon that they use inside political clout to keep the TV networks in line. "We should continue quiet but firm pressure on the media," he advised in a confidential memorandum to the president. "The FCC can keep the networks off balance and worried, as they are now, over possible regulatory measures." He suggested too that the administration feed stories in advance to "friendly or neutral" TV personalities.

After pressuring CBS chairman William Paley to present a more balanced, less antiadministration view, Colson sensed that CBS White House reporter Dan Rather was less critical of Nixon's policies, though he knew neither man would admit to having been influenced. Another senior CBS executive, Frank Stanton, was threatened with contempt of Congress, which would jeopardize the network's broadcasting license. "All we want from you," Colson told him, "is not pro-Nixon coverage, just occasional fairness." Horrified, Stanton asked what Colson meant.

"Just occasional fairness," Colson repeated, commenting later, "I never saw a guy squirm so much in my whole life."

One of Chuck's most ambitious suggestions regarding media was that "solid financial supporters" of the administration buy up radio and television stations. There was even a chance the NBC Radio Network might be for sale. The price under discussion was $55 million, which according to an "extremely knowledgeable" source, could be paid off in eight years using operating profit.

Colson was also fascinated at the potential for a new consumer product, the videocassette, which Sony planned to introduce along with home video players in 1971. The impact of this new system would be revolutionary in two ways: first, it would give political parties a powerful new communication tool for everything from speeches and policy statements to instructions for campaign volunteers; second, it was the beginning of the end of the networks' monopoly on home entertainment programming.

Continuing with his recommendations:

- The Republican National Committee needed a new chairman to lead the charge into the 1972 primary season, and Colson had some very specific recommendations for the president about the kind of man best suited for the job. As the chairman of the party in power, he "ought to be its best technician and the partisan agent of the President . . . Least of all do we need a spokesman who is competing with the President and the Administration for public attention."

Above all, a successful chairman had to have three qualifications Colson spelled out in detail: (1) "Total, exclusive commitment to the president" with no personal ambitions, "egoless and expendable"; (2) able to take on the position as a full-time job; and (3) most important, able to make the party machinery operate efficiently, "a consummate political pro who knows how to organize and use the organization." In a memo to Haldeman, Colson emphasized the point: "The partisan machinery that exists at the Committee can be enormously valuable to us in 1972. The Chairman ought to spend full time making it work in our interest—and the less he is seen on TV, the better . . . I've lived in this town through a lot of chairmen—and I'd like to see us learn from past mistakes."

- In Colson's view the Republicans' relationship with organized labor was "one of the most vital political questions that we face" moving forward. Labor was a Colson specialty, and his friendship with labor leaders in high places was all the more valuable because meaningful ties between blue-collar voters and the Republican Party were so rare. Colson advised that a summit meeting on how to court the labor vote was "not only desirable but essential."

By the end of 1970, Nixon could see the results of the staffing changes made over the summer, and he was pleased with what had been done. He could see that Chuck Colson, in particular, was thriving in his expanded role. Time and again he was the White House insider who gained an understanding of a political liability, formed a plan of action to deal with it, took full advantage of executive branch resources to the extent they could help him, and marshaled outside resources whenever necessary.

There were other young up-and-comers in the Nixon White House that year. One was Tom Huston, former national chairman of Young Americans for Freedom, who joined Bob Haldeman's staff. As past leader of the country's most high-profile conservative student organization, Huston was well-versed in campus politics and had a passion for infusing left-leaning collegiate ideology with Nixon's brand of all-American patriotism.

The violent reaction in academia to the president's Cambodia decision showed how powerful a force liberal student politics were on the national stage. Nixon wanted to get a handle on the campus opposition, and Tom Huston was a man with the credentials, connections, and enthusiasm for the job. He was also a Nixon man in the Colson mold in that he focused on action and results; he wasn't one to stand around worrying about whose toes might get stepped on.

Another young man in a high position at the White House—surprisingly high, in fact—was John W. Dean. When John Erlichman moved from special counsel to the president to the job of domestic policy chief, Haldeman sought a new hire to fill Erlichman's old spot. Erlichman's deputy, Egil "Bud" Krogh, suggested Dean, a friend of his who was an associate deputy attorney general.

President Nixon was on vacation at his San Clemente, California, estate at the time, and Haldeman flew the young attorney out there for a meeting. Approved by the president, Dean became special counsel; he was thirty-one and had practiced law on his own for six months.

Dean, like Huston, had an interest in campus politics and had monitored demonstration activities for the Justice Department. Haldeman had him continue along the same lines at the White House in addition to handling personal legal matters for the president. Unlike Huston, however, Dean had something of a questionable past—one that would have been routinely discovered except that, since he was recommended by Krogh, and Haldeman wanted to sew matters up, the usual background checks were omitted.

Had the chief of staff followed standard procedures, he might never have hired John Dean. And the next three years might have been very different indeed.

Dean had left his first job at a private firm under a cloud. The firm was negotiating to buy a television station license when they learned Dean already owned an interest in it. Though Dean denied any conflict of interest, he and his employer parted company.

Chuck Colson took all these staff changes and additions in stride as his stock continued its rapid rise. His Executive Office Building office was redecorated in blue and gold to match the decor in the Oval Office; his work space and the president's EOB hideaway were separated only by a bookcase. When Colson's father came to visit him shortly before Thanksgiving, he took pleasure in showing off the luxurious furnishings, twenty-foot ceilings, and ten-foot carved mahogany doors.

The elder Colson accompanied his son to a military decoration ceremony in the State Dining Room. Afterwards, Chuck and his father were walking in the Rose Garden when a staff member came up to Wendell Colson and said, "The president would like to see you." Nixon had noticed the old gentleman at the ceremony, asked who he was, and decided to invite him into the Oval Office.

During the course of the visit, the president asked the younger Colson a question or two about some pending business. As he answered, his father realized he was watching his son advising the president of the United States. It was, Wendell Colson decided, the greatest experience of his life. A photograph of the three of them became one of his most treasured possessions.

Through the spring of 1971, Colson continued to refine his position as what the press called "the president's top troubleshooter." Though he invariably declined interview requests, he worked resolutely to bolster Nixon's public image in spite of the mutual feeling of distrust between the White House and the media.

As the president's popularity began a downward cycle in the polls, Colson searched for a spokesman who could defend the administration's viewpoint but would also have credibility within the Washington press corps. After careful analysis, Colson decided the best way to make his case to reporters was with another reporter, someone who knew how the system worked and how to make the rest of the world see administration positions in the best light.

With Chuck himself acting as intermediary, the White House soon hired John Scali, a respected reporter for ABC Television, to handle press relations. Colson also took over key publicity responsibilities from Herb Klein, White House communications director, including the assignment of spokesmen to politically important events when neither the president nor vice president could attend.

On Saturday, June 12, the atmosphere around the president and his associates was unusually relaxed and cordial. The president's older daughter, Tricia, was getting married on the White House lawn. The ceremony was carried live by the networks—a pause in their often stormy relationship with the administration to celebrate a rare moment of unalloyed joy. The president even danced with his wife for the cameras. Colson may well have thought of his own daughter, Emily, just entering her teens, and imagined what he would feel like as the proud father of the bride someday in the future.

The next morning Colson picked up the Sunday *New York Times* and was pleased to see a flattering photo of Nixon and his daughter prominent on the front page, with details of the wedding in an article below. But his brow furrowed in concentration as he read the headline of another story next to the photo, across three columns on page one: "Vietnam Archive: Pentagon Study Traces 3 Decades of Growing U.S. Involvement."

Could this be some damaging exposé? An embarrassment to the administration? As Colson read on, he relaxed. There was nothing here, he told himself, but "a compendium of old memos, position papers, and cables" explaining how President Kennedy got America ensnared in Vietnam in the first place. It was all ancient history; what's more, it reminded readers of shortcomings in the Democrats' foreign policy at a time when the war was finally winding down under Republican leadership.

But when he walked into the White House the next morning, he quickly learned that National Security Advisor Henry Kissinger saw things differently. Before the day was out, Colson saw them differently too.

Hatchet Man

CHAPTER 8

Henry Kissinger was that rarest of successes for the Nixon administration, a highly visible figure who got favorable press. As an emigrant who came to America at fifteen, he had an exotic German accent; as a divorcé, he kept Washington hostesses and their dinner guests spellbound with his charm; as special national security advisor to the president, he was a source of endless information tidbits for reporters; as a master of public relations, he knew how to manage it all for maximum effect.

Though Chuck Colson found Dr. Kissinger's staff somewhat prickly and difficult to work with, and though he wasn't overawed by his relationship with the media, he knew Kissinger was the most important foreign policy figure in the White House next to the president. And he knew that if Kissinger was worried about something, everybody ought to be worried.

On Monday morning, June 14, 1971, at the White House, "Kissinger went into orbit," Colson remembered later. He was as angry as Colson had ever seen him, and fearful besides. The "old memos" the *New York Times* had published the day before were excerpts from the Pentagon Papers, a secret forty-seven-volume report on the history of American involvement in Vietnam. It was commissioned by Secretary of Defense Robert McNamara, and was an exhaustive narrative of political and military action in the region between 1945 and 1968.

Colson had already concluded in his own mind that what the *Times* had printed was harmless and might even hurt the Democrats by spotlighting their foreign policy shortcomings. But Kissinger saw a greater problem: if whoever leaked the information knew those things, they also knew other things that were much more sensitive.

Kissinger had already received diplomatic messages that morning from America's staunchest allies—Australia, Great Britain, and Canada— condemning the release of supposedly confidential information. Colson later recalled Kissinger proclaiming such revelations would "destroy this government," and that if our allies couldn't trust us, "how will we ever be able to negotiate with our enemies?"

As his day in the White House went on, Colson got a more complete picture of the risk publication of the Pentagon Papers represented. The CIA claimed that continued revelations could expose the identities of undercover agents; the National Security Agency reported they might compromise the agents' code-breaking operation.

It seemed to Colson that the real trouble was not in revealing the past, but the risk of derailing the future. President Nixon's great successes continued to be in foreign policy, and one of the greatest of all could be a visit to Communist China that was currently in the works but still top secret. Kissinger was already deep into negotiations with Bejing, and prospects for the journey were promising. But lurking in the forty-seven volumes of the Pentagon Papers was the fact that American U-2 high-altitude surveillance aircraft had flown spy missions over China. China already knew about the flights, but public acknowledgment of them would prompt the Chinese to cancel Nixon's visit in order to save face. That in turn would deny the president an international triumph Colson longed to see him enjoy.

There were other sensitive issues. America was still negotiating the SALT arms limitation agreement with the Soviets, who were furious at the *Times* revelations. And perhaps most damaging of all, Kissinger had returned from secret peace talks with the North Vietnamese in Paris only a month before. With America's self-critical report splashed across the front page, the Vietnamese suddenly had a powerful political and propaganda weapon, whether the facts had any military significance or not.

By Tuesday morning the government had a temporary restraining order against continued publication. Later in the day, the president called Colson to discuss strategy, pulling him out of a meeting he had already convened to brainstorm an administration response to the story.

The special counsel had no idea that their phone call, along with every other call from (or meeting in) the president's office, was being tape recorded.

The tape of that meeting documented the president's suggestion that Colson start drumming up support for the administration from constituent groups, including veterans, and from zealous senators or congressmen eager for press exposure who could "go all out on a thing like this." He also suggested the White House do all it could to label the leaked documents the Kennedy-Johnson Papers. "That's what we're talking about, and that gets it out of our way."

Nixon quickly worked himself up into a heated state, plainly apparent in the recording: "This really involves the ability to conduct government. How the hell can a president, or a secretary of defense, or anybody do anything? How can they make a contingency plan if it's going to be taken out in a trunk and given to a g—d— newspaper?"

Colson quickly soothed and reassured the president: "Well, I don't think there's any question. It's my own feeling that this will backfire against the _New York Times_ and we can help generate this . . . Generate some editorials in other newspapers that are highly critical. The _Chicago Tribune_ ought to give us good play; the _New York Daily News_ should . . .

"I think the _Times_ position is indefensible," Nixon countered impatiently. "It's a violation of security, and they said, 'To hell with you, we're going ahead and publish anyway.' So we would have been very, very remiss in our duties had we not taken whatever legal means were available . . . I think you'll find a great deal of popular support.

"If it were a battle plan for the withdrawal of troops next week that could subject boys to attack, why there'd be no argument at all about it. Now the integrity of the system as a whole is at stake. You simply cannot allow a newspaper to publish classified documents."

The cause of all this commotion was Daniel Ellsberg, a former Marine Corps officer who had worked for Dr. Kissinger in the first year of the administration developing various scenarios that projected how the Vietnam conflict might play itself out. John Mitchell was convinced Ellsberg was a Communist spy, and the president thought he was a traitor.

The label "traitor" wasn't too strong in Chuck Colson's estimation; he knew firsthand the importance of maintaining the integrity of military operations, and he had friends still in the service whose lives could be compromised by grandstanding leaks "in the public interest." He thought it was clear that Ellsberg was trying to embarrass the president to the degree that his authority to prosecute the war would be undermined.

Political fallout was swift and severe. The president's popularity in the opinion polls took a nosedive, the anti-war faction spoke out with new conviction, and the Senate voted for the first time in favor of unilateral withdrawal of American troops. Even more ominous were the North Vietnamese representatives in Paris, who rejected Kissinger's peace proposal four days after the Senate vote. With anti-war sentiment rising and America's allies out of sorts, Colson observed, all the North Vietnamese had to do was wait things out; Ellsberg and the protesters would do the North's negotiating for them.

Colson also saw the president's impatience and disgust over the country's security operations. Nixon repeatedly upbraided the CIA for its inability to establish links between radical campus protesters and Communists, or between enemy infiltrators and Nixon's foes in the press. He was impatient with the agency's director, Richard Helms, and perpetually unhappy with the results produced.

Nixon thought the situation was little better at the FBI, which handled domestic security matters while the CIA operated outside the country. The legendary J. Edgar Hoover, now in his forty-seventh year as director, went his own way and kept the Bureau fiercely independent of the executive branch.

As he so often did when he wanted something taken care of fast and reliably, the president turned to Chuck Colson. "I want him exposed, Chuck," Nixon exclaimed, in reference to Ellsberg while pacing the floor of the Oval Office. "I want the truth about him known. I don't care how you do it, but get it done."

"Yes, sir," Colson answered immediately. "It will be done."

Colson released a damaging FBI file on Ellsberg to a friendly reporter. The public reaction was muted, but the information in the FBI dossier sowed the seeds of another plan to discredit Ellsberg. If the world couldn't be persuaded he was a traitor, perhaps it could be convinced he was some kind of kook.

Bob Haldeman asked Colson and others to recommend people he could hire to form a group inside the White House to plug damaging security leaks. The last name on Colson's list was Howard Hunt, a former CIA agent and fellow Brown graduate Colson knew from Brown alumni gatherings. After a brief interview with John Erlichman, Hunt was hired to work under presidential staff member Egil "Bud" Krogh and assigned a cubbyhole on the third floor of the EOB at the other end of the building from Colson's lavish office.

Soon afterward another ex-security specialist, former FBI agent George Gordon Liddy, joined the operation. Others would follow, all trained in intelligence or clandestine operations. They quickly became known as the "plumbers," since their job was to fix leaks.

A year earlier, Haldeman assistant Tom Huston had chaired an interagency committee set up by President Nixon to see what kind of countermeasures worked best against critical reporters, anti-war activists, and other enemies of the administration. The Huston committee concluded that the best weapon in their arsenal was surreptitious entry. Administration-friendly forces could steal or photograph sensitive documents, or plant bugging devices. The only problem, as Huston admitted in his final report, was that this superior method of public relations hardball was against the law.

"Use of this technique is clearly illegal; it amounts to burglary," the Huston report read. "It is highly risky and could result in great embarrassment if exposed. However, it is also the most fruitful tool and can produce the type of intelligence which cannot be obtained in any other fashion."

In 1970 the risk wasn't worth it. Now it was.

In short order, Liddy came up with an elaborate plan code-named Operation Gemstone that included not only surveillance but wild parties on yachts and high-class prostitutes to blackmail administration opponents. The costs were well beyond what the secret activities budget could support, and so the program was pared down to bugging and photography.

Bud Krogh was in charge of the plumbers. Colson made sure they had an objective and the money they needed to achieve it, but didn't keep tabs on the group day to day. He had no advance notice of specifically what the plumbers would do to stop the Pentagon Papers leaks; as a lawyer he knew that the less he examined the details, the better.

Later commentators would accuse Chuck Colson of developing fantastic plans, including one to bomb the Brookings Institution for the sake of recovering the stolen Pentagon files. The purported plan called for starting a fire at the Institution. When the firemen answered the call and entered the building, all the security systems would be compromised, allowing administration operatives to sneak in along with emergency workers. In the confusion they could reclaim the documents and escape.

However, a more practical job surfaced. Daniel Ellsberg was a patient of Dr. Lewis Fielding, a Beverly Hills psychiatrist. Krogh, Hunt, and Liddy agreed that releasing his confidential psychiatric file to friendly reporters might damage Ellsberg's credibility or embarrass him enough to make him back off. They needed a quick, secret $5,000 to do the job; when the word reached Colson that the plumbers needed cash for operating expenses, he secured it from a political donor. Colson didn't know exactly what the money was for, and he didn't ask. On September 3, the plumbers would break into Dr. Fielding's office looking for damaging information on Ellsberg.

Meanwhile the administration continued fighting the release of the Pentagon Papers in the courts. After the first day's installment in the *New York Times*, the executive branch obtained a restraining order against the publisher prohibiting further leaks. But before the week was out other papers had picked up where the *Times* left off. Finally on June 30, the Supreme Court repealed the restraining order, and publication continued unhindered while Nixon fumed. Ellsberg and his associate, Anthony Russo, freely admitted taking the papers, insisting the public had a right to know America's history of blunders and illegal activities in Vietnam.

Nixon's frank assessment, as recorded in a White House conversation with Colson, was, "They say . . . 'We consider this an immoral war. It's our responsibility to print it.' Now g—d— it, you can't have that in a free country!"

The tape recorder that caught Colson's and Nixon's words in the aftermath of the Pentagon Papers affair was secretly installed on Nixon's order in February 1971. There had actually been a hidden taping system in place when Nixon came into office and he had had it removed. Later his predecessor, Lyndon Johnson, told him the tapes were invaluable in writing his presidential memoirs.

Nixon also saw another advantage. He was irritated when anyone— even his favorites like Dr. Kissinger—told him one thing about a particular issue in private and then said something different in public. If he had the original statement on tape, he would have irrefutable evidence of the shift in position.

Secret taping, Nixon decided, was a good idea after all. He had microphones hidden in his Oval Office and the Executive Office Building hideaway. In the Oval Office there were seven microphones: five hidden in the president's desk and two across the room in the wall lamps on either side of the fireplace. The system was voice-activated, starting the tape whenever there was any sound and turning itself off after a few seconds of silence.

The tapes were poor quality. Every time the tape stopped and started again there was a wowing sound that often obscured the first word or two; the motor of the recorder made a loud, constant hum, and the capstan wheel that pulled the tape through the machine clicked incessantly; words were often indistinct when speakers faced away from the hidden mics or when more than one person talked at once. Transcribing them would be a tedious, headache-inducing exercise for somebody some day. But at the end of his presidency, Richard Nixon would have a historical gold mine.

For all the attention they got in the press, the Pentagon Papers were only a small part of Chuck Colson's world in the summer of 1971. He was busier than ever as a result of the staff reorganization following the midterm elections in 1970.

He was still Nixon's liaison with constituent groups: unions, environmentalists, farmers, homebuilders, aerospace companies—the list seemed almost endless. But now he was also a principle figure in White House communications, having taken the lion's share of PR work from Herb Klein. The president, his private secretary Rose Mary Woods, and Haldeman all consulted Colson on guest lists for state dinners, receptions, and other White House functions. If Colson saw that a person valuable to the administration hadn't received an invitation to an important event, he would make sure they got tickets to a White House gala or a ride on *Air Force One*.

Furthermore, Murray Chotiner left Nixon's staff to return to private practice. He wasn't replaced, and Colson took over most of Chotiner's work as well.

Despite his single-minded devotion to his job and unquestioning loyalty to the president, Charles Colson was meticulous when it came to any overt appearance of impropriety or conflict of interest. Every month he received a bill from the White House Mess for entertainment expenses and snacks charged to his office. Before authorizing payment, he always deducted the cost of his own meals, and paid those out of his own pocket rather than with departmental funds.

When an old business associate from Grumman, a big military contractor and former Colson lobbying client, made inquiries of Colson, he explained very specifically that he could not even talk about business matters as a member of the senior White House staff: "I really have to stay completely out of everything involving Grumman. Even though I no longer have any involvement with the company, I don't want to give even the appearance of trying to help an old friend and client."

When he couldn't find a plasterer to stucco his new house in Virginia, he asked the president of the bricklayer's union for a recommendation, emphasizing repeatedly that he wanted no special favor or discounts, but simply that he couldn't locate a reliable craftsman to do the work. In a file memo he explained this was "the only time that I have asked for any help from anyone with whom I had official dealings in the White House in connection with the home I am building. I made it clear to [union president Tom] Murphy that I was looking for a plasterer that I intended and wanted to pay the prevailing union rate, that I was not seeking any favor or assistance but only trying to find someone competent to handle the job . . ."

When he received presents of even nominal value—frozen steaks or a bottle of whiskey—he always paid for them one way or another. Sometimes he made a donation to charity in the name of the giver. Sometimes he paid for the gift. Sometimes he sent gifts to the office of John Dean, the president's personal attorney, for disposal, always carefully logging and filing the receipt.

Colson well knew the value of running an office that was absolutely beyond reproach. Everything anyone on the president's team did reflected on the president, and nothing was more important than an operation that was as nearly flawless as possible. He saw an essential and inviolable distinction between secret hardball politics and patently illegal activity.

When, on June 22, 1970, the *New York Times* had referred to presidential counsel Murray Chotiner as "the complete hatchet man,'" the sentence was in the last column of a story that began on page 37. In the fall of the following year, the Hatchet Man crown anointed another head. This time the story was page one, column one of the *Wall Street Journal*. The new recipient was Charles Colson, and the title stuck.

"Nixon's Hatchet Man: Call It What You Will, Chuck Colson Handles President's Dirty Work" the headline for October 15, 1971, read. "Evidence is growing," the article began, "that Charles Wendell Colson, President Nixon's 39-year-old special counsel, fits the description pretty well."

The article highlighted Colson's work in muzzling the president's critics even when they were friendly, or members of his own party: AFL-CIO president George Meany for criticizing Nixon's unpopular wage and price controls; Federal Reserve chairman Arthur Burns for his lack of support for White House fiscal policy; even the Council of Economic Advisors for guarded optimism at economic statistics the White House thought should have been praised.

Colson, as was his habit, declined to be interviewed for the article, but insisted he was not responsible for 80 percent of the things he was accused of. Though the article cast Colson generally as heavy-handed, it did display a balance. It quoted one former White House aide as saying, "If you didn't have a Colson you'd have to create him; time and time again, Chuck is there knowing where to press that button." A Republican Party official characterized Colson as "highly professional, practical, tough, bright, balanced and moderate."

The article also repeated a legendary joke Colson had played on presidential press secretary Ron Ziegler. James Doyle, a columnist for the *Washington Star*, had written an article critical of Colson. In reply, Colson drafted a letter to Doyle vowing to "break your g—d— jaw" and sent a copy to Ziegler—but never to Doyle. Frantic, Ziegler ran down to Colson's office to try and forestall a public relations disaster that was actually nothing but a trick.

In the end, the *Journal* concluded, Colson must be pleasing the president or else Nixon wouldn't "keep adding to his responsibilities." And last of all:

"'Chuck is a performer,' says an ex-Nixon aide. 'In the process he may break some bones. But the President likes performers.'

"Another Nixon man says Mr. Colson doesn't do anything different from a number of other White House aides, 'except maybe he's the guy that gets caught.'

"Finally, it's safe to say that in the tightly organized Nixon White House, Mr. Colson is doing little that hasn't been ordered or cleared by his superiors. He once told a visitor: 'I would do anything Richard Nixon asks me to do—period.'"

"Let's Get On It"

CHAPTER 9

Wendell, Chris, and Emily Colson were all teenagers now, still living with their mother in Massachusetts. As busy as Chuck was as an advisor to the president, he also took seriously his responsibility as advisor to his children.

In the fall of 1971 Wendell was beginning to think about college, and wondered whether he should consider a Navy scholarship, which would require several years of military service after graduation. The question brought one of the most publicized and divisive issues of the time down to a personal level in the Colson family.

Even though the number of American troops in Vietnam was steadily decreasing, soldiers were still being killed there, young men were still being drafted, and anti-war sentiment was still strong on college campuses. Wendell and his father had a long discussion about his options. There was a chance he would be drafted, though it wasn't likely. But should he volunteer by accepting a military scholarship?

Colson hesitated at first to give advice on such an important and personal decision, but followed up soon after their talk with a letter to Wendell reviewing his options. The ex-captain was proud of his service in the Marine Corps and thought it had taught him invaluable lessons. He also saw volunteering for duty as a valuable service to the nation.

"I believe in this country," Colson wrote to his oldest child.

> For all of its faults and imperfections, no people in the
> history of the world have created a better society or a better
> system of Government. As we pass through life, each of us

has a *duty* to give as much as we receive. One way to give is to work for our Government, to help improve it and to help perform the services of Government for our people—this service can be as a lowly private in the Army or as a counsel to the President . . .

You will learn and you will toughen yourself and have discipline, physical and mental. Self-discipline is hardly taught in our colleges today; yet it may well be the most important facet of your character. *You cannot succeed in life without it* . . .

If there is one thing I would like to instill in you it is the appreciation of our country, what it means to each of us and indeed to the hope that some day we can achieve peace in the world and a more civilized life for people everywhere. This country is man's best hope and if those of us who enjoy the benefits of life here aren't willing to work for it, not just enjoy its riches, it will not endure.

That same month Chuck and Patty bought shares of stock for Chuck's sons under the provisions of the Uniform Gifts to Minors Act. Chuck wrote a letter of instruction to his banker and a detailed memo (longer than the letter) for his personal file listing exactly what was purchased and how it was accounted for.

Nineteen seventy-two showed every sign of being a wonderful year for Richard Nixon, and therefore a wonderful year for Charles Colson. The president's most likely opponent in the '72 campaign, Senator Edmund Muskie of Maine, had lost momentum after sharply criticizing Nixon's Vietnam negotiations. Colson had convinced Secretary of State William Rogers to blast Muskie and imply he was a traitor. The ploy was an unqualified success, and Muskie's support evaporated. Meanwhile, upstart Governor George Wallace of Alabama was mounting the most serious third party effort since the Bull Moose candidacy of Teddy Roosevelt, which would probably fracture the Democratic vote and further enhance Nixon's chances.

Nixon's rocky relations with the media had also improved, partly on account of a visit by First Lady Pat Nixon to Africa. Colson thought the newfound appeal for the First Family on the part of the press "may well be one of the most important political developments" of the entire first term.

In a memo to the president three weeks into the new year, Colson was delighted at the new image Nixon's family lent his chief by association:

> As you know we have tried hard for 3 years to project "color" about you, to portray the human side of the President, the personal warmth, the compassionate, considerate qualities you have. Because of the hostility of the media it has been an exceedingly difficult, frustrating and not especially successful undertaking. Mrs. Nixon has now broken through where we had failed. She has come across as a warm, charming, graceful, concerned, articulate and most importantly, a very human person. People, men and women, identify with her—and in turn with you. In many cases, these are the people we have found it the hardest to reach. It would be hard to overestimate the political impact of this.

In February Nixon enjoyed one of the greatest foreign policy triumphs and most historically significant events of his career when he became the first American president to visit China (and, not coincidentally, to return home the night of the first presidential primary). Though the Chinese were allies of North Vietnam, their changing perception of the Soviets had prompted them to embrace overtures from the U.S. for a deeper dialogue on world issues. Communist Russia had controlled the Communist sphere of influence unchallenged since the end of World War I. Now China, an emerging giant lumbering into the twentieth century at last, home to the world's largest population, wanted respect and even fear from the Soviets. Showing signs of friendship to capitalist Americans was the way to do it.

The Cambodian crisis was long past, China was a political grand slam, and soldiers were pulling out of Vietnam at a steady rate. On the surface the political situation could hardly have been better. But in the inner circles of the White House, Chuck Colson was hard at work on damage control over a secret operation he needed desperately to keep secret.

For years the Justice Department had been involved in a huge antitrust action against the International Telephone and Telegraph company. The administration secretly offered ITT a deal: contribute $400,000 to Nixon's reelection efforts and the charges would be dropped. By design the president knew nothing about the arrangement; if he was kept in the dark there was no way he could be tainted should the facts somehow come to light.

To Colson's dismay, newspaper columnist Jack Anderson, a longtime Nixon opponent, published the news—Colson called the column a "Jack Anderson stiletto"—that a memo written by ITT lobbyist Dita Beard pointed to the arrangement and implicated the White House.

Colson leapt into action, taking charge of internal damage control. He sent Howard Hunt, one of the leaders of the secret Pentagon Papers plumbers group, to visit Beard in a Denver hospital, where he appeared disguised in sunglasses and a dime store wig. The plan was to have the memo declared a forgery. Colson also prepared a detailed analysis for Haldeman on the political fallout of the Beard memo plus a list of other potentially damaging memos in the White House ITT file: the story in the White House records was far different from what the public had been told.

Hearings had already been held on the controversy, and the authorities were getting very close to uncovering the role of Deputy Attorney General Richard Kleindienst in the ITT operation. Kleindienst was in the middle of confirmation hearings for appointment as attorney general, replacing John Mitchell, who was leaving to head up Nixon's reelection campaign. If it looked like Kleindienst's involvement was about to be discovered during the confirmation process, Haldeman and Colson decided the White House would withdraw his nomination.

Noting the rumblings from the press in the wake of Anderson's revelation, Colson warned Haldeman, "There is the possibility of serious additional exposure by the continuation of this controversy." The most damaging documents, Colson reported, were between domestic affairs advisor John Erlichman and Attorney General Mitchell. These notes mentioned Kleindienst by name.

There was, Colson said, a September 1970 memo "from Erlichman to the A[ttorney] G[eneral] referring to an 'understanding' with [ITT president Harold] Geneen and complaining of McLaren's actions. [McLaren was the justice department prosecutor.] There is a May 5, 1971 memo from Erlichman to the A. G. as to the 'agreed upon ends' in the resolution of the ITT case and asking the A. G. whether Erlichman would work directly with McLaren or through Mitchell. There is also a memo to the President in the same time period . . . This memo would once again directly contradict Mitchell's testimony [in the official ITT inquiry] and more importantly directly involve the President."

Colson engineered a system of "deniability," making sure people in the public eye were denied access to key information that could lead investigators to the truth. "I have deliberately not told Kleindienst or Mitchell," Colson continued. Only [John Dean's assistant] Fred Fielding, myself and Erlichman have fully examined all the documents and/or information that could yet come out." He also set out systematically to track down and destroy all copies of the memos in circulation.

Kleindienst deferred the government appeal to the Supreme Court, and eventually a settlement was reached out of court. The whole ITT story remained secret for more than a year; by the time the truth came to light there would be far bigger distractions in the White House.

With the Dita Beard crisis contained, Colson moved on to other projects designed to keep the president's approval rating up through the election season. Nixon himself came up with a number of schemes, invariably calling on Colson to carry them out.

In a television interview, CBS White House correspondent Dan Rather grilled the president with what Colson described as "a string of snidely worded questions." Afterwards, Nixon summoned his counselor to his office. "Get a hundred people to call Rather and complain," he ordered, and then dictated specific complaints for them to use. Before long the Republican National Committee assigned an employee full-time to organize letter writing campaigns and other responses to such negative reporting.

The president was a great admirer of evangelist Billy Graham, and called him or invited him to the White House on occasion. With the help of Colson, among others, the president persuaded Graham to assemble other high-profile evangelical leaders for a meeting with him in the Roosevelt Room. The purpose was, as Colson later admitted, to do a "snow job" on them and convince them to publicly endorse the president's policies. The administration also repeatedly asked Graham for his mailing lists, which would include literally millions of traditionally-minded people who were prime prospects to be Nixon contributors. Though always respectful, Graham invariably turned them down.

Another assignment was to popularize a book critical of TV coverage during Nixon's 1968 campaign. *The News Twisters* was, by Chuck's estimation, a well-researched, scholarly, and rather boring book without much popular appeal, but it had reams of proof that the television networks and reporters were biased against the Republicans in '68. "Chuck," the president exclaimed, "I want this on the best-seller list!"

At a meeting of his staff later that morning, Colson asked if anybody knew how to turn a book into a best-seller. Someone learned that the best-seller lists were made based on weekly telephone surveys of certain key New York bookstores. From that point on, as Colson later wrote, "it was a matter of logistics. I sent eight thousand dollars from campaign funds to one of our stalwart supporters in New York. He in turn recruited several young volunteers who roamed the streets, buying out one by one the total supply of a dozen stores. The following Monday I proudly strode into the Oval Office and laid *Time* magazine on Mr. Nixon's desk. There on the best-seller list was *The News Twisters*."

Howard Hunt left the White House in the spring of 1972 to work for Nixon's reelection committee; hundreds of copies of *The News Twisters* soon ended up stacked in his deserted EOB office.

As the '72 campaign began gearing up, Colson spent even more time working on assignments he received directly from the president. Haldeman never grew comfortable with the arrangement but was powerless to do anything about it. However, the situation did make Haldeman more likely to jump on Colson after a rare slip-up. One day Haldeman gave Colson a dressing-down for a mistake he had no choice but to acknowledge. Reflecting the locker-room spirit that sometimes inflected their relationship, Colson later sent Haldeman two walnuts in a paper bag with a handwritten note that said simply, "You got 'em."

In the middle of primary season, on May 8, the Vietnam conflict returned to center stage. Responding to enemy action, Nixon ordered resumption of bombing over North Vietnam as well as the mining of Haiphong Harbor. The president considered his action essential in order to continue troop withdrawals even though it put ongoing disarmament talks with the Soviets in jeopardy.

Colson was at the White House with the president and other members of the innermost circle of advisors until after midnight. Nixon's announcement of the bombing, carried live by all three television networks, made Colson nauseous. The election was five months away; if the Russians canceled the upcoming U.S.-Soviet summit, the president's popularity would go into a free-fall and the Democrats would whip them. The '68 election had been won by a hair in the popular vote. Bad momentum now could result in realizing one of Nixon's abiding fears: that he would be a one-term president.

Fortunately the Russians, though protesting loudly at Nixon's actions, eventually went ahead with the summit. The president's approval rating soared.

During his visit abroad he called Colson almost every day, some days several times a day. Only when the president was away from Washington could Colson usually depend on having any uninterrupted personal time. Enjoying a rare free evening at home with Patty, Chuck had had a couple of stout cocktails when the phone rang: it was the president calling from Spaso House, the VIP guest quarters at the Kremlin.

Chuck seldom drank in the evenings just because he never knew when the president would call asking for advice about something and he wanted to be sure he stayed sharp. But now it was late at night (early the next morning in Moscow) and Nixon had called to chat. Caught off guard, Colson succeeded in steering the president away from serious policy decisions not only because he was feeling a little lightheaded, but because he was sure the Russians had tapped the telephone line. When the president returned to Washington, Colson explained he hadn't wanted to discuss sensitive policy decisions over the phone because he figured there were eavesdroppers listening in.

"Oh really?" the president answered sarcastically. "Of course I knew I was being listened to. I wanted the Russians to know I was still running the government."

Throughout the spring and summer, Colson continued doing everything in his power to build the president up, and to use the power of the presidential office to thwart his enemies. A representative memo of the time, written to John Dean on June 12, read:

"I have received a well informed tip that there are some income tax discrepancies involving the returns of Harold J. Gibbons, a Vice President of the Teamsters Union in St. Louis. This has come to me on very, very good authority.

"Gibbons, you should know, is an all out enemy, a McGovernite, ardently anti-Nixon. He is one of the 3 labor leaders who were recently invited to Hanoi.

"Please see if this one can be started on at once and if there is an informer's fee, let me know."

Colson also promoted bogus special-interest groups that supposedly supported Senator McGovern, who, to the Republicans' delight, became the Democratic candidate rather than the more moderate Senator Muskie. In an operation reminiscent of Nixon's 1950 Senate race, Republican operatives fanned out around Washington to distribute handbills promoting a "Gays for McGovern Fund-Raising Party."

While the final Democratic platform had not contained prohomosexual language, the topic had been debated at length. The flyer announced that "the Democrats have adopted a Gay Rights plank as a Minority Report."

The text continued: "George McGovern had the courage to put his a— on the line—risking more than we shall probably ever have to risk— to support us. Now he needs our support. He needs those Gay dollars to fill his war chest."

Colson was so proud of it that he sent a confidential copy to Nixon's best friend, Florida financier Charles "Bebe" Rebozo, in Key Biscayne.

On Saturday, June 17, 1972, the president was on vacation in the Bahamas with another friend, Robert Abplanalp, when the first early-morning news bulletins reported that five burglars were captured breaking into the Democratic National Committee headquarters in the Watergate Hotel. This elegant hotel and office complex, Washington home to numerous senators, congressmen, and members of the Supreme Court, overlooked the Potomac next to the just-completed Kennedy Center for the Performing Arts. The five men broke into the office of Lawrence O'Brien, chairman of the DNC, and had been arrested carrying electronic bugging gear.

Colson heard the details that afternoon as he was getting ready for a swim in his backyard pool. Answering the special White House phone on his bedside table, he heard John Erlichman's voice. "Where is your friend Howard Hunt these days?"

Hunt had left the White House months before to work for the Committee to Re-elect the President (which its opponents gleefully referred to as CREEP). Colson had last seen Hunt back in the winter, when he and Gordon Liddy came to see him about getting Magruder to approve an intelligence plan.

Surely this wasn't it.

The headline in Sunday's *Washington Post* proclaimed, "Five Held in Plot to Bug Democratic Party Office." One of the burglars had a slip of paper in his pocket with Howard Hunt's name on it. Once investigators found Hunt they soon traced the trail to his old White House friend, Chuck Colson, Nixon's hatchet man.

By Tuesday Colson himself was in the headlines, and profoundly upset that any connection with him might reflect poorly on the president. Nixon had flown back to Washington, and called his special counsel into the presidential office to reassure him. Chuck suggested that he and everyone else on the senior White House staff give a sworn statement to the FBI. For once, as far as he knew, they had nothing to hide. The president's secret taping system captured Colson's words: "Everybody [on the White House staff] is completely out of it . . . This is once when you'd like for our people to testify."

The Watergate bugs had been installed on May 28, when the five operatives sneaked into the DNC Watergate headquarters, planted the devices, and escaped undetected. The burglars were caught when they reentered the office to replace a telephone bug that was inoperative. They had taped open a lock on the door to the stairwell; a security guard discovered the tape and removed it. When the lock was taped a second time, he called the police and the intruders were arrested.

One question that came up both then and later was why whoever ordered the bugging chose to infiltrate DNC headquarters. Party headquarters handled logistics for the Democratic Convention and other bread-and-butter matters: security, hospitality, travel for delegates, and so forth. All the strategic political decisions and planning came from the candidate's headquarters. To most observers, that was where bugging made sense—and after all, campaign spying was as old as campaigning itself; nothing unusual about it.

Of all the theories about why DNC was wired instead of McGovern's offices, one of the most intriguing came in time from Fred Emery, a BBC Television producer and an Englishman with no direct stake in either political camp. One issue that had haunted Nixon during his unsuccessful campaign to be governor of California was that his brother Donald had received a loan from billionaire recluse Howard Hughes. The implication was that since Hughes loaned Donald money, brother Richard would do him favors as governor.

The fact was that Hughes had loaned the money, though Richard Nixon insisted his mother's house was pledged as collateral. Even so, the connection was that much more fuel for his critics' fire. Now, ten years later, the party opposing Nixon's reelection was headed by Lawrence O'Brien, who had himself once been on Howard Hughes's payroll—and for all anybody knew, might still have close contact with him.

The president was determined to prove a connection between O'Brien and Hughes in retaliation for the Donald Nixon-Hughes relationship that had been such a personal embarrassment in '62. That was why the burglars bugged O'Brien's office and O'Brien's phone; that was why they risked detection with a second break-in to replace the broken bug on O'Brien's phone even though the rest of the bugs throughout the office suite were working.

(Numerous variations of this theory developed over the years, all revolving around the assumption that the point of the break-in was to expose a relationship between O'Brien and Highes.)

Colson knew the president was out to get some dirt on O'Brien, yet had no advance warning that the plumbers were breaking into the DNC. But as with the Pentagon Papers operation, Colson was key on two crucial points.

First, it was a man he had recommended, Howard Hunt, who helped mastermind the Watergate break-in, even though Hunt no longer worked in the White House, but had transferred to the Committee to Re-elect the President.

Second, it was Colson who pressed for approval of an unspecified clandestine operation when it seemed that no one else would. Early in 1972, Gordon Liddy had been trying for months to get the official go-ahead for a simplified version of his Gemstone surveillance operation. Finally he asked Hunt for a meeting with Hunt's "principal," Chuck Colson.

The two met in Colson's EOB office. Liddy launched into his story, but Colson cut him off. "All you need is a decision, right?" Colson asked, according to Liddy. When Liddy said that yes, that was what was keeping the political intelligence team from getting to work, Colson called Jeb Magruder with Liddy in the room and said, "Gordon Liddy tells me he can't get a decision out of you people on his intelligence program. I don't want to get into a debate of the merits; it just seems to me that after all this time somebody ought to be able to make a decision. Let's get on it."

Later when Hunt offered to give Colson the details of the plan, Colson insisted he didn't want to hear them. By April, Hunt and Liddy had a budget of $300,000 approved from a secret cash campaign fund. They had known whom to go to; Colson was the guy who got things done, especially if they were important to the president.

If Hunt and Liddy hadn't been on the payroll, would somebody else have concocted the Watergate break-in? If Colson hadn't pressed for release of the operational funds, would somebody else have done so? These hypothetical questions would long hang in the air of history.

As the summer of 1972 rolled around and with an election to win, Watergate soon faded to a distant corner of Chuck Colson's mind. Returning from the Republican National Convention in Miami Beach on Friday, August 28, he was shocked to see about half of his staff had taken a long weekend. Stern-faced, he dictated a memo on the spot that left no doubt as to his dissatisfaction. By the following Monday the memo had been leaked to the press and several major dailies published the whole thing.

He had written it tongue in cheek, and knew his staff would take it that way. He had even repeated a quote attributed to him in an earlier news item saying he would walk over his grandmother if necessary to get Nixon reelected. The fact was Colson never said that; a campaign worker had said it in an effort to describe Colson's intensity and drive. The old story had been inaccurate, but Colson played it up in this supposedly private memo to his personal staff.

He began by reminding everyone that there were seventy-one days until the election and that each day had twenty-four hours. He hoped that everyone would have time during that period to "recharge the batteries; an occasional Sunday afternoon may be possible but don't count on it."

It was crunch time. "No one should ever be out of reach of the telephone . . . each individual member of the staff should insure that he or she can be reached at any time of the day or night . . . Make every day count. Think to yourself at the beginning of each day, 'what am I going to do to help the President's reelection today?' and then at the end of each day think what you did in fact do to help the President's reelection."

Personal feelings took a back seat to performance. "I am totally unconcerned with anything other than getting the job done. If I bruise feelings or injure anyone's morale, I will be happy to make amends on the morning of November 8 assuming we have done our job and the results are evident."

Then there was the grandmother comment. "Just so you understand me, let me point out that the statement in last week's UPI story that I once was reported to have said that 'I would walk over my grandmother if necessary' is absolutely accurate."

Now Nixon's hatchet man was going after grandmothers, and the press played up the comment in story after story. Network TV commentator Eric Sevareid and syndicated humorist Art Buchwald both picked it up—Buchwald twice. Colson got a mountain of letters from angry grandmothers; even his own mother criticized the comment (though both of Colson's grandmothers had been dead many years).

One of the few people who was delighted at all the furor was President Richard Nixon. Beaming with pride, he told visitors, "Colson—he'll do anything!"

No Air of Triumph

B etween the end of the Republican National Convention and election day, Colson kept the pressure up as promised—on his staff, on the press, on the opposition—even though McGovern was fading badly. In a briefing to the president, vice president, cabinet, key Republican congress-men, and senior White House staff members, Colson admitted the most recent polls gave Nixon a 34 point lead, but that this was no time to

> play it safe, to stress the positive lines, to ignore our oppo-
> nent, perhaps not even to mention his name and to ride the
> high road of talking only about our grand accomplishments
> from now to November.
>
> Well, ladies and gentlemen, that might just work—if
> we were a majority party or if we had a friendly or even
> reasonably neutral media. But neither of those conditions
> exist. One thing is clear. The campaign which keeps the
> momentum, the campaign which stays on the offensive has
> always [the prepared text had "generally" here; Chuck
> scratched it out and wrote "always"] been the campaign in
> American presidential politics that has won and there is
> one thing that is absolutely clear about the '72 campaign:
> George McGovern cannot win this election if we—those of
> you in this room—succeed in keeping him and his cam-
> paign on the defensive.

One development that kept the Democrats guessing was the effect George Wallace's third party candidacy would have. Even though the candidate, an ardent segregationist as governor of Alabama, had been wounded in May by a would-be assassin, his American Independent Party had qualified for a ballot position in all fifty states. When news first broke of the shooting on May 15, Nixon's immediate worry was that the suspect, Arthur Bremmer, was "some right-wing nut" and a Nixon supporter. "It would be great," the president said, "if this guy were a left-wing fanatic."

Nixon ordered Colson to call Howard Hunt and tell him to find out what he could about Bremmer. Plans were discussed for Hunt to go to Bremmer's apartment in Milwaukee and see what he could learn about the suspect's political ties. Colson told Hunt to stand by for instructions. But the FBI got to the apartment first, and Colson never called Hunt back.

Keeping the Wallace attack in the news and McGovern off balance were two ways to minimize the political fallout from Watergate. Nixon characterized the DNC break-in as a "third-rate burglary," and others in politics and the press freely admitted that one team trying to steal the other's signals was all part of the game. Still, the break-in kept percolating just under the surface.

Shortly before the Miami Beach convention, a Washington newsletter called "The American Political Report" observed that while no presidential challenger had overcome the kind of lead McGovern was struggling against, "Nixonmen are nagged by only one possible Achilles Heel: the Watergate bugging-and-payoff episode and the kindred issue of influence-peddling.

"Administration strategists are nervous about the Watergate bugging mess, and the *sotto voce* question is: How far up the Nixon hierarchy do the expected indictments reach? Probably not far enough for the sort of voter outrage the Democrats need."

The same issue also reported that "Chuck Colson has approached his old law firm about returning to the fold." Colson went out of his way to counter any appearance of conflict of interest. He also wrote to Gadsby & Hannah, his old firm, to underscore his dedication to Nixon's reelection effort. "I have made no decision as to what I will do or indeed can do after November 7. Nor do I intend to make such a decision until *after* the election."

Even in his private affairs, Colson observed, press leaks were a treacherous liability. A partner from Gadsby & Hannah had leaked news of an earlier discussion between Colson and the firm, generating the story.

Nixon was a runaway winner in the polls, Vietnam negotiations continued on a promising track, and Colson began to sense a smashing victory in November, though he never wavered in his aggressive political offense. The *Boston Globe* called him "the No. 1 hardnose of the Nixon administration."

Lawrence O'Brien filed a civil suit against Colson over the Watergate bugging, but a court order kept its contents out of the newspapers. The fact that O'Brien was Nixon's enemy made him Colson's enemy too, but Colson was shocked and disappointed that the Democratic chairman would take such an action. Privately he admitted his respect for O'Brien even though they had long been on opposite sides of the political fence, but he accused O'Brien of hitting below the belt by filing a lawsuit against Colson personally.

Publicly Colson continued his habit of staying out of the news as much as possible. He reasoned, "Once any guy around the White House becomes concerned with his own image and his own press, he's no longer concerned with the President's." Under the circumstances, the less the media spotlight shone on Colson the better for Nixon. "In the midst of the Watergate typhoon," the *Globe* declared, "his star is steadily rising."

Other, more public figures were already getting caught in the Watergate web. John Mitchell resigned as Nixon's reelection chief in July. The campaign treasurer, Hugh Sloan, also resigned, and Gordon Liddy was fired from his "official" position as counsel to the reelection finance committee for failing to cooperate with the FBI when their investigation led from the burglars to him. Mitchell's replacement, Clark MacGregor, got in hot water immediately for acknowledging that Liddy spent campaign contributions on secret security projects, the nature of which were still not entirely clear.

On August 30, President Nixon announced that an internal investigation led by his personal White House lawyer, John Dean, had been completed and that no one in the administration had done anything illegal. The

Nixon team held fast to their story even as the five Watergate burglars plus Hunt and Liddy were indicted on September 15, 1972, for the break-in.

As summer turned to fall, the media published reports that Colson "may leave the administration." This was true; he had told the president privately in July that he planned to return to his law practice, though he continued to insist publicly he wouldn't make any decision until after the election. He relished his position near the center of power in the White House, but serving the president was costing him a fortune in lost income compared with what he could be earning as a Washington lawyer. As high as his income had been before, he could command even greater fees with his new connections as a recent administration insider. He was mindful of the fact that he had three children to put through college; he was also supporting his parents.

Despite the best efforts of the McGovern organization, Watergate made barely a ripple in the hearts and minds of voters during the last weeks before the election. On October 24, Henry Kissinger returned from Paris after concluding a peace accord with the North Vietnamese. Nixon planned to keep the deal quiet to avoid any feeling on the part of the enemy that he was negotiating for political gain. The news leaked out anyway, and Nixon announced to the nation and the world that "peace is at hand."

When it was all over, Nixon would amass 47 million votes to 29 million for McGovern—a landslide that gave Nixon the electoral votes of every state except Massachusetts and the District of Columbia.

After the polls closed, Chuck, Patty, and young Wendell Colson went to celebrate with senior staffers and major contributors at the exclusive Shoreham Hotel in Washington. Considering Nixon's huge and historic victory margin, Chuck expected a happy crowd ready to celebrate—an even more joyful occasion than the one following their white-knuckle win of '68. But something was wrong. The atmosphere was unaccountably sour. Patty and eighteen-year-old Wendell picked it up as clearly as Colson himself. People were drinking heavily. Some were grousing about the fact that their $25,000 contribution hadn't even gotten them a handshake with the president. Others were reminding presidential insiders, including Colson, about jobs they expected. There was, Colson decided, "no air of triumph here."

Colson's White House pager went off. The president was in his EOB office and wanted him at once. The Colson family left the packed ballroom and climbed into a waiting limousine. In minutes they were walking down the elegant marble hallway of the Executive Office Building. Colson settled his wife and son in his own office adjacent to the president's, assuring them he'd just be a few minutes.

Entering the presidential hideaway office, Colson saw Nixon puffing the pipe he often smoked in private, and Bob Haldeman scrutinizing election returns at a small table nearby. The president's valet brought two scotch and sodas (Haldeman never drank), and the newly reelected chief proposed a toast: "Here's to you, Chuck. These are your votes that are pouring in, the Catholics, the union members, the blue-collars, your votes, boy. It was your strategy and it's a landslide!"

As Nixon rambled on he called his valet and ordered something to eat. It was nearly 3 A.M., but Colson dutifully joined the boss in a predawn snack, realizing that Patty and Wendell had been waiting next door for more than an hour. Even in this moment of triumph Nixon and Haldeman seemed unfulfilled; Nixon carped over the wording of his reply to McGovern's telegram conceding the election, and Haldeman grumped that he couldn't get accurate election returns. Finally, when Haldeman's assistant reported the wire services had shut down for the night, Nixon concluded the conversation and Chuck escorted his exhausted family home.

It was only 8 o'clock on the morning after election day when the White House phone on Chuck's nightstand rang, summoning him back to another presidential meeting. As he dressed and downed a couple of cups of coffee, he thought to himself, *It's nice of the president to want to thank us, but he could have waited until tomorrow.*

Arriving in the Roosevelt Room, Colson joined the rest of the senior staff in applauding the president as he entered. To everyone's surprise, Nixon spoke only briefly, mostly to tell a story from British political history when challenger Benjamin Disraeli defeated incumbent Prime Minister William Gladstone, despite Gladstone's successes in office, because, Disraeli claimed, Gladstone was "an exhausted volcano."

The president then turned the meeting over to Haldeman and left the room. After the half-hearted applause died down, Haldeman said, "I will expect resignations from every member of the staff to be delivered to the staff secretary by noon on Friday." Colson was shocked. He had flogged his staff of thirty mercilessly for months, promising them vacations and the prospect of better positions if the president were reelected. Now he had to tell them the president expected them to resign so the administration could "start fresh."

A few minutes later Colson was summoned to the Oval Office where the president assured him he wasn't in the same category with the rest of the staff, and asked him to reconsider his own resignation. But the offer rang hollow. Maybe Colson was an exhausted volcano after all. Haldeman's rude and chilling display had only perpetuated Colson's impression from the night before that something wasn't right. Doing his best to salvage the situation, Colson called his staff together, explained that the resignations were a traditional formality at the beginning of a new administration, and gave everybody vacations. He recovered sufficiently from the shock to defend the president's resignation policy in a speech to the New England Society of Newspaper Editors a few days afterward.

On November 13, the Monday after the election, Colson, Haldeman, Erlichman, and the president met for dinner at Camp David. In a private moment, Nixon asked Colson to stay in the administration for a second term. Colson answered that he had written a memo at Haldeman's request detailing what he would be interested in: the Secretary of Labor appointment, Republican Party chairman, or White House counselor in charge of reorganizing the administration for the second term.

The president asked if he would stay on as special counsel for legislative affairs. Probably the president knew, and certainly Haldeman and Erlichman knew, that Colson would never accept such a bureaucratic job. It was an offer for appearance's sake only. But then Nixon suggested Colson could be general counsel to the Republican National Committee and part of the president's informal "kitchen cabinet," and afterward came back around to the idea of Colson reshaping and streamlining the White House for the second term.

A few days later, though, Haldeman called and told Colson that the president had changed his mind and that "we think you really should go and start the law practice." It seemed obvious to Chuck that the president would have been glad to have him stay, but that Erlichman and Haldeman had talked him out of it.

(Colson would see other evidence of Haldeman's and Erlichman's scheming. Once after a flight in *Air Force One*, Chuck's son Wendell met him at the airport. Thinking the plane was empty, Chuck took Wendell on board to see the president's office. But when he opened the president's door, Haldeman and Erlichman were inside having an intense discussion, which stopped abruptly as soon as Colson appeared. From their expressions and actions, there was no doubt in Chuck's mind that they were talking about him.)

Colson submitted his official resignation letter on November 20. Seasoned communicator though he was, the special counsel to the president labored over seven rough drafts before he could put into words what he felt about his years of service to a man he deeply admired:

> The opportunity to serve you has been the greatest
> privilege of my life. I shall always be deeply proud to have
> had a part in the great undertakings of your Presidency.
> History will record these, I am convinced, as epochal
> advances by a gifted leader in moving our nation strongly
> and realistically toward a generation of peace—not only
> peace abroad but also peace at home for all citizens.
>
> Speaking in a personal vein, I leave the White House,
> I believe, a better man, inspired by your example. I have
> learned first hand from you what most people can only
> know in the abstract—the truth that one must never be
> deflected or disheartened by captious criticism or the tem-
> porary tide of opinion from persevering in what is right
> and just. I have watched you in moments of crisis making
> the hard decision—the decision you knew to be in the
> long-term best interest of the country, rejecting the expe-
> dient and the self serving. Time and again I have watched

you do this with total disregard for the political consequences to yourself. I have seen you act with strength of
spirit and courage that is the hallmark of greatness. In so
doing you have brought about in this country a resurging
national confidence and sense of purpose.

Thirty years later, Charles Colson's feelings about President Richard
Nixon would remain unchanged.

Among the other letters he wrote near the end of his White House
tenure were two to Henry Kissinger. One was an official letter of farewell.
The other was a personal letter that gave Colson a platform for expressing
his deeper feelings:

"I cannot find words adequate to describe my personal admiration for
your accomplishments. Having been exposed just slightly in recent weeks
to what you have been up against and the burdens you have carried
[another Vietnam policy crisis at Christmas], I perhaps know more than
most of the great strength, courage and perseverance that was required on
your part. It has been a remarkable performance and when all is finally
written, I hope others will appreciate, as I do, how brilliantly you handled
it under the most difficult circumstances."

Colson expected his resignation to be effective December 31, but the
president asked him to stay on staff until March 1, 1973, to help get the
new term under way. Colson agreed, but this put him in an awkward situation. Presidential press secretary Ron Ziegler announced the sixty-day
extension on December 2, and now there was a muddy conflict of interest
issue to deal with. Clearly Colson was leaving and had to make prepara-
tions at whatever law firm he would be joining, but at the same time he
would remain part of the White House inner circle for another two
months.

On December 12, the *New York Times* published an editorial critical of
Colson's reported plan to leave the White House and become a consultant
to organized labor. Colson had long been the friend of numerous unions,
especially the Teamsters. He had been involved in the president's decision,
carried out by George Shultz, to commute the thirteen-year prison sentence of former union president Jimmy Hoffa for jury tampering and mail

fraud after the parole board had refused three times to do so. The *Times* labeled the union's relationship with the firm Colson was reported to be joining as a conflict of interest.

Colson wrote a memo to John Dean asking for advice. Dean had well established himself as the White House authority on fine points of the law involving anything touching the president, and Colson wanted to prepare for his career move while avoiding "any embarrassment to the President and myself."

Colson was not inclined to re-join Gadsby & Hannah. His old friend and original law partner, Charlie Morin, had left that firm on October 1 for a new firm subsequently known as Morin, Dickstein, Shapiro & Galligan. This was the firm Colson had every intention of joining, though he was scrupulously careful not to ask for a position at the moment, and they were equally careful not to offer him one.

Chuck Colson's last season in the White House was filled with moments of personal and historic significance. In December 1972 Nixon resumed bombing in North Vietnam when the peace agreement began to unravel; just before year's end the Vietnamese reaffirmed their commitment to ending the war and the bombing stopped. Three days after the inauguration, Nixon made the historic announcement that "peace with honor" had been achieved. Colson sensed that the end to the Vietnam War meant even more to the president than his reelection. To celebrate the news, Nixon invited Colson for a private luncheon in his office—just the two of them, enjoying Dubonnet on the rocks and cottage cheese and pineapple salad. It was, Colson wrote, "no triumphant V-E day," but it meant a long dark chapter in American history was over; soldiers would stop dying and prisoners would start returning home.

Looking back later, Colson wondered whether he had let a crucial window of opportunity close on him and his president during what came to be known as "the Christmas bombing." Nixon was "enormously distracted" by the war during that period, which kept him from concentrating on the launch of his second term, and also kept him from spending much time at all on Watergate. He just didn't believe it was important enough to pull him away from his duties as commander in chief.

Colson's future law partner, David Shapiro, advised Colson to make it plain to the president that, based on what little Colson had told him, there was a real danger of obstruction of justice in the Watergate business. But Colson couldn't discuss the break-in at length, because Nixon was "too consumed with Vietnam." Yet there was one time in January, when Colson was beginning to put the pieces of Watergate together on his own, that he finally confided to the president his fear that the break-in could involve people in the White House, though he had no proof.

As Colson later remembered: "When I got nowhere with Haldeman [in convincing him there was a problem, not knowing Haldeman was a key player in the conspiracy], I went to Nixon and said, 'I'm concerned. This could stretch into the White House.' And he looked at me and said—in a very low voice, now as I think about it [they were in the president's EOB office]—'You mean Bob and John?' And I said, 'Yes.'" Nixon never brought the conversation up again, and the window of opportunity closed for good.

As a last hurrah to finish out his presidential service, Colson was commissioned to travel to Moscow, accompanied by Patty, on an official visit to appeal for the right of Jews to emigrate from the Soviet Union. At the end of their long flight on a government 707, Colson and his entourage of diplomats were greeted by a brass band, awaiting them stoically on the runway apron at 11 P.M. on a foggy Moscow February night.

Chuck and Patty stayed in the American ambassador's residence, Spaso House, which became their headquarters for a whirlwind week of meetings and sightseeing excursions. The ambassador warned them not to say anything anywhere that the Soviets shouldn't hear—their limousine, and even their room at Spaso House, were certainly bugged.

Finally came the time for the key meeting of the trip between Colson and Soviet Minister Vasiliy Kuznetsov. Colson tried to explain the American position on emigration. "We are all immigrants, a whole nation of them. One of my grandfathers came from Sweden, the other from England. To us the right of a person to emigrate is a fundamental human right. We can't bargain it away. It's nonnegotiable. It's God-given to everyone."

After a good deal more back-and-forth discussion, Kuznetsov said curtly, "Mr. Colson, we will do our part. You can tell the president." A novice at international diplomacy, Colson had no sense of the minister's meaning until an American diplomatic official happily told him later, "We got what we came for!" In the next year, more than thirty thousand Jews were allowed to leave the USSR.

On Colson's last day in Moscow the ambassador arranged a news conference for Western journalists. Colson had dealt with a series of questions about his meetings and a few about Watergate (the Senate committee to investigate Watergate—later known as the Ervin committee—had been unanimously voted into existence on February 7), when someone asked him to comment on reports that he had sent Howard Hunt to visit Dita Beard the year before in connection with the ITT scandal. Taken completely off balance, Colson uttered a quick quip and the ambassador rapidly brought the conference to a close.

And there were more signs that White House political intrigue was becoming a front-burner issue. During a stopover in Vienna on the way home, Colson saw an article in *Newsweek* connecting him with all sorts of Watergate misdeeds—accusations that would eventually prove to be false but that were devastating nonetheless. He had just achieved an important breakthrough in international diplomacy, yet here he was reading falsehoods about himself that supposedly took place halfway around the world. Colson cut his trip short by two days and flew back to Washington.

The White House Colson returned to was a different place from the White House he had left. The creation of the Ervin committee had caused panic in the executive branch. John Dean, until this point a relatively minor player in Colson's view, had appointed himself to take over some of Colson's old responsibilities and was seeing the president, he claimed, several times a day.

In his last official meeting with Nixon as special counsel, Colson entreated the president to purge the White House of the Watergate business. The hidden taping system captured his words of February 13, 1973: "Whoever did order Watergate, let it out! Let's get rid of it now, take our losses!" But the president "seemed almost paralyzed by

Watergate, unable or unwilling to face harsh realities," Colson reflected afterward. The presidential counsel had no idea what his chief knew, or how deep his secrets ran.

A few days later Chuck Colson cleaned out his EOB office and moved a block down the street to elegant and expensive quarters at his new law firm, now renamed Colson & Shapiro. The Teamsters had already signed on and other clients were lined up at the door. To welcome their newest and most famous rainmaker to the fold, the partners presented him with a Lincoln Continental and a full-time chauffeur. Charles Colson was forty-one, at the top of his game, and, according to the *New York Times*, "well on his way to becoming one of the busiest and best paid lawyers in Washington."

A Sinking Ship

=== **CHAPTER 11** ===

The most valuable commodity in Washington is influence: the closer anyone is to the people at the center of power, the more influential he is, the more respect he commands, and the more money he makes. Charles Colson was the first member of the White House senior staff to leave the Nixon presidency in the wake of the '72 reelection, and that made him an instantly hot commodity. Before joining the administration in 1969 Colson was already a very successful, well-connected, and well-paid lawyer-lobbyist. After spending three years in the EOB office immediately adjacent to the president's, his stock had skyrocketed.

Colson & Shapiro, with nineteen lawyers and offices in Washington, Boston, and New York, had new clients all but pacing up and down the sidewalk waiting to transfer their business. Predictions were that Colson, whose salary at the White House topped out at $42,500, could expect to make between $300,000 and $400,000 his first year at the firm.

The aspect of his old White House job that he missed the most was regular contact with the president. Typically they talked several times a day; Nixon almost always called Colson at home in the evening to follow up on some earlier event or to ask his opinion about a point. Chuck missed the man, the friendship; he also missed the power.

The one part of the job he hoped to leave behind, the expanding investigation into Watergate, stayed stuck to him like a spider web on the fingertips. Colson had no prior knowledge of the Watergate break-in and believed the president had no knowledge of it either. But there was that direct link between Colson and the burglary: one of the burglars had Howard Hunt's White House phone number in his pocket, and Hunt had been hired by Colson.

Rumors kept appearing in the news, and the more Colson protested the more strident the accusations became. He combed through his memory for recollections of meetings or memos or anything else that could help him prove his position and his innocence in the approval chain that led to Watergate. The very intimacy with the president that had given Colson so much clout both in and out of the White House was now working against him. How could someone the president knew so well and called on for advice so frequently not know about the break-in?

John Dean asked Colson to talk with Howard Hunt, who on January 11, 1973, had pleaded guilty to the Watergate burglary, and see what his current attitude was toward the White House. Colson's law partner David Shapiro convinced Colson not to go, and saw Hunt himself instead. Hunt told Shapiro that he wanted money to keep quiet, and that Colson should pass his demand on to the White House. Shapiro reported the news, along with the caution that if Colson relayed the message he would be guilty of obstruction of justice. Sensing Colson's rising concern for the president and the president's potential for further involvement, Shapiro suggested that if he wanted to help Nixon, he should tell him to hire "the best criminal lawyer in the business."

Colson and Hunt had spoken before about commitments real or imagined in the aftermath of the break-in. Colson had gone out of his way at first to avoid knowing any details about Hunt's and Liddy's surveillance operation, but as Watergate grew in scope and its potential to harm the president, the facts were becoming more unavoidable.

Just after the election, Colson called Hunt and took the precaution of recording the conversation on his office dictation machine. Hunt insisted he and the other defendants, indicted on September 15, 1972, had been promised money. "Commitments that were made to all of us at the onset have not been kept," he complained. "There's a great deal of financial expense here that has not been covered and what we've been getting has been coming in very minor drips and drabs."

Colson interrupted him. "Don't tell me any more." It wasn't the first time Colson had insisted he say nothing else. Yet Hunt forged ahead.

"We think that now is the time when some moves should be made and surely your cheapest commodity available is money. These lawyers have not been paid."

Hunt asked Colson if he would "receive a memorandum from me" on Watergate to read and then destroy. Colson declined, saying the only way he could help Hunt was to stay "as completely . . . unknowing as I am" about exactly what went on.

Colson made no promises, and in fact said very little, though he was relieved to hear Hunt say he had told his lawyer that, regarding Watergate, Colson "had absolutely nothing to do with it."

For all the trouble stirring around them, Colson told Hunt that at least "we got the president in for four more years, and thank God for the country we do."

"Exactly," Hunt replied.

On January 8, 1973, the day the Watergate trial started in Judge John Sirica's courtroom, the president called Colson into his hideaway EOB office to discuss clemency for Hunt. Their conversation was recorded. The president told Colson that Hunt had decided to plead guilty.

Colson already knew this, and confided to the president, "He's doing it on my urging."

Of all the defendants, Colson and Nixon agreed that Hunt was in the most precarious shape, both financially and emotionally. His daughter suffered from brain damage caused by a car accident years earlier, and his wife had been killed in a plane crash a month earlier to the day. Colson said Hunt objected "violently" to reentering the DNC headquarters to replace the inoperative bug, but that Liddy had insisted on it.

The president introduced the idea of clemency for Hunt. "Hunt is a simple case. I mean after all, the man's wife is dead, was killed; he's got one child that has—" he paused and Colson finished the sentence "—brain damage from an automobile accident."

After his later conversation with Shapiro about Hunt's continuing demands, Colson passed along to the president the suggestion that he should hire a criminal lawyer. The next week, Bob Haldeman called and invited Colson to meet him in his White House office. The atmosphere of the meeting was bizarre. Colson entered the room and headed toward the conference table where the two of them always sat, but Haldeman abruptly directed him toward a pair of chairs across the room flanking the fireplace. Then the taciturn chief of staff, notorious for his disdain of small talk, was uncharacteristically chatty, asking Colson about his new practice and hesitating to get to the point.

Finally he asked Colson what he thought the president should do to "get rid of this Watergate mess."

"Bob," Colson replied frankly, "I told the president last week to hire a criminal lawyer, someone who can get all the facts, piece the whole mystery together and give the boss cold-blooded, hard advice. Then get rid of the culprits. It's the only way."

It would be months before Colson knew that Haldeman seated them where they were in order to secretly record their conversation. Or that one of the chief culprits who ought to be sent packing in this case was sitting across from him at that moment.

Haldeman laughed off Colson's suggestion. This wasn't a legal problem, he insisted, but a PR matter. If they could just get some fair coverage in the press, the whole controversy would dissolve into a mist.

On March 19, James McCord, the convicted leader of the Watergate burglary team, wrote to Judge Sirica claiming the defendants perjured themselves and had been pressured not to tell the truth. When Sirica made the letter public four days later, all eyes were on Colson again. Who else was in a better position to demand silence of the burglars or reward them for it?

The headline in the *Washington Post* read, "McCord Links Mitchell and Colson to Watergate Bugging Plan." The fact was that Colson and McCord had never met, and Colson had never heard of James McCord until the break-in was reported. The questions and allegations were big stories, but Colson's denials were seldom reported and usually dismissed with a knowing smirk.

It was Chuck's partner and friend David Shapiro who came up with the idea of taking a lie detector test. Colson balked at the idea. Results weren't admissible in court; everything depended on the skill of the operator. He had nothing to gain and everything to lose. But Colson studied the idea further, and when Shapiro found a respected New York operator who could do the job, Colson agreed to go through with it. Besides, if he failed he could keep the test a secret.

And so on a rainy April 4, Colson found himself standing, drenched to the skin, in a run-down New York office building near the theater district, being wired up to a frightful looking machine that would reveal all his secrets. He was soaked because he happened to share a cab from the train station with an ABC News reporter and couldn't risk having him learn his true destination; he had given the cabbie a false address and walked the rest of the way. It was his ninth wedding anniversary. He should have been home with Patty, he thought, but here he was sneaking around New York like some character in a B-grade detective movie.

Just the process made him nervous: wires taped to each fingertip, an inflated rubber pad encircling one arm, a metal chain around his waist. "Now tell me every lie you've ever told and anything you've ever done you are ashamed of," the operator began.

"You're kidding! We'll be here all day!" Colson replied.

But that, the operator explained, was the first step to an accurate reading. Colson talked for an hour. The machine was calibrated and the real questions began:

"Did you order the Watergate break-in?"

"No," Colson answered. He felt his heart racing. His skin was ice cold.

"Did you know about it in advance?"

"No."

At each question Colson felt his face flush. He was so sure he would fail that he decided not even to wait a few minutes for the results. He took the elevator down to the street and stood under the entrance canopy waiting for a taxi. As a cab pulled to the curb Colson made a dash for it through the rain. Just then he heard Shapiro's voice: "Chuck, Chuck—Stop!"

Colson paused on the sidewalk, taxi door open and rain pouring down on the two of them.

"You passed with flying colors!"

Tears welled up in Chuck's eyes, then cascaded down his cheeks. *Thank God it's raining*, he thought as he climbed into the cab and slammed the door. *What would Shapiro think if he saw me blubbering like a baby?*

At first it seemed that passing the test gave Colson the clean slate he so badly wanted. "Colson Reported Passing a Lie Test on Watergate" trumpeted the *New York Times* in a front-page story on April 8. But it was less than two weeks later that the same paper saw the test in a different light, as an "overt sign of continuing concern about guilt and possible recrimination within the President's close circle of advisors." Now rather than putting stock in the positive results, the press seemed to be saying that the very act of taking a lie detector test branded him as guilty.

Privately, Colson took comfort from his recording of the phone conversation with Hunt in November. The words "you had absolutely nothing to do with it" were surely his ace in the hole. Howard Hunt, a key Watergate defendant who had already confessed his guilt, had unequivocally affirmed Colson's innocence. He played it for Dean, Erlichman, and Haldeman with a sense of great relief, despite the obstruction of justice issue it raised, unaware that the trio of presidential insiders harbored far darker secrets of their own, and that by the end of the month all three would be out of a job.

He had no way of knowing about another recording that preserved a recent conversation between Dean and Nixon in which they agreed they could come up with a million dollars in cash over two years to keep the Watergate criminals quiet. Even though what he knew was only the tip of the iceberg, Colson suggested to the president that he appoint an outside special counsel to work through the Watergate mess. This, he explained, was important because it seemed that John Mitchell was already on the hook for obstruction of justice and others close to the president could follow. As soon as Dean got wind of the recommendation, he began distancing himself from Colson, and likely intensified actions to cover his own position. As Chuck Colson redoubled his efforts to protect the president, the president himself and a handful of confidantes were making that task all the more impossible.

Just before leaving the White House, Colson had advised the president to come clean on Watergate. Though Nixon chose repeatedly not to act on Colson's advice, the president and his men kept soliciting it. Colson was now officially an unpaid consultant to the president, in part so Nixon could keep tapping into his ex-counsel's store of information and advice, but also because it provided cover for a claim of executive privilege to keep Colson from testifying before the Ervin committee if such a claim became necessary.

On April 12 John Erlichman called Colson in Boston and told him the president would like a summary of his Watergate recommendations. Nixon had actually called Colson already with the same request: the pace of developments was picking up. The president's inner circle of support was coming apart.

It was apparent that John Dean had decided to cut a deal with the prosecutors. He had hired an attorney and was now angling to save his own skin. There were rumors that Jeb Magruder had been sounding off about White House involvement in the cover-up at a bar association convention in Bermuda. John Mitchell was in the crosshairs as a high-ranking member of the team who might take the fall for all of them. Colson had already suggested Mitchell was the most deeply involved in cover-up payments and could rightly be singled out.

In a phone conversation with the president, Colson tried to help his former boss focus on the "extraordinary accomplishments" of his administration. The White House taping system caught the president worrying that some of his closest advisors were convinced Watergate was "going to destroy the presidency." Colson replied that they might remember the name, but that Nixon still had a shot at a shining legacy: "They'll remember the g—d— Watergate but it won't destroy the presidency, not if the president acts fast."

Colson held tightly to memories of triumphant moments in the Nixon presidency that he thought would live on long after Watergate became a historical footnote. Earlier in the year he had assured the president, "Everyone I've talked to has said, 'Congratulate the president on the [release of the American] prisoners [in Vietnam].' The impact of that is the equivalent of a thousand Watergates."

The morning after Erlichman's call, on Friday the thirteenth, Colson met with him in his White House office at 11:30 as requested to review Colson's recommendations. There had been some strategic discussion of using the Watergate spotlight to charge the Democrats with campaign law violations. That effort, Colson predicted, would be "only a marginally successful tactic." Committee chairman Sam Ervin wouldn't stand for it; neither would Republican committee member Lowell Weicker, an ideological liberal and no fan of the president. Both houses of Congress were controlled by the Democrats, and the public mood was turning more hostile by the day.

Colson was convinced there was no wiggle room in their position. Continuing to hide the truth would subject them to hearings that would be "a fiasco, highly damaging politically" that might well "result in revelations involving other than Watergate that could have an extremely adverse PR impact." Colson consistently said he saw the danger in Watergate as a legal matter; here he played to his audience by couching the issue in political and public relations terms. He was trying everything he could to get the president to act, and act fast.

"I am also convinced," Colson continued, "that either the grand jury or the Ervin hearings will expose any 'higher ups' who had foreknowledge in involvement in the Watergate."

Sticking with his previous recommendation, Colson advised the White House to come clean and get it over with.

> If those who did in fact have knowledge of the
> Watergate or who were in any other way involved in
> the Watergate, are now exposed, there is a chance at least
> to avoid the Ervin hearings and to terminate the grand jury.
> It *may* be possible to avoid a subsequent investigation
> into a conspiracy to obstruct justice and a conspiracy
> to commit perjury. On both of these counts there is a
> much greater danger of wider involvement and indeed of
> much more serious criminal charges being sustained
> against a number of people who are very close to the
> President . . .

My recommendation therefore is that those involved in authorizing, planning, or approving of the Watergate operation either come forward or be exposed now. To wait only incites other more serious charges and/or politically embarrassing disclosures, *as well as* revelations of those involved in the Watergate itself.

He was also in favor of suspending executive privilege under very specific and tightly controlled conditions, and restated his belief the president should appoint a special outside counsel. As for in-house advice, "Remove John Dean and make Fred Fielding [Dean's assistant] or someone else counsel to the President. Dean's usefulness has been destroyed and so if he remains in his present position it makes all of the actions of the President suspect."

"If it is necessary to find a means to expose the guilty parties," Colson concluded, "I can develop a plan to do this." At the bottom of the page he wrote in longhand, "Mitchell."

Unknown to Colson but recorded by the secret White House taping system, the president met with Haldeman and Erlichman in the Oval Office on April 14, 1973, to discuss pardons for the Watergate burglars plus Liddy and Hunt. Nixon said he couldn't grant pardons right away (though Liddy later claimed they had all been promised pardons within two years), but had to wait until "a reasonable time had expired, and before I leave office they'll get off."

"You get them full pardons. That's what they have to have, John," Nixon continued to Erlichman. "Do you agree?"

"Yep, I sure do," Erlichman responded.

By the following Monday the Watergate dam had burst. Dean went to the U.S. attorney seeking immunity from prosecution in exchange for his testimony; Jeb Magruder, Mitchell's deputy, decided the prosecutors knew everything anyway and resolved to plead guilty; Fred LaRue, an advisor to Mitchell, was also implicated in paying hush money to the burglars; Pat Gray, acting director of the FBI, admitted to burning Watergate evidence in his back yard.

In a flurry of meetings and phone calls over the next week, Colson and Erlichman discussed reports that as a result of information the prosecutors received from Dean, Howard Hunt would be asked under oath about the Pentagon Papers assignment as well as Watergate. Colson jotted down that the defendants had already received $350,000 from LaRue by way of Dean, money taken from a fund set aside for polling expenses.

Colson underscored to Erlichman that the Pentagon Papers business involved "highly classified national security matters," and that no one was to testify about them. President Nixon insisted that the 1971 burglary of Dr. Fielding's office in order to discredit Daniel Ellsberg "was classified highest national security, that it had been ordered by the President and that J. Edgar Hoover had known and approved of it at the time."

At one point Erlichman suggested sneaking Hunt out of the country but, as Colson wrote in his notes, "cooler heads prevailed."

Colson was ever mindful of his desire to protect the president without legally conspiring to obstruct justice. He recalled an earlier meeting with Erlichman and Dean when the three of them suggested, in response to continuing pressure from Hunt, that Colson meet with Hunt's lawyer, William Bittman, but that Colson would not offer "intercessions of any kind—or even seem to." Bittman pressed Colson for a commitment on a pardon and other assistance, but Colson reported that he "gave no assurances."

On April 27, 1973, Judge Matthew Byrne revealed in court that Hunt and Liddy arranged a break-in of Dr. Fielding's office. Three weeks later Byrne dismissed all criminal charges against Ellsberg. The president's position on national security was utterly defeated, and the heat on the administration edged up a notch.

Also on April 27 the media continued its unrelenting criticism of Colson with a story in the *Washington Post* headlined "Aides Say Colson Approved Bugging." In an effort to spin the facts in their favor, various Watergate figures had concluded that Chuck Colson approved the whole operation. The facts were that Colson had broken the approval logjam that was delaying Operation Gemstone but that he knew nothing ahead of time about the Watergate break-in. He'd learned about it by phone from John Erlichman the day after it happened, standing in his swimming trunks.

But facts were lost in the scramble as the accused abandoned the sinking White House ship, saying whatever they could think of to minimize damage to themselves.

Colson's side of the story was buried at the bottom of the fourth column in the *Post*: "If Colson had known about and pushed for the bugging, as Magruder and LaRue have told prosecutors, it is unclear why he would have urged the President to find out more about the conspiracy.

"Colson publicly denied last week that he had warned the President," the reporter admitted, but that "associates of Colson . . . asserted that the electronic surveillance had the appearance of a Colson operation particularly because of Hunt's involvement." The reporters also reminded readers of "a memo to some members of the White House staff before last year's election that he would 'walk over my grandmother if necessary' to reelect the President."

Desperate to salvage some remnant of his presidency, Nixon ordered the resignations of his closest and most faithful staff, Haldeman and Erlichman, along with Dean; Attorney General Kleindienst also resigned the same day, April 30. Erlichman and Haldeman were dismissed at Camp David where, Erlichman wrote later, Nixon sobbed uncontrollably and offered the men money. "That would just make things worse," Erlichman said, refusing the funds. Haldeman asked only that their "resignations" be announced separately from Dean's (a request Kleindienst also made), which Nixon promised to do, though he did not—all were announced together.

There were two legal processes now under way, the Senate investigation and a criminal investigation through the Justice Department. On May 3, Colson appeared before Ervin committee staffers, and around the same time endured a confrontational interview with Earl Silbert, chief assistant U.S. attorney, who accused Colson of a variety of acts totally unrelated to Watergate.

To his relief, Colson was informed that he was not a grand jury target of the U.S. attorney; furthermore, there was no evidence that Colson had any advance knowledge of the Watergate break-in, or that he had participated in a cover-up. But the former special counsel wasn't off the hook for long. On May 25, Harvard law professor Archibald Cox was sworn in as the special prosecutor in the Watergate affair. In his first meeting with Silbert, who had been handling the case up to that point, Silbert gave Cox an eighty-page summary of the investigation which, among other things, completely exonerated Colson.

After Silbert finished reviewing the case, Cox's first question reportedly was, "But where's Colson?" When he realized the investigation found Colson innocent, the new prosecutor, a long-time friend of the Kennedy family and staunch liberal, decided there hadn't been enough digging. At the first press conference after his appointment, Cox announced there would be more detailed inquiries into the activities of Charles Colson.

In the Crosshairs

========= **CHAPTER 12** =========

O ne of Colson's few real friends in the media was ABC correspondent Howard K. Smith. Colson had invited Smith to lunch at the White House staff mess several times over the years, and they and their wives enjoyed socializing together. Colson was frustrated at the continuing barrage of rumors and half-truths that appeared in the media. No matter what he said or how strenuously he denied any claim, he seemed to make little headway in presenting his side of the story to the press.

Finally Charles Colson had his chance. Smith invited him to tell his story to a nationwide audience, and though Colson had steadfastly refused lengthy interviews in the past, he agreed to this one. On June 5, 1973, Smith hosted a 30-minute ABC Television network special titled *In the Matter of Watergate: A Conversation with Charles Colson.* Colson was the only guest and Smith the only questioner.

One of his first statements on the program was to explain why he was doing it. "I couldn't sit by any longer idly watching while the president of the United States was being tried in the press on third-, fourth-hand hearsay, on opinion, on the wildest kind of charges. I know that the president of the United States was not involved in the Watergate. I know that the president of the United States was not involved in the Watergate coverup. And I think that the sooner we get to the heart of that matter, the sooner we get to that critical question, the better for the country."

Colson continued by deftly responding to allegations by burglar James McCord ("a convicted felon") and John Dean ("concerned about his own culpability from a criminal standpoint"), explained his relationship with Hunt at the time of the break-in (his secretary initialed Hunt's timesheets), discussed the difference between the Pentagon Papers burglary and Watergate (national security versus campaign intelligence), and spoke on a range of other issues. According to Smith, John Dean declined an invitation to be interviewed for the program.

In the days following the broadcast, Colson and the White House received a flood of admiring letters and telegrams. One viewer wrote, "Thank God someone spoke positively in defense of our president" and had finally made a powerful response to the "hysterical slander" of recent press coverage. Another observed, "The circus on TV daily is sickening and the main purpose is to try to implicate [Nixon] and discredit the good work he has done while in office. I'm sure the President will not resign—we need him!" Even the president, who never admitted to watching television, had a set wheeled into his office for the broadcast and called Colson afterwards to congratulate him.

On June 25, John Dean testified before the Ervin committee that the president knew of the Watergate cover-up nine months before, beginning with a meeting between the two of them on September 15, 1972. He also implicated Colson in the cover-up. The public saw Dean's testimony as a desperate attempt to save himself—columnist Joseph Alsop branded him "a bottom-dwelling slug"—yet the information was shocking. It also directly contradicted the president's own statements. (Years later Nixon would admit that Dean's account was "more accurate than my own.")

Early the next morning after Dean's appearance, Colson appeared for a solid hour as a guest on the *Today* show. To Dean's allegation that Nixon knew about the cover-up, Colson replied, "I think that's preposterous. One of the most tragic sights that I think I've ever seen on American television was John Dean standing yesterday before the committee saying, 'I hope the people will forgive the president.' Forgive the president for what? For what John Dean did and his colleagues conspired to do? Forgive the president because John Dean participated in a conspiracy to lie to the president, to keep information away from the president?"

On the issue of clemency for Hunt, which Dean had also laid at Colson's feet, Colson repeated the facts about his January 8 meeting with the president, categorically denying Dean's charge that he had discussed executive clemency for Hunt. He also acknowledged the earlier meeting with William Bittman, pointing out that he had prepared a memorandum for Dean on the meeting and subsequently offered it to federal prosecutors and the Watergate committee—a fact Dean had omitted from his testimony.

Colson insisted he had nothing to hide. He acknowledged recording the phone conversation with Hunt, and said he gave the recording to Dean and encouraged him to get to the bottom of it, but that Dean only played the recording for Haldeman and Erlichman. Colson also defined the difference between Magruder's testimony—that Colson ordered the plumbers to "get the information from O'Brien's office"—and the truth, which was the far more general statement that Magruder's organization needed to "get cracking on Mr. Liddy's plan for security and intelligence."

"But not on bugging?" asked NBC reporter Carl Stern.

"No, no. And Mr. Magruder in his own testimony says that I never mentioned bugging or any other illegal activities."

In his 248 pages of Watergate testimony, Dean mentioned meeting after meeting to discuss Watergate with senior White House staff members over a period of several months. "Curiously enough," Colson pointed out, "I wasn't in any of those meetings." Dean and the others didn't want to tell Nixon the truth, Colson explained. They were the ones who were breaking the law and endangering the presidency.

New charges, often having nothing to do with Watergate, kept appearing in the press and Colson kept trying to defend himself against them. The papers would run a story—Hunt accusing him of falsifying documents; labor union leader George Meany accusing him of sending goons to a union convention in 1971; claims that he interfered with the Ervin committee—then Colson would draft a response and his secretary would call the source of the story, along with other major media, and read it over the phone, logging the calls as she went. More often than not, the rebuttal was ignored.

Dean revealed the existence of a White House "enemies list" and credited Colson with developing it. Colson released a statement explaining that a member of his staff, since deceased, "was responsible for maintaining lists of supporters of the administration as well as opponents of the administration." These were used by the social office, personnel office, and other components of the White House organization for preparing guest lists for dinner parties, receptions, appointments to federal commissions, and other similar purposes.

"I don't think it is particularly unusual, unprecedented or offensive," Colson continued, "for a President's staff to want to know when extending invitations to the White House or making appointments to boards or commissions whether people under consideration had been friendly or unfriendly. It is tragic that Mr. Bell [who compiled the lists] is not available for comment, a fact no doubt Mr. Dean realizes."

On June 28, during the Ervin committee hearings before a live network television audience, Senator Lowell Weicker, who had emerged as one of the administration's most strident opponents even though he was a Republican, accused Colson of trying to influence the committee by planting a story that Weicker had mishandled campaign contributions in the 1970 election. The same day, Colson prepared a reply for his secretary to call in to the media which said in part, "I do not know what Senator Weicker is talking about . . . I know of nothing improper or in any way out of the ordinary with respect to any assistance Senator Weicker received from any Republican organization in 1970—nor have I ever suggested there was."

The next morning, a Friday, Colson and David Shapiro called on the senator in an effort to get at the truth and clear the air. Weicker had refused to take a telephone call from Colson and insisted he come to his office. Arriving at eight o'clock sharp, Colson asked if Weicker had some sort of grudge against him. If anything, Weicker was even more enraged than he had been the day before. "I don't have any grudge against you," the six-foot-six senator roared. "I don't know you . . . but I do know what you stand for, Mr. Colson, and we live in two different worlds. I deal in hard-nosed politics; you deal in bull—."

Colson tried to reason with the senator, who angrily grilled him about a memo written months before requesting a secret IRS investigation of a labor leader unfriendly to the president. John Dean had given it to the committee. Yes, Colson admitted, he had written the memo. After all, this was hard-nosed politics. But the IRS matter had nothing to do with Watergate. What about the accusation that Colson had tried to smear Weicker? The fact was that a White House staffer named Jack Gleason had been assigned by Larry Higby, Bob Haldeman's chief assistant, to dig up the dirt on Weicker. Colson had nothing to do with it and hadn't known anything about Higby's order. Even as Colson and Weicker were meeting, the wire services were straightening out the story.

But Weicker was furious beyond appeal. The senator stood up and came around his desk until he stood nose-to-nose to the former Marine Corps captain. "You can just get your ass out of my office because you make me sick and I don't even want you in here!"

Colson left the room in a daze. One witness said he looked "like a punchdrunk fighter." The papers, which characterized Colson as the alleged "master dirty trickster," carried a short excerpt of Colson's denial at the bottom of page 10. The page one headline read, "Angry Weicker Orders Colson from His Office."

Two days later, Sunday, July 1, Colson appeared on *Face the Nation*. Throughout all the accusations in the press against him, his problems with Weicker, the president turning on Haldeman and Erlichman, and the host of disturbing and potentially devastating events of the previous six months, one aspect of Colson's life remained absolutely unchanged: his unqualified and unwavering support of Richard Nixon.

In the opening minute of the broadcast, Colson declared that "the proudest moments of my life were serving this president, who I think will go down in history as one of the greatest presidents of all time."

Again he tackled the accusations made by Dean. "It is perfectly clear now in hindsight that people did not tell the president the truth, people who knew the facts. Now I think at the very center of that conspiracy to keep the truth away from the president was John Dean."

He agreed that the circumstantial evidence against Mitchell and Magruder was significant, but refused to speculate on the outcome of in-vestigations about them, or about Erlichman and Haldeman, until they had the chance to defend themselves in their own words.

"There is a fundamental question that is before the American people," Colson said with conviction, "and that is, was the president involved or wasn't he? I think it's imperative that the American people know immediately the truth about the president of the United States . . . I'll stake my credibility against Mr. Dean's any day of the week. I've known the president since 1956. I know his integrity. I know his determination, his courage to do what is right for this country, and I'll stand for what I know to be the truth against Mr. Dean's accusations."

A week later on a radio show hosted by Chicago personality Irv Kupcinet, Colson explained why he had taken up the challenge to become the president's defender.

> I was driving home one night from bringing my son home from college, and I heard on the car radio James McCord, who was one of the convicted Watergate burglars, one of the original conspirators, one of the ones who conceived and planned and executed the idiocy we now know as the Watergate break-in. I heard him on the radio saying that he had come to the conclusion that the president had set in motion the Watergate, had been responsible for the Watergate. This is so utterly preposterous . . . Someone who is under a provisional sentence and therefore it is very much in his interest to say the most sensational things possible. Someone who has reportedly sold his memoirs for a million dollars . . .
> I made up my mind that night after listening to the radio. I really didn't have a choice. I couldn't sit by and allow the president of the United States to be tried on innuendo, third-hand hearsay, on the most bizarre charges for something I know the president didn't have anything to do with.

He covered the same ground again: Hunt, Dean, clemency, what Nixon knew and when; and he refused again to comment on the veracity of statements from Mitchell and others. "I don't think it's right, Kup, to speculate," he explained. "I've been for the past year the butt of so much press speculation about myself I'd characterize as 90 percent false, that I really don't want to contribute to it on the part of other people. Let them have their day in court."

In his testimony, Dean had made much of a March 21, 1973, meeting when he told the president there was "a cancer on the presidency" and that the whole story had to come out. In fact, Colson said, Dean was under pressure from Colson to step aside for a new special counsel, but Dean refused, knowing that telling the whole story would destroy him personally. Resigning then would have been "a perfect opportunity if Dean really did want to get the truth to the American people."

Furthermore, the president had told the American people on April 17 that real progress had been made in getting to the truth. Colson was certain that Nixon said this because Dean told him an investigation had been made. But in his Watergate testimony Dean said he had never carried out an investigation.

"I'd hate to have it on my conscience," Colson continued, "that I took this man who had done such magnificent things for the American people over the past four and a half years and I tried, out of a desperate attempt to stay out of jail, desperate attempt not to be prosecuted, a desperate attempt to save my own skin, that I would try to drag the president of the United States down. To me, if he can live with himself, I'll be very surprised. I couldn't."

Nixon's daughter Julie had been quoted as saying the president discussed the possibility of resigning with his family. Kup asked about that.

"Knowing the president as I think I know him, the last thing he would ever do is resign," Colson responded. "He's not a quitter and the president deeply believes in what he is doing for the country . . . I don't think for a moment that that's a realistic possibility."

Colson worked tirelessly to defend Nixon's position. News reporters staked out his luxurious Virginia home, and he talked with them almost every day. They interviewed him on the way to work. But the Watergate story took on a life of its own. Chuck Colson was screaming the truth into a howling gale of rumor and testimony and leaks. He still had not had the opportunity to tell his side of the story to the Ervin committee, though his lawyer had repeatedly requested he be allowed to speak.

Newsweek ran an article headed "Whispers About Colson" that declared "the man increasingly in the crosshairs is the president's special counsel, Charles W. Colson." Another article titled "The Colson Connection" sported a photo with the caption, "Colson: Calculated ignorance" and the conjecture from Magruder that Colson "must have known about Gordon Liddy's wiretapping scheme in advance."

On July 9 Colson wrote to Sam Dash, counsel to the Watergate committee, to complain about repeated leaks to the press of confidential testimony before the committee. (There were persistent rumors that Senator Weicker selectively leaked information to reporters.) Colson had asked time and again for access to the original material the testimony (and thus the leaks) were based on, but Dash refused to share them.

"I hope you appreciate how difficult it is to try to answer a charge by a newspaper under these circumstances," Colson wrote. "A reporter apparently can see the allegation contained in a committee staff report, but the person accused cannot."

Colson then requested a letter from him be read into the record, which Dash also refused because it would "establish a very unfortunate precedent;" yet on the same day a letter from a congressman was read into the record. Colson again asked to testify before the committee and was again denied.

On Monday afternoon, July 16, Colson was at work in his law office— or trying to work; like everybody else in the city he was mesmerized by the Watergate hearings and keeping one eye on the TV. Alexander Butterfield, a former member of Haldeman's staff in charge of keeping the president's daily schedule, now chief of the FAA, was on the witness stand.

As viewers from coast to coast watched in astonishment, Butterfield told the committee that Nixon had secretly recorded every meeting and phone conversation in his office for more than two years. Butterfield had told committee staffers about the system during his preliminary interview behind closed doors the Friday before, assuming that Haldeman or Higby, who had both been interviewed, would have mentioned it.

This news changed everything. Colson and Shapiro looked at each other, wide-eyed. "Some friend you've got," Shapiro said flatly.

Colson's first reactions were shock and betrayal: shock that something so important and incredible could be going on in the White House without his knowledge, and betrayal that all his private counsel and unguarded opinions were recorded without his knowledge. A president already in grave peril over a bugging incident was also bugging himself and everybody around him. Only Nixon, Haldeman, and a tiny circle of Haldeman's staff knew the system existed. There were 3,700 hours of tapes in all, kept in storage by the Secret Service.

But feelings of despair soon turned to feelings of almost unimaginable relief. After all the slander he had been forced to endure, here, like a miracle, were recordings of meetings and conversations that would prove Colson's innocence. (The evidence was even better than he knew. On June 20, 1972, the White House system recorded a Watergate strategy meeting between Haldeman and the president where Haldeman said categorically, "I don't think Chuck knew specifically that, you know, this project was under way or that these people were involved.")

Entering the White House the next day, Colson expected to feel a sense of vindication and sense the smell of victory in the air. But what he saw instead was worried expressions that "indicated more and greater troubles were ahead." The president was in the hospital with pneumonia; the whole White House was paralyzed with fear.

On August 7, the Ervin committee took a recess without ever giving Chuck Colson a chance to defend himself on the record. Silbert's detailed preliminary investigation had turned up nothing connecting Colson to Watergate. But the leaks and accusations kept flying at him like flaming arrows. His friend the president was under increasing attack. Colson had been falsely accused by Senator Weicker on network television, then browbeaten in his office. Now the secret tapes added a new and unprecedented level of madness to life in Washington that Colson had never known in more than twenty years there, "reducing political morality to the level of bayonet warfare."

Looking ahead, Charles Colson—high-flying Washington lawyer with his own chauffeur—saw nothing but black desolation. He felt empty, rudderless. Was this all there was to life? Was this the view from the top?

He canceled the press interviews on his calendar. He needed to think. He found himself wondering about his purpose in life, what it was that would give him happiness and fulfillment. He recalled the unanticipated emptiness of election night the previous November; the lack of genuine excitement over his trip to the Soviet Union in February.

And he found himself thinking more and more about a remarkable visit he'd had in March with an old friend from Massachusetts.

The Great Sin

CHAPTER 13

M aybe he was just tired. Chuck Colson had worked ten- and twelve-hour days, six and seven days a week, for three and a half years; then with scarcely a break he had plunged into his new law practice, while at the same time continuing to advise the president on Watergate and trying to keep his own name out of the mud. It was an inhuman pace, maintained in the face of a deluge of false accusations and looming uncertainty about the future.

At an important meeting in New York just after he had returned to his law practice, Colson couldn't keep his attention focused on the presentation. Millions of dollars were on the line—his young associate was eagerly taking notes—but Colson could hear nothing, and sat watching mouths around the table moving in silence, as though there were a soundproof glass barrier separating them. It was the first time in his life he'd ever been unable to concentrate on a meeting. He thought he was having a blackout.

It hadn't been that long since he and Patty returned from their official visit to the Soviet Union. Maybe his system was still scrambled by the time change and the unfamiliar food. And he must have done things well enough at the meeting: Colson & Shapiro got the business.

In March, Colson went to Lexington, Massachusetts, outside Boston, to renew a business relationship he had especially enjoyed during his pre-White House career. Raytheon Company had been one of his favorite clients at Gadsby & Hannah, and now they wanted Colson & Shapiro to handle their legal affairs.

Raytheon was an electronics manufacturer and defense contractor, and the largest employer in New England. Its executive vice president,

Brainerd Holmes, was first in his class at Cornell, the former head of the NASA manned spacecraft program, and an old friend of Colson's. Just before the election, Colson had invited him to the White House for a meal; both men looked forward to reviving their business relationship.

After a full day of meetings with an assortment of vice presidents and engineers, Colson received word that Tom Phillips, president of the company and Holmes's boss, wanted to see Colson before he left. Colson and Phillips had met in the mid-1960s when Paul Hannah, former general counsel for the company, joined Colson's law firm.

Holmes stopped him as he started for Phillips' office. "Chuck, maybe there's something I should tell you about Tom before you go in there. He's had quite a change—some kind of religious experience." Holmes paused awkwardly, then continued. "I don't really understand it, but it's quite important to him. He might come on, well, a little strong."

This news was a surprise to Colson. Tom wasn't the religious type, but whatever he did, he did with passion. Maybe it was some kind of fund-raising program. High-profile executives were always being asked to do things like that, and it would be right in line with Tom's character if he had agreed to chair a foundation or a building committee for something.

At first he seemed just the same as the last time Chuck had seen him, but after a minute or two he sensed a genuine difference. Rather than the customary executive circus of phones ringing constantly, secretaries flying in and out of the room, and subordinates hopping on one foot in the doorway, the whole atmosphere was unexpectedly calm. There was the same efficiency and singleness of purpose as before, but the whole process was so much more relaxed—certainly a far cry from the nonstop controlled explosion in the EOB.

Phillips asked Colson how he was. "I'm doing fine," he lied. He was wound up and miserable. "A little tired."

"You really should get some rest, Chuck," Phillips replied. Though he had always been a courteous and thoughtful person, Colson was struck at the new sincerity in his friend's voice.

After a while the talk turned to Watergate. "It looks to me like people are trying to drag you into it," Phillips observed.

In reply, Colson began a long-winded recitation of the facts but Phillips cut him off. "Don't explain," he said. "If you tell me you weren't responsible, that's all I need to hear."

Brainerd Holmes had warned Colson that Tom Phillips had had "some kind of religious experience." He hadn't said anything about it so far, yet clearly he was a different man: more confident, assured, relaxed, and content than Colson had ever seen him, though no less a successful business executive. Finally Colson's curiosity got the best of him.

"Brainerd tells me you've become very involved in some religious activities."

Phillips smiled. "Yes, that's true, Chuck. I have accepted Jesus Christ. I have committed my life to Him, and it has been the most marvelous experience of my whole life."

Colson was completely dumbfounded. How could one of the country's most successful business executives, one who dealt in the realities of science and electronics, one who climbed to the top based on real-world performance, commit his life to someone who lived two thousand years ago?

He stuttered a reply and the conversation moved on to other things. But as the two of them walked toward Phillips's office door at the end of their visit, Tom put his arm around Chuck's shoulder and came back to his accepting Christ. "I'd like to tell you the whole story some day, Chuck. I had gotten to the point where I didn't think my life was worth anything. Now everything is changed: attitude, values, the whole bit."

They shook hands and Chuck headed back to Washington, but he couldn't get his friend's statement, or his new attitude, out of his head. Tom had to be making a million dollars a year. How could he think his life wasn't worth anything? But he'd seen the proof with his own eyes: the new sense of genuineness, the confidence, the serenity, the sheer joy that Tom radiated in the room, yet without any loss of business drive or creative energy. Raytheon was more profitable than ever.

In the months that followed, Colson doggedly fought the weary emptiness that sometimes threatened to overpower him, and revisited his discussion with Tom Phillips time and again. How could he of all people feel bad about his life? If anybody had a reason to feel bad, it was Charles

W. Colson, Watergate punching bag. But sometimes, sitting alone in his office or late at night after Patty had gone to sleep, Chuck drifted back and latched on to that March conversation and to Tom's words: "I have committed my life to Him, and it has been the most marvelous experience of my whole life."

Colson could surely use a marvelous experience. After the Ervin committee declared a recess on August 7, Chuck and Patty planned a short vacation to a favorite hideaway in Maine with a stop to visit Chuck's parents in Dover, Massachusetts, on the way. Dover wasn't far from Tom Phillips's home in the Boston suburbs. For reasons Colson could never explain, he called Phillips and asked if he could stop by. His friend said he would welcome the visit, and Chuck was surprised at his own excitement at the thought of hearing the rest of the story about Tom's new life.

(It wasn't until long afterward that Chuck learned Tom had worried about their meeting, stewed mightily about what to say, and practiced his remarks repeatedly in order to make them as clear and compelling as possible because it was the first time he had spoken to anybody on the topic.)

On Sunday night, August 12, 1973, Chuck left Patty at his parents' house in Dover and drove to Tom's spacious New England Colonial clapboard house in Weston. He didn't feel like trying to explain what he was doing, so he told Patty he had to go to a business meeting. Sunday meetings were commonplace, and Patty had no reason to think this night was anything out of the ordinary.

Chuck found the house and headed for what he thought was the front door. It was the kitchen instead, but Tom's wife, Gert, welcomed him warmly as she finished cleaning up the supper dishes. Tom was playing tennis with their two teenage children, she explained, and, drying her hands on a dish towel, she went out the back door to call them.

The three players soon came bounding into the kitchen, cheeks flushed and shirts dappled with perspiration after a game in the unusually hot and humid New England summer night. Gert handed the two men tall glasses of fresh iced tea, then Tom led Chuck from the kitchen through the house to a screened porch at the other end. Chuck removed his dark gray suit jacket and tie (which would have been required for any "business meeting," even on the weekend) and Tom mopped his face and neck with a towel.

Tom began the conversation with the same question he had asked in March. "Tell me, Chuck, are you okay?" Colson deflected the question. Raytheon was one of his biggest and most important clients. This was no time to admit he had any personal problems that could in any way compromise his performance.

So his host began to talk, first about his rise through the corporate ranks. He had been extremely successful by any measure and had made it to president at age forty. But, he continued, something was missing. He felt "a terrible emptiness" that robbed him of sleep and made him feel worthless and powerless to do anything about it.

There was, he said, "a big hole in my life" that nothing he knew could fill. After he had looked everywhere else for answers, he looked in the Bible. "Something made me realize I needed a personal relationship with God, forced me to search," he went on.

Colson had goosebumps. Maybe his problem wasn't all that unusual, but the answer was something he hadn't thought of: religion. He didn't have any idea that a personal relationship with God was even possible. He asked Tom to tell him more about his thoughts on what seemed to be a conflict between monetary and career success and the hollow emptiness he felt.

"All the material things in life are meaningless if a man hasn't discovered what's underneath them," Tom explained. He went on to describe a business trip he'd made to New York when he noticed there was a Billy Graham Crusade in Madison Square Garden. Out of curiosity—and perhaps the sense of a glimmer of hope—he went to the crusade. "What Graham said that night put it all into place for me. I saw what was missing, the personal relationship with Jesus Christ, the fact that I hadn't ever asked Him into my life, hadn't turned my life over to Him. So I did it— that very night at the Crusade."

"That's what you mean by accepting Christ? You just ask?" Colson queried.

"It's as simple as that."

This was unfamiliar ground. Colson knew Jesus as a historical figure, but never imagined Him as somebody he could give his life to today, somebody actually a part of contemporary daily living. He was profoundly moved by Tom's story, but he couldn't imagine something as simple as accepting Christ could change a man's life so completely. Even so, there was no doubt the change was there.

The conversation moved back to Colson's life in Washington and the Watergate fishbowl. Colson spoke at length about all the false accusations that were flying in every direction. After he finished, Tom gently but firmly told him the whole uproar was completely wrong, and completely unnecessary considering the size of Nixon's victory.

"If only you had believed in the rightness of your cause," Tom said, leaning forward with his elbows on his knees, eyes fixed on Chuck's, "none of this would have been necessary. The problem with you is that you had to destroy your enemies because you couldn't trust your instincts."

Tom was right on target. But, Chuck explained, politics was a world unto itself. It was dog-eat-dog; it was war. Nixon was slammed mercilessly by the press and had no choice but to fight back.

Yet even as he spoke those words, Colson felt different somehow about them. The words sounded unexpectedly empty and tired—just like Colson felt himself. As he wrote later, "I was describing the ways of the political world, all right, while suddenly wondering if there could be a better way."

Then Tom cut to the heart of the matter. "Chuck, you guys brought this on yourselves. If you had put your faith in God, and if your cause were just, He would have guided you."

As he spoke he reached for a small paperback book on a nearby table. "Chuck, I don't think you'll understand what I'm saying about God until you're willing to face yourself honestly and squarely. This is the first step." He held up the book for Chuck to read the title: *Mere Christianity* by C. S. Lewis.

Handing it toward him, Tom suggested Chuck read it while he was on vacation. Then he paused and withdrew his outstretched arm. "Let me read you one chapter first."

Lewis was an Anglican, the mother denomination of Colson's own Episcopal Church, and, like Colson, a keen intellectual. By trade a professor of literature at Oxford and then Cambridge, Lewis had gained a wide following as a Christian layman writing everything from theology to children's books. His death ten years earlier, on the day President Kennedy was shot, had gone virtually unnoticed.

Tom angled the book to catch as much light as he could from the small lamps on the porch, opened it to a chapter titled, "The Great Sin," and began to read aloud. Lewis had adapted the text from radio talks he had given during World War II; rather than render the words irrelevant, the intervening years had instead underscored their wisdom and multiplied their power:

> There is one vice of which no man in the world is free; which every one in the world loathes when he sees it in someone else; and of which hardly any people, except Christians, ever imagine that they are guilty themselves . . . There is no fault . . . which we are more unconscious of in ourselves. And the more we have it ourselves, the more we dislike it in others.
>
> The vice I am talking of is Pride or Self-Conceit . . . Pride leads to every other vice: it is the complete anti-God state of mind . . . As long as you are proud you cannot know God. A proud man is always looking down on things and people: and, of course, as long as you are looking down, you cannot see something that is above you.
>
> For Pride is spiritual cancer: it eats up the very possibility of love, or contentment, or even common sense.

As Tom read, Colson saw scenes from his life flash before him "as if projected on a screen." Pride was at the center of every signal moment: giving the valedictory speech at Browne and Nichols; thumbing his nose at a Harvard scholarship; being "good enough" for that Marine Corps recruiter; all the way to the White House: "Mr. Colson, the president wants to see you right away."

As Tom continued, Chuck grew ashamed to the point of agony. His whole life was built on pride, "The Great Sin." Everything he did was for more influence, more power, more praise, and lately, more money. As he later recalled, "In those brief moments while Tom read, I saw myself as never before. And the picture was ugly."

Chuck scarcely knew his friend had finished. His mind was a maelstrom.

"How about it, Chuck?" Tom's words brought him back to a dimly lit screened porch on a humid summer night.

Tom was asking him if he was ready to accept Christ himself. But it was too much, too soon. "I can't tell you I'm ready to make the kind of commitment you did." He had to be certain, had to read up on it and get past his "intellectual hang-ups."

Chuck had seen too many foxhole conversions in the Marine Corps. He hesitated to make a commitment when it might turn out to be a crutch.

"I understand," Tom said quietly.

Chuck almost wanted Tom to press his case, but Tom handed him his copy of *Mere Christianity*, suggesting he read it and the Gospel of John in the Bible as well. He also jotted down the name Doug Coe, a man in Washington who "gets people together for Christian fellowship—prayer breakfasts and things like that."

Tom read a few verses from Psalms—they felt to Chuck like "a cold, soothing ointment"—and then offered to pray for the two of them. Outside of a church service, Chuck had never prayed with anyone in his life except for grace before a meal. Tom leaned forward in his chair, bowed his head, and prayed with simple sincerity for Chuck and his family, that Chuck's heart might be opened to the saving knowledge of Jesus Christ. The prayer was so natural and personal. The only praying Chuck remembered was stilted and formal, peppered with "thee" and "thou"; Tom was talking to his best friend.

As he listened, Chuck felt a surge of energy pulse through his body, then a wave of emotion that made him want to cry. Tom finished, and Chuck knew he was expected to say something now. But he didn't know what to say; besides, it was all he could do to fight back the tears.

Tom walked Chuck back through the house to the kitchen door. "Let me know what you think of the book, will you?" He put his hand on Colson's shoulder. "I'll see you soon."

Alone in the driveway, Colson could feel the grip on his emotions slipping rapidly. The tears he had held back earlier now rimmed his eyes as he fumbled for the car key. Reflexively he brushed them away. "What kind of weakness is this?" he muttered aloud. His only answer was the sound of crickets in the breeze of an August night.

Tears came again, this time spilling over and cascading down his cheeks before he could stop them. Suddenly he felt an overwhelming desire to go back inside and pray with Tom. Why hadn't he done it before? He turned off the engine, got out, and walked briskly back toward the house. But before he reached the door he saw the downstairs lights go off one after another, then watched Tom and Gert walk through the hall and start up the stairs. The hall light went out. He had missed his chance.

Returning to his car, Chuck started the engine, headed down the driveway, and turned onto a quiet road laced between rows of towering pines. The tears were flowing harder now; street lights and headlights began to blur, then ran completely together. He pulled off the road onto the mounds of pine needles that covered the shoulder and stopped the car. He cried uncontrollably; great, heaving sobs piercing the darkness and tears streaming unchecked down his face, rendering little soft, moist circles in the starch of his shirt. He leaned forward and cupped his face in both hands, wondering whether his cries were audible inside the Phillips house. His whole body shook; his hands were drenched.

Then from deep within the core of raw emotion that enveloped him came the sensation that water wasn't running only down his face but coursing though his entire body, flooding it with a sense of cleansing and cooling and relief. He had no idea what it meant to "accept Christ," but he sensed a presence and a power unlike any he had ever known.

And he prayed.

"God, I don't know how to find You, but I'm going to try. I'm not much the way I am now, but somehow I want to give myself to You. Take me!

Charles Wendell Colson and his parents, Wendell and Inez Ducrow Colson, c. 1945. Both parents were from immigrant stock, his father's family from Sweden and his mother's from England. The family was enjoying a period of relative prosperity after Colson's father had spent twelve years earning accounting and law degrees in night school.

Freshman Colson in his high school football uniform.

Colson as a student at Brown University, Providence, Rhode Island. He turned down a full scholarship at Harvard because he thought it was too haughty and accepted an offer from Brown instead.

The student government board at Brown hears testimony on a violation, Judge Chuck Colson presiding.

Lieutenant Charles W. Colson, U. S. Marine Corps. Though he enlisted too late to fight in Korea, Colson served in Puerto Rico and Guatemala.

One of Colson's first high-profile projects as special counselor to the president was smoothing the transition from the old Post Office Department to the new quasi-independent Postal Service. In the Oval Office (l. to r.), Bob Erlichman, presidential domestic advisor; aide Henry Cashen; Colson; James Rademacher, head of the postal employees union; President Nixon.

Colson and President Nixon in the White House Cabinet Room with a trade association group. As a lawyer and lobbyist, Colson developed important ties with a long list of trade groups and labor organizations that helped the president appeal to broad constituencies. Colson boasted that the president never refused to see a group he recommended.

Colson meeting with his staff, which he did at 9:15 every morning, right after his 8 A.M. meeting with Nixon's chief of staff and other key advisors. In a city where proximity to the president is a sign of power, Colson had the ultimate position: in the Executive Office Building immediately adjacent to Nixon's private hideaway office.

The president often invited Colson to sit in on White House meetings that might have an impact on trade groups or unions. Here he advises the president during a discussion with (l. to r.) Secretary of Transportation John Volpe, presidential assistants Bryce Harlow, Dick Moore, and Peter Flanigan, and Undersecretary of Commerce Rocco Siciliano.

President Nixon and his friend, Charles "Bebe" Rebozo, followed by Colson, celebrating Nixon's 1972 re-election at La Hasta Restaurant in Miami. According to one report, the president and Rebozo were "as drunk as skunks."

Sidewalk press conference on June 21, 1974, moments after being sentenced to one to three years in prison. Against the advice of his defense attorneys, Colson insisted on pleading guilty to a charge stemming from the Pentagon Papers case. Based on punishment imposed on other Watergate figures, Colson had hoped for a suspended sentence.

Between the time of his sentencing and the day he reported to prison on July 8, Colson was busy putting his finances in order and making arrangements for his wife, Patty. Even so, he took time out for a "going into prison party" at the Palm Restaurant in Washington, where he recreated the widely but incorrectly quoted promise that he would "walk over his own grandmother" to get Nixon elected.

Chuck and Patty Colson at home after Colson's release from prison, early 1975.

Colson began making notes for his first book, Born Again, *while he was still in prison. It was an instant best-seller when it was published in 1976, and Colson used the royalties to begin Prison Fellowship. In 1978* Born Again *was made into a feature film. This is a prison mug shot staged for the filming.*

A protest scene from Born Again.

NO
PARDON
FOR
COLSON

Colson and former president Jimmy Carter help build a Habitat for Humanity house in Chicago, 1985.

Colson visiting prisoners in the early 1980s.
Within a week of his release from Holabird Prison in January 1975, Colson returned as a visitor to Maxwell Prison, where he had also been housed, to visit members of his Bible study group.

Early 1980s prison visits.

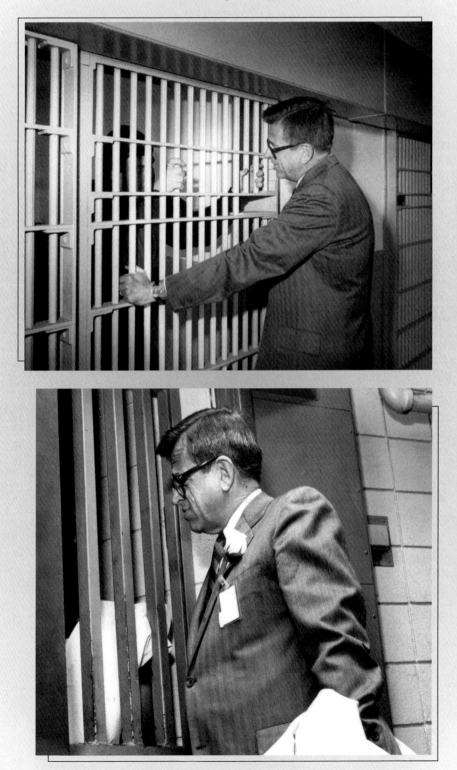

Colson at Lorton Prison near Washington, one of the toughest facilities in the federal system.

In prison during the late 1980s.

The Colson family at home in Florida, 1988: Chuck; Patty; his children, Wendell, Christian, and Emily; their spouses and children.

*Founder of
Prison
Fellowship
Ministries*

Sharing the good news of Christ

Colson with HRH Prince Philip upon receiving the Templeton Prize for Progress in Religion. Colson donated the entire $1 million cash award to Prison Fellowship Ministries.

Colson delivering the Templeton Address in recognition of his award at McCormick Chapel, University of Chicago, September 1993.

Colson with evangelist Billy Graham at the National Prayer Breakfast in Washington. A sermon by Graham inspired Colson's friend Tom Phillips to accept Christ; Phillips later witnessed to Colson and led him to Jesus.

Though some Christian leaders have opposed the idea, Colson has made a case for evangelical Protestants and Catholics to join forces in outreach through the "Evangelicals and Catholics Together Statement" of 1994 and a book of essays published the following year. Here he meets with Pope John Paul II in New York, 1998.

Recording a radio broadcast with James Dobson of Focus on the Family. Colson's own daily radio program, "BreakPoint," launched in 1991, is syndicated in more than one thousand markets and also available on the Internet.

Patty and Chuck at a Prison Fellowship retreat in Palm Springs, around 1995.

"Take me! Take me! *Take me!*"

It was some time before he got back onto the road and headed for his parents' house in Dover. But the Chuck Colson that pulled onto the pavement at last was a different man from the one who had pulled off it. He had spent a lifetime single-mindedly dedicating his energy, intellect, and talent to getting ahead. To making a reputation for himself. To becoming financially secure. To building his business, providing for his family, protecting the president of the United States. Now the transforming journey had begun toward using that same rare and remarkable energy, intellect, and talent in the service of Jesus Christ.

It was not to be a quiet road lined with stately pines, but a dark path through fiery trials such as the Kingdom's newest disciple could scarcely imagine.

A New Perspective

=== **CHAPTER 14** ===

Chuck stared out the window at the restless Atlantic. He and Patty had found a quiet cottage on the ocean in Boothbay Harbor, Maine, a world away from the frenzied stress of Washington. Hoping for a few days out of the spotlight, he was surprised when the clerk in the rental office recognized his name.

"Is Watergate still going on?" the craggy-faced young man asked.

"Yes, it's still going on," Chuck replied, disappointed that his notoriety had followed him even to such an isolated place.

"Well I'll be!" the clerk said. "I thought it was over in June. My TV's been busted."

Fantastic! Colson thought to himself. *We've found a place where the TV doesn't work!*

He unpacked his suitcase, pulled out *Mere Christianity*, and arranged a yellow legal pad on the table in front of him as though he were getting ready to plot out his argument for a case. At the top of the page he wrote, "Is there a God?"

His mind flashed back to the night off the coast of Guatemala when he'd looked up at the stars and been suddenly struck by the massiveness and magnificence of the universe. He remembered, too, a summer day years later when he took his younger son, Christian, out on the lake in a brand new sailboat. From the tiller Chuck had watched Chris hold the mainsheet, his eyes sparkling as he felt the wind against the sail and realized he was controlling the boat. Without knowing how or when it happened, he had found himself talking to God: "Thank You, God, for giving me this son, for giving us this one wonderful moment. Just looking now into this boy's eyes fulfills my life. Whatever happens in the future, even if I die tomorrow, my life is complete and full. Thank You."

It was the same kind of one-on-one conversation Tom Phillips had with God when he prayed for Chuck on the porch.

Opening the book, Colson started reading and making notes, grateful that he had never had to face Lewis in court. His arguments in favor of Christianity were meticulously presented and intellectually airtight, and soon Chuck was filling page after page with thoughts pro and con. The lawyer in him responded to Lewis's argument supporting the existence of moral law, yet the realist countered that nothing invisible and undetectable could be so powerful.

But was what Chuck felt on Tom Phillips's porch and afterwards in his car undetectable? On the contrary, there was power in that moment unlike anything he had ever experienced. The love of God was invisible and no scientific method could detect it, yet Chuck had felt its power firsthand. It was as real as the crickets in the pine trees; as real as the surf crashing now outside his window.

He read with interest Lewis's answer to the question of why, if God was good, was there so much evil in the world. It was because selfish, sinful mankind had the freedom—within the limits of authority set by God—to act any way it wanted to, and human pride resulted in sinful, destructive decisions.

The second day of their vacation, Patty had become aware that Chuck wasn't himself. Typically he attacked vacation with all the restless energy he put into his days at the White House, constantly on the go, endlessly looking for the next surprise or diversion. But on this trip he was completely different, holed up with a borrowed paperback book and obviously distracted. As the two of them were reading on the deck of the cottage, Chuck looked up from his book and turned to Patty.

"You believe in God, don't you?"

In the nine years of their marriage they had never discussed God. Chuck was a nominal Episcopalian; she was a Roman Catholic. His Protestant faith and his divorce had prevented them from being married in Patty's church, but that had been the last significant religious issue in their life as a couple.

"You know I do."

"But have you really thought about it? Like who God is and why He created us?"

Patty's face wore an expression of surprise mixed with confusion. "What's in that book you're reading?"

Chuck gave her an overview of his meeting with Tom—leaving out the emotional epiphany in the car—and explained that he was looking for answers to his questions about God. And that the little book Tom gave him was terrific.

Patty's natural reaction was to suggest her husband talk to a priest. Her husband thought to himself that forty years of priests and ministers had failed to do what one little paperback was accomplishing. He was understanding Christianity, and feeling his desperate need for it as the answer to all the uneasiness and dissatisfaction that had haunted him since election day.

"Jesus Christ is God," Lewis wrote, citing John 10:30 ("The Father and I are one"). This, Chuck sensed, was the essence of Lewis's message. "Not just part of God, or just sent by God, or just related to God. He was (and therefore, of course, is) God."

Colson found a striking point of comparison between Lewis's thinking and his own career in public service. As a government official, he defended the right of the state to encroach upon the rights of individuals for the common good. If it protected the state it was good policy, even if a few people suffered as a result.

The key to the issue, Lewis claimed, was that individuals were the important ones, not the state, because their souls were immortal and the very existence of a state was transitory.

"If individuals live only seventy years," Lewis explained, "then a state, or a nation, or a civilisation, which may last for a thousand years, is more important than an individual. But if Christianity is true, then the individual is not only more important but incomparably more important, for he is everlasting and the life of a state or of a civilisation, compared with his, is only a moment."

With a knot forming in his stomach, Colson acknowledged that meant the rights of Dr. Daniel Ellsberg were more important than the secrets in the Pentagon Papers.

He could no longer sidestep the question. Now he knew the facts, and the only question was what he would do with them. Delay was pointless.

At the end of the week Chuck Colson stood alone on the deck of his rented cottage watching and listening as the ocean breakers roared and hissed on the rocks below. The last words in Lewis's little book rolled around in his head:

"Submit to death, death of your ambitions and favourite wishes every day and death of your whole body in the end: submit with every fibre of your being, and you will find eternal life. Keep back nothing. Nothing that you have not given away will be really yours. Nothing in you that has not died will ever be raised from the dead. Look for yourself, and you will find in the long run only hatred, loneliness, despair, rage, ruin, and decay. But look for Christ and you will find Him, and with Him everything else thrown in."

Unfamiliar words formed on Colson's lips and he spoke them aloud into the sea breeze blowing across the New England shore. "Lord Jesus, I believe You. I accept You. Please come into my life. I commit it to You."

Newfound strength, serenity, and purpose coursed through him, driving out the fears, tensions, and animosities of a lifetime. He looked at the future with new eyes. Confident though he was, he sensed a difficult road ahead.

But before his tribulations resumed, Colson made some new friends whose support would be essential in the months to come.

Colson returned to his law practice seeing life from a new perspective. It was almost like he'd never noticed the people he encountered every day as individuals before. His driver, the people in the lobby, junior staffers at the firm all made a fresh impression on him. They saw that he smiled and took notice of them like he never had in the past.

A few days after he returned from Maine, Colson took an odd message from his secretary. There was a Mr. Coe waiting to see him, she said over the office intercom, and he wouldn't identify himself. This was the fellow Tom had mentioned to him. Colson had written Tom about his decision, but there would scarcely have been time for him to get the letter.

Doug Coe sauntered into Colson's office like the two of them were old friends, draped his arm over Colson's shoulder and said, "This is just great, just great, what Tom has told me about you." Tom had read Chuck's letter over the phone to Doug, and asked him to get in touch.

Doug gave Chuck a little background on himself. He had come to Washington at the invitation of Oregon Senator Mark Hatfield. Before that he had been at Willamette University, and had a staff position with Young Life, a Christian campus organization. He now worked with the Fellowship Foundation, which sponsored an annual prayer breakfast in Washington and provided meeting facilities and other hospitality in the name of Jesus to public figures in the capital. Chuck responded with the story of his experience at Tom's, his week of contemplation at the shore, and his decision to accept Christ. It was the first time he'd ever shared the whole story with anyone, and it felt strange. But it felt wonderful.

Coe was delighted. "You'll want to meet Senator Hughes," he declared. Colson didn't think so. Hughes was a liberal Democrat who despised Nixon.

"That doesn't matter now, Chuck," Doug said easily. Chuck couldn't imagine that by accepting Christ it would turn sworn political enemies into friends.

"You'll have hundreds of people all over this city who will want nothing more than to help you. Some of them know we're meeting and are praying for you right now."

This seemed unbelievable to Chuck. For months he had fought against a tide of hostile media and a public thirsting for blood in the Watergate affair. No one, not even his former colleagues at the White House, had ever offered to help him or asked if he needed anything. Now this acquaintance of thirty minutes was telling him perfect strangers cared about him.

Doug suggested that they pray together. Chuck hesitated: he had never prayed in front of anyone like this before, and furthermore he wondered what would happen if someone came into the office and caught them at it. But Doug seemed so natural and encouraging that Chuck agreed. Doug thanked God for bringing the two of them together, then Chuck stammered haltingly through the first group prayer of his life.

As Chuck struggled to sort out his feelings over the next several weeks, the wheels of justice ground on in the glare of television lights. Before the month was out, David Shapiro and another partner and friend, Judah Best, learned that the grand jury hearing evidence on the Ellsberg break-in was going to hear evidence against Colson. Colson's immediate response was to ask to testify before the jury and tell his side of the story— something he had been denied in the Watergate hearings. Shapiro and Best were against it, fearing he might say something that could be used against him if there were eventually a trial.

But Colson prevailed, and on August 30, found himself in a Washington courtroom being questioned by the assistant special prosecutor, William Merrill. "I am here at my own request," Colson informed the grand jury, "because I have felt from the beginning that I would like to be in a position to tell as much as I know about the events, anywhere I can."

Colson's initial confidence soon turned to concern. Merrill asked about alleged dirty tricks in the 1972 New Hampshire primary; about his attitude toward the candidacy of Robert Kennedy; about homosexuals supporting George McGovern. The questions had nothing whatever to do with Ellsberg.

After a lunch break and a discussion with Shapiro, Merrill focused more on the Ellsberg break-in. The jurors, all eyes and ears as long as the prosecutors had been asking juicy questions about campaign tricks, lost interest. Some read newspapers while others dozed.

Colson returned the next day for a second session, but this time the jurors seemed even less engaged. With all the prejudicial publicity, it would be impossible for President Nixon's hatchet man and biggest cheerleader to get a fair hearing. A few days afterward Colson received word that he would be indicted in the Ellsberg break-in case. Then two days later, Sam Dash, the chief counsel of the Watergate committee, called to schedule Colson's appearance there. Colson and his legal team had been trying for months to get the committee to let him testify. Colson was convinced that the reason Dash kept putting him off was that his story would present such a compelling defense of Nixon that it might cost the committee some momentum in building the public case against the president.

Now that Colson was being indicted in the Ellsberg case, he couldn't testify about any aspect of it before the Watergate committee without jeopardizing his legal defense. Of course Dash realized this; for the sake of appearance he argued that Colson hadn't actually been indicted, but that the indictment was "imminent." Shapiro said it was a technicality, and that it was essential in the name of fairness for his client to be spared testifying in one case while under indictment in another. In the end, the committee refused and ordered Colson to testify.

Colson appeared voluntarily before the Ellsberg grand jury for the third time on September 6. He went again on September 10, but terminated his appearance when it became painfully obvious, according to a statement Colson released to the press, that "the Special Prosecutor was determined to prosecute regardless of the facts I could testify to. I will have nothing further to say . . . other than to state as I have today that I am innocent of the charges that have been made."

With the crescendo of negative publicity rising unchecked, Colson also announced he would take a leave of absence from Colson & Shapiro beginning September 11, 1973, and that the firm would be renamed Dickstein, Shapiro & Morin.

"Regardless of how rough the road ahead may be," Colson's statement concluded, "I have faith that in the end the truth will prevail."

Colson's appearance before the Watergate executive committee, the closed-door prelude to his public and nationally televised testimony, was September 19. He and his attorneys arrived at the Capitol and found the steps crawling with journalists crowded so close to the car that they could scarcely open the doors. With the help of the Capitol police, the group waded through the shouting mob, past clusters of tourists, and into the anteroom of the richly decorated caucus chamber.

Colson's legal team insisted that he take the Fifth Amendment. They said it was the only way he could protect himself from compromising his defense in the Ellsberg case. Colson adamantly opposed the idea. In the eyes of the American public, taking the Fifth was an admission of guilt. If you had nothing to hide, there was no reason to hide behind the Constitution. Refusing to testify meant you didn't believe in yourself, Colson thought. It was a cop-out, and he couldn't imagine doing it.

As they waited, Shapiro decided they should try again for a delay. If they didn't get it, he insisted Colson was to take the Fifth. To the former presidential counsel, it didn't seem possible that such a nightmare could be unfolding. He had waited months for the chance to tell his side of the story, and now it looked as if that chance would come under the only conditions that would make giving his testimony impossible.

The session began with Dash admitting an indictment in the Ellsberg case was likely, and that Colson would probably be on the list. Shapiro argued that Colson's constitutional right to a fair trial was at stake. The committee asked Colson and the others to leave them while they debated the issue. Through the massive mahogany doors of the room they could hear the senators in heated debate, especially Howard Baker supporting Colson's position and Lowell Weicker vigorously opposing it.

Finally after a long hour's wait, Colson and his group were called back into the room. A stern-faced Senator Ervin looked at Colson. "The committee has denied your request. Stand up and raise your right hand."

Still unsure what he would do when the moment came, Colson put his hands on the table to rise. Shapiro leaned toward him and said, "You have to do it or you can get yourself another set of lawyers."

Dash began the questioning. "Mr. Colson, are you acquainted with E. Howard Hunt?"

Colson opened his mouth but for an instant nothing would come out. "I never thought I would be in this position where I felt that my own legal rights were being prejudiced and that I had to avail myself of my constitutional privilege. I do not like doing this. I very much dislike it. I hate it. I am going to, Mr. Chairman, follow the instructions of my counsel, which I have to say are not the instructions of my conscience . . . I decline to answer."

The next day's *Washington Post* carried the news on page one with the headline, "Colson Won't Reply to Watergate Quiz." The following week's *Time* magazine breathlessly reported, "*Time* has learned that the former White House special counsel not only may be among the first former officials to be indicted by Special Prosecutor Archibald Cox's grand jury but that he is under investigation as the possible source of the White House pressure that kept the Watergate wiretapping plan alive until it was finally approved."

It was true that Archibald Cox desperately wanted Colson indicted and leaned heavily on his subordinates to make a case against him. In a file memorandum following a telephone conversation, Colson noted a private report from Ellsberg prosecutors that Cox was "convinced that I was involved in the Ellsberg affair and that they were very anxious to have me indicted so as to vitiate the national security defense which would otherwise be raised."

It was also true that the information the media based their stories and suppositions upon was patently false and planted by the CIA. In time Colson himself would see portions of the top secret files that included compelling evidence of a CIA plan to implicate him in the Watergate affair in order to divert attention from the agency. Because Howard Hunt had worked first for the CIA and then for a CIA front, the organization feared that the public spotlight might get too close to them in the process of the investigation. In one file memorandum, a CIA operative repeatedly boasted about planting derogatory stories in the *Washington Post*, the *Los Angeles Times*, *Newsweek*, *Time*, and other places. (Eventually even Senator Baker, in one of his final reports on behalf of the Ervin committee, revealed that the CIA "took relish in implicating Colson in Hunt's activities.")

As the Watergate landscape grew bleaker, Chuck Colson sought the light of Christian counsel among his new circle of friends. In October, Doug Coe and his wife, Gretchen, arranged a small party for Chuck and Patty with Senator Harold Hughes (D-Iowa), Congressman Al Quie (R-Minn.), former Texas congressman Graham Purcell, and their wives at Quie's home in Virginia. Colson could scarcely imagine sitting down with a political enemy like Hughes, but Coe assured him once again that they were all brothers in Christ and that nothing else was important.

The conversation was far more relaxed and cordial than any other Washington social event the Colsons had attended. Instead of backbiting and gossiping about politics, the conversation revolved around Quie's horses, what everybody's kids were doing, and other nonpolitical topics.

Then out of the blue Hughes turned to Colson and said, "Chuck, they tell me you have had an encounter with Jesus Christ. Would you tell us about it?" Senator Hughes, as Chuck had already learned, had a remarkable story of his own. He was a World War II veteran, former truck driver, and one-time alcoholic who had beaten the bottle by the grace of God, then gone on to serve three terms as governor of Iowa before being elected to the Senate.

Momentarily flustered at Hughes's request to discuss his conversion experience, Chuck began his narrative after a brief pause, haltingly but without embarrassment, even though he found himself wondering, "Will these people think I'm nuts?" He told the story about his visit with Tom Phillips from beginning to end, then about his week at Boothbay Harbor.

He finished and the room was silent. Then Hughes slapped his knees with both hands and declared, "That's all I need to know, Chuck. You've accepted Jesus and He has forgiven you. I do the same. I love you now as my brother in Christ. I will stand with you, defend you anywhere, and trust you with anything I have."

The next minute the whole group was on its knees in prayer. Then as they all rose to their feet, Hughes wrapped his arms around Colson in a big bear hug. *This,* thought Colson, *is what Christian fellowship is all about.*

There was no time for Chuck Colson's new faith to take root and grow strong. It was tested immediately by legal and political forces now swirling out of control in Washington.

Early in the fall Colson received a phone call from the president assuring him of his support. "I know they've been after you, Chuck, but it won't work. There is no way I am going to let them do it to you. You are innocent in this. I know that, and from now on the president is in charge."

Only a few days later, however, the president called not to offer help but to ask for it. Like old times, Nixon needed something done that no one else seemed able to accomplish, and he wanted Colson to handle it. Along with all the other crises in Washington, allegations had been made that Vice President Spiro Agnew, virtually the only member of the administration who had avoided even the slightest taint of Watergate, had accepted bribes while governor of Maryland, and that the bribes continued after he became vice president.

Evidence was mounting that Agnew was guilty. The vice president wanted Congress to impeach him, which would block a criminal indictment; he figured his chances of acquittal were better in Congress than in court. The previous summer, Nixon had called Colson and asked him to represent the vice president. Colson agreed to take the case, though his partner Judah Best did most of the work. Now the president wanted Agnew out, and he wanted Colson to break the news. Colson was stumped. It was an inappropriate request. How should he respond as Agnew's counsel? Moreover, what was the Christian response? To Chuck, the latter was an unfamiliar question.

Then Colson learned from Nixon that both the Speaker of the House and the minority leader in the Senate would oppose an impeachment resolution against Agnew, exposing him to criminal charges. They would only have taken that position at Nixon's direction. The president had betrayed his own second in command.

Colson agreed to carry out the president's request. The meeting was awkward for both of them, and Colson could see the hurt in Agnew's eyes when he realized his boss had turned on him. After days of deliberation, Agnew concluded that the Justice Department offer of no prison time and a plea of no contest was the only choice he had other than a felony conviction.

On October 10, 1973, Agnew resigned the office of vice president, an event unprecedented in American history. Less than two weeks later, however, another historic political upheaval took place that propelled Watergate—and the political career of Chuck Colson—faster than ever toward their final ends.

"If Christianity Is True . . ."

CHAPTER 15

It became known as the Saturday Night Massacre.

Archibald Cox, the special Watergate prosecutor appointed by Nixon, irritated the president almost from the moment the secret White House taping system was revealed. He had subpoenaed nine of the tapes, Nixon refused to turn them over on the claim of executive privilege, and a tug-of-war had continued ever since. Besides, Cox had been poking around into other matters, particularly the question of $17 million in government money spent on improvements at Nixon's homes in Florida and California.

As pressure to release the tapes mounted, Nixon offered what he called the Stennis Compromise. Mississippi Senator John Stennis, the seventy-two-year-old chairman of the Senate Armed Services committee, was a Democrat respected on both sides of the aisle who had spent a quarter century in Congress. Nixon proposed Stennis listen to the tapes, then certify edited transcripts for accuracy and completeness as they pertained to Watergate. After days of intense negotiation, Cox refused.

In response, President Nixon insisted Attorney General Eliott Richardson fire the special prosecutor. Richardson resigned rather than carry out the order. When his deputy, William Ruckelshaus, was subsequently ordered to do the job, he balked and was either fired or resigned (accounts vary). Robert Bork, the solicitor general, was then brought in to fire Cox. Alexander Haig, who had replaced Bob Haldeman as Nixon's chief of staff, called in the FBI to seal off Cox's office. The whole process from Richardson's resignation to Cox's termination took less than four hours. The office of the special prosecutor was abolished.

Heavy-handed though it was, Cox's departure brought new hope to Charles Colson that he might not be indicted. There was little doubt in Colson's mind that Cox had been gunning for him from the start, was frustrated over not finding sufficient evidence to indict him, and kept threatening to do so to keep him on the defensive. In response to overwhelming negative publicity after Cox's firing, the special prosecutor's office was reestablished on November 2, and a new prosecutor sworn in three days later. Cox's replacement was Leon Jaworski, 68, a distinguished Houston attorney and former president of the American Bar Association who had earned his law degree from Colson's law school alma mater, George Washington University, in 1926.

During the summer, Colson had been so sure he would be indicted by Cox that he had prepared a press release responding to the accusations. The months of waiting had been hard on him, and, he thought, even harder on his family. Wendell was a sophomore at Princeton, Christian was in his last year of high school, and Emily was in the tenth grade. They loved their father and trusted him, but it was hard to deal with the endless stream of critical press reports and the taunting from their classmates.

Patty saw her husband gaining new strength from his faith, and felt both relieved and threatened by it. The two of them had gone to her Catholic church for years, but now Chuck's personal religious expression had taken a new tack. Would he want to pull her away from her Catholic beliefs and practice? What would happen if and when his conversion became public?

People who knew him well were already sensing a difference in the man. After a bruising day of legal sparring with the special prosecutor's office, Dave Shapiro noted how calm and unruffled his client looked. "I don't know what you've found, Chuck," he exclaimed, "but I sure wish I had it."

Since their night of fellowship at the Quie home, Harold Hughes, Graham Purcell, Doug Coe, Al Quie, and Chuck Colson had started meeting for breakfast every Monday at Fellowship House, an elegant but unassuming building on Washington's Embassy Row run by volunteers as a place for Christian prayer and fellowship. They ate and prayed together, encouraging and supporting one another with no regard for political alignment. To Colson's surprise, the man who most often suggested praying for President Nixon in these troubled times was Senator Hughes, the liberal Democrat and unalloyed opponent of Nixon's politics. And it was Hughes who first suggested they invite the president to pray with them.

Even without Watergate, Richard Nixon would have had a difficult six months. In the summer he was stricken with pneumonia, the first illness of his presidency; Haig found him in bed coughing up blood. Then came six days of war between Israel and her neighbors during Yom Kippur in October. America's continued rapprochement with China made the Russians nervous enough to authorize massive troop movements that put the United States military on nuclear alert. Middle Eastern oil producers declared an embargo on the United States, doubling the price of gasoline almost overnight and creating maddening fuel shortages. The president also watched helplessly as the South Vietnamese, now without American support, steadily lost ground on the battlefield against the Communists.

Colson mentioned the offer to pray at Fellowship House in a phone call to the president after the Cox firing and heard only silence in return—Nixon's nonconfrontational way of saying no. He approached Nixon's private secretary of twenty-five years, Rose Mary Woods, to see if she would help convince him. "You've got to be kidding, Chuck," she said, certain that Hughes and Nixon in the same room would produce nothing but fireworks.

In spite of his opposition to presidential policies, Hughes shortly received an invitation to breakfast at the White House—not with the president, but with a group that met once every other week in the basement of the West Wing to pray for one another and their country. In the more than three years Colson had sat upstairs in the Roosevelt Room every morning for his senior staff briefing, he'd had no idea that some of those mornings there were people he didn't even know, including some who despised his politics, praying for him downstairs.

Because tensions in the city were so high, Harold and Doug suggested Chuck accompany them to the breakfast in case Hughes encountered a clutch of unfriendly Nixon loyalists; he could calm the waters if need be. The morning of December 6, 1973, Colson entered the conference dining room in the White House and saw Hughes already at his place, and already surrounded by pro-Nixon men. As Colson took a seat and started eating, the door opened and Arthur Burns, chairman of the Federal Reserve, walked in and took his place at the table.

"What's Arthur Burns doing here?" Colson asked the man on his right, remembering how he had embarrassed Burns years before by planting the false story that he was asking for a raise during a time of government budget cuts. "He's Jewish."

"Not only is he Jewish," Colson's table mate replied, "he's the chairman of this breakfast meeting!"

The only empty place was beside Colson. Burns took a seat, barely acknowledging Colson's presence.

Hughes had been invited to talk about his plans to leave the Senate for full-time lay ministry. He spoke with simplicity and power about how Christ had changed his life, his decision to leave public office in order to serve his faith, and then closed with a few words about getting to know his brother in Christ Chuck Colson.

The audience was absolutely stunned. Nixon's hatchet man a Christian?

Fighting back tears as a result of Hughes's powerful testimony, Chairman Burns thanked the senator for his visit. Then he rose, taking Colson by the hand. "Now I would like to ask Mr. Colson to lead us in prayer."

It was a minute before Mr. Colson found his voice. When he did, he prayed that everyone assembled there would live their lives and carry out their responsibilities with humble reliance on God.

As the group broke up, many of them spoke to Colson, shook his hand, or embraced him. There were no politics in this room, no Watergate, only brothers in faith who loved and cared for one another. Colson had never experienced anything like it.

Saying goodbye to Hughes, Colson ran down the basement corridor hoping to catch Burns before his limousine pulled away. Spying him in the cloakroom near the door, he stepped in. "Doctor Burns, I want to apologize . . ."

He scarcely finished his thought when the chairman replied, "You don't need to apologize. All that is behind us. I've never, never felt—I've never known—well, this has been quite a morning!" He squeezed Colson's arm and walked outside into the bright winter morning.

At 11 A.M. Jerry Warren, the president's assistant press secretary, held the daily White House press briefing. He made a series of routine announcements, then opened the floor for questions, expecting the customary onslaught about Watergate. But CBS White House correspondent Dan Rather pursued a different line of questioning.

"Jerry, what is the president doing continuing to see Charles Colson?"

"I don't think he is," Warren answered.

Rather probed on. "What was Mr. Colson doing at the White House today?"

"Well," Warren said hesitantly, "he was attending a meeting in the dining room downstairs which is held every other Thursday. A group of White House staff members get together for a prayer breakfast and Mr. Colson was attending that."

"Prayer!" someone yelled, incredulous. "Is he going to be the next preacher?"

The press room exploded in laughter. When the noise died away, Rather continued.

"I would like an answer."

"That is the answer."

"That he was attending a prayer breakfast?"

Warren explained the nature of the breakfasts and that Senator Hughes had been the guest speaker. But Rather was suspicious.

"Jerry, isn't this a little unusual, to have a full-time paid lobbyist for very large associations and individuals in and out of the White House to attend things such as a prayer breakfast?"

"No, I don't think so at all . . ."

Rather insisted he wasn't anti-prayer breakfast but thought the issue was important. "While Charles Colson was, at one time, a member of the White House staff, he is now operating for people such as the Teamsters Union. Now we all know the way Washington works. These people ingratiate themselves with people in positions of power, and at such things as, yes, prayer breakfasts, they do their business. Isn't someone around here worried at least about the symbolism of this?"

Warren reiterated that it wasn't a problem. The jokes then resumed, and Warren brought the press conference to a close. But Chuck Colson's Christian conversion was out of the bag.

Just before lunch the switchboard at Dickstein, Shapiro & Morin sprang to life. Every reporter in Washington, it seemed, wanted a statement from Chuck Colson. This was what happened every time some big announcement was made. *At last*, Colson thought, *the indictments have come through.*

The first call he took was from Aldo Beckman, Washington bureau chief of the *Chicago Tribune*. There were reports on the news wires about Colson attending a prayer meeting at the White House, and Colson and Hughes becoming friends. "And then there's something else here about your having found religion."

Colson's face flushed with anger. "My religion is my own business and I'm not about to talk about it in the public press."

"Jerry Warren announced it. It's already public."

As calls poured in, Colson asked his secretary to make a list of them. Then he thought about what had happened that morning. He had been to the White House many times since resigning from the presidential staff. Why had Rather decided to ask about this particular visit? Why hadn't Warren brushed the question aside?

Colson briefly supposed it could be a one-in-a-thousand coincidence, but then had another thought: this was all God's doing. He was recognizing Chuck's commitment and at the same time making sure he couldn't backtrack on it. Chuck Colson was now locked into living his life for Jesus. He couldn't deny it, couldn't soft-pedal it, so he did his best to explain it, calling back all the reporters and telling them he had accepted Christ.

The press was unconvinced and merciless. "Colson Has 'Found Religion'" read the headline in the next day's *New York Times*. An editorial in the *Boston Globe* intoned, "If Mr. Colson can repent his sins, there just has to be hope for everybody." Columnist Harriet Van Horne spoke for many when she declared, "I cannot accept the sudden coming to Christ of Charles Colson. If he isn't embarrassed by this sudden excess of piety, then surely the Lord must be."

Sudden? Hardly. Chuck had pondered the question of religion off and on since that starlit night off the coast of Guatemala twenty years before, and had been saved for four months. Excess of piety? Colson had not offered any statement or made any effort to identify himself as a Christian; in fact he had done just the opposite. It was the media who went looking for the story.

Soon however, even the press had to face the fact that Chuck Colson was a changed man. An article in the *Washington Post* read, "Colson's spiritual awakening may not remedy any of his problems with the Watergate Grand Jury, but it does satisfy one group, the men who meet with him regularly for prayer at Harold Hughes' home."

Perhaps the best recognition of Colson's new life came from seasoned CBS reporter and commentator Eric Sevareid. On December 17 he spoke of the issue on the evening network news to an audience of thirty million.

"The new Colson does not claim the capacity to walk on water, but he has given up walking on grandmothers. A good many people here, anxious to believe in something, are quite willing to take Colson's change of heart as real. After all, that kind of change is what innumerable critics have been demanding all along . . . Mr. Colson is clearly on the right track in more ways than one."

Letters poured in to Colson first by the hundreds, then by the thousands. Some of them took issue with his politics, but all of them conveyed the writers' gratefulness for Colson's speaking up on behalf of Christ. One of the most gripping was written on plain lined tablet paper by a sergeant in the Air Force who had seen an article about Colson in his local newspaper.

Churches and preachers, he wrote, had never been able to reach him in the past.

> After reading you article (the article on you) it has help
> me more than anything in my entire life. It is Christmas
> morning. I'm usually drunk or trying to get drunk by now,
> but here I am watching the children open up their presents
> and thinking about going to church somewhere . . . I didn't

even buy any 'booze' this year. Its people in position like yours who confess their past (maybe not so good life— wrongs) or whatever it may be called sure do help people in position like me. I truly feel free within my inner self this morning and I pray that God may help both of us in all of our trying efforts. I going to try and find that book "Mere Christianity" down here and read it my self.

Tears streamed unchecked down Colson's cheeks as he read. In all his years as a Senate staffer, big-time lawyer, and special counsel to the president, he could not point to a single person whose life he had changed for the better. Now he could. The words of C. S. Lewis came rushing back: "If Christianity is true, then the individual is not only more important [than the nation] but incomparably more important." Here was a man celebrating Christmas with his family as a direct result of Colson's conversion— with essential help from the very media the administration so despised.

Early in January Colson and his lawyers met with the new special prosecutor, Leon Jaworski. Still faithful to his old boss, Colson had agreed to let the president use James St. Clair, who had been handling Colson's affairs, as his own lawyer, and be represented instead by the three top principals at his old firm, David Shapiro, Judah Best, and Sid Dickstein.

One thing Jaworski was curious about was whether or not Colson's religious conversion would prompt him to change his testimony. Now that he was a Christian, would he come clean and tell all? Colson was sorry to disappoint, but he was telling the truth already. There was nothing Chuck Colson the Christian could tell them that Chuck the unsaved could not.

On January 17, 1974, in a meeting held at Colson's request, Jaworski threw him a life preserver as the ship of Watergate sank ever faster. "Mr. Colson, unless my staff can show me a lot more evidence I would not include you in the Watergate cover-up indictment. Of course . . . there's still this Ellsberg thing."

The news made him feel both relieved and apprehensive: relieved that he would be spared being charged in Watergate, but apprehensive because this was the first time the Watergate prosecutors had ever directly suggested there was even a chance he might be indicted. He'd expected an indictment in the Ellsberg case that had never come, but he had never thought there was any possibility of being charged in Watergate.

Jaworski went on. "I think Mr. Colson really wants to wipe the slate clean and look forward to a useful career as a citizen and as a lawyer."

It was a clear signal to an attorney as astute and experienced as Colson. If he pled guilty to a misdemeanor in the Ellsberg case ("there's still this Ellsberg thing") and implicated others, he could get off with a minimum sentence—probably only probation—and retain all his civil rights, including the right to practice law. If he refused, Jaworski was intimating, he would be charged with a felony; if convicted he would be disbarred and prevented from earning a living.

The great impediment to taking the special prosecutor up on his offer was that there was nothing in the indictment Colson could honestly plead guilty to. He was charged with the Ellsberg break-in, but had known nothing about it. A guilty plea would be a lie.

But it would be such a relief to get the whole nightmare behind him! He thought of Patty and his children and all they had been through, first with the accusations and then with the public cynicism—and questions of their own—about his conversion experience. One little yes, and it would all be over.

Deeply conflicted, Chuck went to Harold Hughes for advice, laying out all the options: Nixon's most faithful champion seeking advice from one of his most intractable political opponents.

"Did you do what you'd have to plead guilty to?" Hughes asked. They were alone in front of the fireplace in Hughes's modest den.

"No. I didn't know about the burglary until it was over. But I'm not sure there's much moral difference. I would have done anything the president ordered."

"That's not the point, Chuck. Is what you have to say in court true in your own heart? True between you and God?"

"No. I'd have to say I knew and approved of the break-in. This would not be true."

"Well brother, you're going to have to ask Christ to give you the answer."

Hughes buried his face in his hands. Colson stared into the fire. To the both of them the answer was only too clear.

Innocence and Guilt

CHAPTER 16

Chuck wondered how he would explain his decision to Patty and the children. They had been completely supportive through the long night of Watergate. Here was his chance to end the misery, avoid jail, and keep his law license. But it meant telling a lie, and he knew before God that he couldn't do it.

He talked it over with Patty as soon as he came home from Harold's and, as he hoped she would be, she was with him all the way. Then he flew to Boston to share his decision with the children. He explained that the biggest risk was turning down a misdemeanor plea only to be found guilty of a felony.

It was Emily who framed the entire issue in its simplest form. "Did you do what they want you to say you did?" she asked after a detailed discussion.

"No, I didn't," her father answered.

"Well then, don't say you did."

Chuck said a quiet prayer of thanks for the courage of his children. A few days later he wrote the three of them a letter walking them through his decision process in detail. He recalled their decision as a family for him to leave his law practice and go to work for the president. "I don't for one minute regret having made that decision" he told them. "I'm proud of having served my country and there was nothing I did while I was in the White House that I am ashamed of. That doesn't mean there aren't things I would not do over again, but my only motive throughout the three and a half years was to help the President of the United States and to try to do what was right for our country."

Criticism and risk in life were the price of getting involved as opposed to remaining a spectator. "Those who have tried to do difficult jobs have very often been misunderstood . . . If you set goals, especially difficult goals, and if you really try to change things that you find around you, if you pursue things you believe in and they are controversial, then inevitably brickbats will be thrown at you."

Jaworski's offer was "a very attractive and tempting proposal, especially when I remember how hard I worked for four years at night to earn a law degree and how much that means to my economic future and therefore, to your economic future . . . Among other things I would have been able to look forward to spending a lot more time with each of you and doing some of the things we would have done had I not gone into the White House in the first place."

Absent his plea bargain, he saw slim prospects for vindication. "I don't know what the outcome will be of trials that will be highly publicized at a time in our history when public attitudes are so ugly and when there is such a terrible desire for retribution. I don't think it will be really possible to get a fair trial, but I have to have faith, first in God, and second in the American judicial system . . . I believe in God and in my country and if I were to compromise my own belief in what is true, then I would be admitting that I did not believe in one or the other and I can't do that.

"I know that I have your love and understanding and that's all I'll ever ask for. I hope you can be proud of me and that you will keep your faith.

"Love, Dad."

There was another round of lie detector tests, which Colson passed easily. Another grand jury summons. Another protest by Shapiro since his client was clearly a target. Another subpoena. Once again Colson took the Fifth as the press and public smirked knowingly.

The Watergate indictments were handed down March 1, 1974. Seven men were named, including Charles W. Colson, special counsel to the president, as well as Erlichman, Haldeman, and Mitchell. President Nixon was named as an unindicted coconspirator; the jury vote to name the president was 19–0.

On March 7, indictments were handed down in the Ellsberg case. There were six on that list, Colson and Erlichman once more among them, along with Liddy and three of the burglars.

The arraignment for both cases was scheduled for Saturday, March 9. Colson arrived at the courthouse, threaded his way once again through a jostling crowd of news reporters, political protesters, and curious onlookers. Colson greeted Mitchell, Erlichman, and Haldeman with genuine warmth. There had been tensions and disagreements among them all in the past, especially between Colson and Mitchell. But this was the time to support one another, not open old wounds.

One of the defendants was Gordon Strachan, Haldeman's bright-eyed twenty-seven-year-old assistant. Colson saw him sitting at a table alone and lost in thought, holding back tears. He had been so eager to serve, and now he had followed his boss right into a federal indictment.

Strachan looked up and saw Colson. He smiled. "I understand you're reading the Bible."

"Yes I am, Gordon."

"I'd like to hear about your experience."

"I'd like to when we can talk. Hang in there, Gordon. God will give you the strength if you ask." Strachan smiled again, bit his trembling lower lip, and turned to face the bench as Judge Sirica entered the courtroom.

The seven defendants were ordered to the front, and stood in a row facing the judge. Chills coursed through Colson's body as he heard "The United States of America . . . charges Charles W. Colson." It was like a dream. Captain Charles Colson, USMC; Charles Colson, Esquire, Special Counsel to the President; here was a man patriotic to the bone who loved his country and had made substantial personal and financial sacrifices to be of service. Now he was the enemy. A wave of nausea swept over him.

It was his turn to plead. His mouth was so dry he wasn't sure the words would come out. He licked his lips and finally rasped, "Not guilty to all counts."

His knees felt weak. Snatches of a Bible verse flashed into his head: "Neither death nor life, nor angels nor rulers, . . . nor any other created thing will have the power to separate us from the love of God that is in

Christ Jesus our Lord" (Romans 8:38–39). Even as he stood there with the others the words were a comfort. Somewhere he knew Doug and the rest of his new Christian brothers were praying for him.

The next Monday, Colson attended his regular breakfast meeting at Fellowship House. The arraignment had been front-page news in the Sunday papers, and Colson was apprehensive in spite of himself about what the rest of the men would think. Maybe they'd be willing to counsel and pray with him privately, but not be publicly associated.

"Brother, look at it this way," Doug Coe cheerfully advised. "We've got a Christian in the news." Rather than shun their newest member, the group pledged its unqualified support.

"If you're indicted, we all are," Al Quie added.

Graham Purcell chimed in Texas-style, "You're stuck with us, podner."

Discussing what they could do to help, the men learned from Chuck that the Ellsberg trial was scheduled for July and the Watergate case in September. There was no way his legal advisors could prepare for the both of them so close together. Ken Adams, an associate at Colson's former law firm, suggested collecting all the clippings they could about the Ellsberg and Watergate affairs that mentioned Colson to show that there was no way he could get a fair trial on account of all the publicity. Surely one judge or the other would issue a stay or move the trial to a different city, or both. The problem was the sheer volume of old newspapers and magazines to go through. Even with everybody in the firm volunteering nights and weekends, they would never finish compiling the clippings by the judges' May 1 deadline.

One night Doug Coe arrived at the office with an ex-Marine Corps captain named John Bishop to take charge of the operation. He brought in volunteers from Fellowship House—college students, secretaries, retirees—eventually almost eighty in all, and organized them into work squads. They set up shop in a conference room piled high with newspapers and attacked them like a battlefield opponent. Some worked days, others worked nights. They dubbed themselves Christians for Colson. Office regulars, including Shapiro, couldn't believe the dedication and selflessness of these people. More than one confirmed grump found a new beginning and new hope during that time in what C. S. Lewis called the "healthy infection" of Christianity.

With one day to go before the deadline, Christians for Colson heard the news that President Nixon had released transcripts of key Watergate tapes. In making them public he proclaimed, "The documents will once and for all show that what I did with regard to the Watergate break-in and cover-up were just as I have described them to you from the very beginning."

They would also prove his own innocence, Colson thought. Obtaining an advance copy of the transcripts just ahead of their public release, he skimmed through them eagerly at first, then with shock and sadness. The president had concealed the truth from him time after time; he came off here as a shallow, petty, indecisive politician, not the inspiring, patriotic leader who opened historic negotiations with China and ended the Vietnam War, who won reelection by one of the biggest landslides in history. It was not the Richard Nixon that Colson knew and still admired.

The next day, Shapiro entered his motions for moving the trials and giving the defense more time, accompanying his request with a stack of carefully clipped and catalogued press stories that stood seven feet high. All motions were denied. "It was a bitter disappointment," Colson later recalled. "But for me no outcome in the courtroom could sour the sweet taste of Christ's love from eighty otherwise complete strangers."

In their attempts to pin as many accusations as possible on Watergate figures, Jaworski and his team had begun questioning former members of Colson's White House staff. While the transcripts were still in the news, Colson got a call from Dick Howard, who had served admirably as Colson's administrative assistant. He was preparing to leave government service for a prime job in the private sector. Now, he informed his old boss, the prosecutors were threatening to charge him with perjury.

They had questioned him repeatedly about the rumor that Colson had hired thugs to beat up Daniel Ellsberg. As they had done with others on Colson's staff, the questioners had applied strong pressure to Howard to make him say something under oath that would confirm their theories.

Colson assured him that as long as he was telling the truth, he wouldn't be indicted.

Yet Colson himself was hardly an example of that strategy.

Chuck went directly from his office to Doug Coe's home to ask his advice on the Howard matter. Colson thought he should just give in and plead guilty to the indictments if that's what it took to keep his own loyal staffers from having their careers ruined.

Coe counseled against it. "Stop worrying about Dick. There are brothers who can help him. You are being tested. Now open yourself, and God will supply the answer."

A member of the British House of Commons whom Colson had met at Fellowship House reminded him of a short crisis prayer used by King David. Colson adopted it for the situation at hand, and used it every time another former staffer was called to testify: "Lord Jesus, please turn the counsel of my enemies into foolishness. Help me find Your answer. Show me Your will."

On May 9 the judiciary committee of the House of Representatives began debating articles of impeachment against President Nixon. The same week, Chuck accepted an invitation to appear on *60 Minutes* in an interview with CBS television reporter Mike Wallace. He was nervous about it, seasoned speaker and interview subject though he was, because he was afraid of saying something that would jeopardize his Christian witness. It was a dilemma he had been wrestling with for months now in one way or another. What he decided would determine Dick Howard's future: tell the truth and Howard gets indicted; tell a lie and he gets off. As a Christian Chuck was called to speak the truth in love; but as a defendant in a federal court case he had to be careful if he wanted to keep his freedom and his law license, and help others keep theirs. He had one foot in the old world and one in the new.

The *60 Minutes* session was scheduled for May 16 in Harold Hughes's basement den, the same place where the two of them had prayed for guidance on how Chuck should plead. Chatting with them both before the cameras rolled, Mike Wallace seemed sympathetic and quite friendly. But as soon as the director gave the signal, he suddenly transformed into the incisive, aggressive investigative reporter TV audiences loved.

Early in the interview, as broadcast on May 26, Wallace laid his groundwork by reviving the "hatchet man" and "walk over his grandmother" connections, and making the statement that Colson put Hughes on the White House enemies list.

Colson disowned the enemies list, though he joked that if he'd made one Harold would probably have been on it. He also acknowledged Wallace's skepticism over the reports of his conversion. The public criticism he had endured, Chuck said, was "one price that you have to pay to be true to your own convictions and your own beliefs."

Nervous as he was, Colson found a moment during the interview to articulate the change in his thinking as a result of coming to Christ. Wallace had challenged him on whether or not he had apologized recently to people he had wronged before he was a Christian.

He explained that he had been apologizing to people when the opportunity arose, since his view of what was right had changed so dramatically. "In politics there is a kind of feeling that anything goes because you've got to win and you've got an objective. And you're going to do what's necessary to win that election, or you're going to do what's necessary to get your point of view across. I think when you stop and reflect on a lot of it, you realize that maybe you would have been better to put your faith in the Lord to be on your side if you were right, and not if you weren't, and trust more in Him and less in your own wits."

Wallace moved on to Nixon and the revelations in the tape transcripts. He asked Colson whether they reflected moral standards he—and by implication, Christians—wanted to see in the White House.

"I'm not going to characterize how I look at those transcripts, because I don't think you can," Chuck answered.

Wallace pressed further and finally said, "You say that you are a new man in Jesus Christ. It seems to me as though your prior faith takes precedence over your new faith."

One foot in one world and one in the other.

Hughes came to his friend's rescue. "I want to interrupt, for a very simple reason. Your questions are attempting to take the material and the spiritual and to divide a man from whom his loyalties have been for a long period of time." Chuck was "new in Christ, a baby in Christ," and just beginning to reconcile his life with his new spirituality.

Chuck picked up the thread. "The meaning of the faith, Mike, is very simple. It's a relationship between God and myself, and between myself and my brothers and my fellow man. And I will judge myself by the standards I think Christ has set for us, but I don't really think it's my business to judge others."

Colson remembered his statement the next week during pretrial motions in the Ellsberg case before federal judge Gerhard Gesell. Dave Shapiro opened with an impassioned argument on the importance of national security in the case. Ellsberg was risking America's safety in publishing top secret diplomatic and military information.

Gesell interrupted him to deliver a lecture on the constitutional rights of individuals. To Chuck, the judge sounded remarkably like C. S. Lewis in his reasoning: the individual, with his immortal soul, was infinitely more important than civilization's transient states and empires.

No, Chuck thought to himself, he hadn't known about the Ellsberg break-in, but if he had, he would have approved it. That being the case, what difference did it make *in God's eyes* whether he learned about it before it happened or after?

Judge Gesell adjourned the session without ruling on the motion to allow a national security defense. For Colson it was the darkest moment of the whole sad Watergate business. He had tried to slander Ellsberg in the press the way others, including the CIA, slandered Colson. He had not been a party to damaging a man's property, but was part of a more serious crime in God's economy: damaging a man's spirit.

He had not broken man's law, but he had broken God's. The point tortured him. Would his Christian witness and sincerity always be suspect?

As a favor to Doug, Chuck had agreed to speak at the annual YWCA prayer breakfast in Owosso, Michigan, on May 23. Preparing frantically for two federal trials, Colson had no time to spend speaking in the hinterlands. But he had promised Doug and resolved to make good on that promise. It was one of the biggest events of the year in Owosso, with hundreds of people enjoying platters of baked eggs.

After the meal and some Bible readings, Chuck was introduced and began to speak. It was his first public audience of Christian believers, and he wondered what pressure he would feel as he talked. But he had silently asked the spirit of God to speak through him, and as he stood there was no pressure at all. His explanation of his spiritual transformation was the clearest and most confident ever.

Near the end of his remarks, he thought he should say something about the indictments and affirm his innocence of the charges. "I know in my own heart that I am innocent of many of the charges—"

The sound of his own words stopped him cold. Many of the charges? Was he guilty of some of them?

He looked down at his notes in vain for help. He felt his face flush. "—innocent of all the charges that I stand accused of."

He finished his speech, but the passion was gone.

Flying back to Washington, he mused over the words he had spoken. There was no doubt about it. As long as he was a criminal defendant, he decided, his conversion would remain incomplete and his testimony would be suspect. He remembered the words of Dietrich Bonhoeffer in *The Cost of Discipleship* about what he called the Great Divide: "The first step which follows Christ's call cuts the disciple off from his previous existence . . . To stay in the old situation makes discipleship impossible." Chuck knew Bonhoeffer had lived by those words, and died at the hands of the Nazis to uphold them.

He went through all the points again. Mike Wallace had tripped him up asking about Nixon's language on the Watergate tapes. He hadn't wanted to criticize the president, but he couldn't endorse his profanity. And he couldn't talk about anything that could be used against him during a trial.

He knew many people were convinced that his Christianity was a sham, a scheme to get him out of his Watergate jam, and that as long as that cloud hung over him, his Christian witness would be ineffective. The trials might take two years, and then there would be appeals after that. He would never be free to live his new life as long as the legal process dragged on. And would he, one of Richard Nixon's closest advisors, ever get a fair trial in the

District of Columbia, where the jury pool was heavily Democratic? They would convict him with relish whether he was guilty or not.

The last straw was the prosecutors' hounding of Dick Howard, a fine, capable young man—completely innocent—with a great career ahead of him; an indictment would destroy him professionally

Colson couldn't plead guilty to something he hadn't done, but there was something he had done that he could plead guilty to: attempting to affect the outcome of Ellsberg's trial by destroying his credibility. He wasn't even sure it was a crime to the lawyers; but he had no doubt it was a crime to the Creator of lawyers and courts and everything else in the world. What was more, admitting it was the only way he could be free to talk about his experience with Christ. And that, in the end, was all that mattered.

Patty was thunderstruck at the news. "Why do you have to do it?" she implored, trying her best to understand. "Dave says you'll be acquitted. Then our lives will be normal again."

"It will never be the same," Chuck explained, knowing it was the most difficult thing he had ever asked of her. "I just have to do it." And Patty agreed.

Next he told Harold Hughes, who shouted "Hallelujah!" when he heard the news; and Dave Shapiro, who responded with "You are nuts!"

Shapiro thought his friend had gone over the edge. "What you've done isn't a crime."

"It ought to be. My guilty plea will set a precedent and stop it in the future."

"You are an idiot, and you're going to end up in the slammer."

"I know."

The prosecutor was as shocked as Shapiro had been. He called Judge Gesell at his summer home in Maine. The judge reminded Shapiro that his policy with high government officials was to impose a prison sentence, and that there was no deal expressed or implied in the guilty plea.

Bud Krogh had gotten six months for his confession in the Ellsberg break-in, and Colson's crime was less serious; therefore the punishment should be less serious too, except that Colson was higher on the totem pole and might get a relatively greater punishment as a result. Maybe six months for him too. Colson insisted he'd never been so sure in his life that he was doing the right thing.

Patty struggled to understand her husband. He had fought so long—and others had fought and argued and prayed for him—to avoid prosecution for something he didn't do; now he was pleading guilty to something he wasn't accused of, something his lawyer said wasn't even a crime. It was so hard to imagine Chuck away from her. They had never been apart more than two or three days in the ten years of their marriage. And what about his children? His career? The family finances?

Chuck suggested they pray silently together, and they both drew strength from their prayers. Patty was so brave and faithful. She would follow her husband without hesitation even if she couldn't see the road ahead of them.

Chuck also confided in his Christian brothers, sharing what he had revealed to Patty, the judge, and to William Merrill, the deputy special prosecutor who had pursued Colson so venomously. "Once this is over," he'd said to Merrill, "will you guys try to do something about the system, not just the people? There are abuses in the CIA and the FBI and the courts too, as well as the White House. For the good of the country there's a lot of cleaning up to do."

There was heartfelt discussion at first among Purcell, Coe, Hughes, and Colson—Quie was out of town—over the best course of action. Finally Colson said, "I want you to pray that the judge will accept my guilty plea."

Graham Purcell was the last to come around. "If this is what it takes to give you freedom of the spirit, then I'm with you. But it hurts, man. It hurts."

Late into the night they prayed with all their hearts that Chuck Colson would be convicted of a felony. And Chuck Colson prayed hardest of them all.

The Gavel Falls

O n Monday, June 3, 1974, Charles Colson entered a Washington court-room filled with the now-familiar collection of reporters, courtroom sketch artists, and curious onlookers. The other Ellsberg defendants were there as well. None of them had any idea what Colson was about to do. The only people who knew besides Chuck and his attorney were Patty and his Christian prayer group. He had tried to call the president earlier in the morning, but Nixon had had visitors in his office and couldn't take the call.

The bailiff announced Judge Gesell, and the room rose as one. As the spectators took their seats the judge announced there would be a disposition before arguments began. This meant one of the defendants had entered a guilty plea. Everyone eyed the men; the lawyers and their clients all sized one another up warily.

Merrill, Colson, and Shapiro approached the bench. Colson tried on the spur of the moment to take the measure of Judge Gerhard Gesell; as far as the temporal world was concerned, he was placing his life solely in this man's hands.

Merrill began reading the charge: that Charles W. Colson was guilty of obstructing justice "by devising and implementing a scheme to defame and destroy the public image and credibility of Daniel Ellsberg and those engaged in the legal defense of Daniel Ellsberg . . . to influence, obstruct, and impede the conduct and outcome of the Ellsberg trial." Gasps of astonishment echoed through the room.

How did the accused plead?

"I am guilty of the crime charged," Colson said, barely above a whisper. He had written the charge himself, a violation of Title 18, United

States Code, Section 1503, which makes it a crime to "influence, obstruct or impede the due administration of justice" by way of "any threatening letter or communication."

The judge asked Colson if he understood that he was waiving his constitutional right to a trial, and that all that remained was to impose sentence.

Colson affirmed that he did understand. "I have come to believe in the very depths of my being that official threats to the right of a fair trial for defendants such as those charged in this information must be stopped; and by this plea, your honor, I am prepared to take whatever consequences I must do to help in stopping them."

The judge set sentencing for June 21. Colson was free on his own recognizance until then. A momentary hush enveloped the courtroom; then the reporters bolted for the telephones. Colson was the first White House insider to plead guilty, and there had been no indication whatever that it would happen.

Prosecutor Merrill shook the accused's hand. "Good luck, Chuck. I mean it."

In a small anteroom Colson prayed with Doug Coe and the brothers. Then outside on the sidewalk Colson read his statement to the press. "I have watched with a heavy heart the country I love being torn apart these past months," he said. "The prompt and just resolution of other proceedings, far more important than my trial, is vital to our democratic process. I want to be free to contribute to that resolution no matter who it may help or hurt—me or others."

No one cared about him pleading guilty so he could speak the truth, or so future defendants would be assured a fair trial. Fred Graham of CBS asked the only question anybody cared about: "Are you going to testify against the president?"

The public assumed the worst for the embattled commander in chief. The *Washington Post* headline read, "Colson's Plea Worries White House." There was also a strong strain of cynicism. A *Time* magazine photo of Chuck and Patty talking with reporters after the plea was captioned, "Was it repentance or the most clever ruse of all?" An unidentified lawyer for another defendant was quoted in the accompanying story. "Any man who would walk over his grandmother for Nixon would go to prison for him too." It seemed there had to be a trick. Colson was going to prison to protect the president.

The House Judiciary Committee, now debating articles of impeachment, let it be known they would be interested in any dirt Colson wanted to throw at the president in the process of cleansing himself. Alexander Haig visited with Colson to gauge what he was up to and how it would affect Nixon. It seemed almost nobody could take Colson at his word. All he wanted to do was tell the truth.

The president wrote Colson a note on June 3 encouraging him to "keep your faith in the fact that as time goes on your dedicated service to the nation will be remembered long after the indictment has become only a footnote in history." But by the time the president called Colson the next evening, the customary combative spirit had returned: "It's a crime that Ellsberg should go scot-free while you plead guilty," Nixon fumed. "You weren't involved in these things! You are innocent!"

Colson told Nixon that it was because of his courage and leadership that Wendell and Chris didn't have to worry about fighting in Vietnam. History, Colson thought to himself, would record the great accomplishments of this man; but his moral compass took him in a direction Chuck could no longer follow.

As part of the presentencing process, Chuck and Patty met with a parole officer whose recommendations were supposed to guide the judge in passing down his sentence. The interview was almost over when the officer stretched back in his chair and asked something he admitted wasn't a part of the official report. "Tell me about your religious experience and Senator Hughes and the fellowship."

"Well it's not really relevant to what we're doing here, is it? Maybe some day I can come back . . ."

"No, I'd like to know right now. Just explain it the way it happened."

Colson tried at first to give him an abbreviated account, but the man wanted more. As he talked, he watched a bored and battle-weary bureaucrat transform into an eager seeker of the truth. In an account written later, Colson recognized, "Here was a thirsty man looking for the Giver of fresh water. My role was to pass the cup." The man wished aloud that Senator Hughes could visit with him. The next day Hughes spent three hours talking and praying with him. Even in the dreary office of a court bureaucrat, Christ could renew a life.

Another step in the sentencing process was to gather letters of support from people who knew or worked with Colson. With less than three weeks between the date of his plea and the sentencing hearing, he and his legal team had to work fast. They assembled lists and scrambled for addresses. Some on the list wanted Colson to help them write the letters; others wanted suggestions on copy points. Everyone wanted to do anything they could to keep Chuck out of prison. Attorney General Richard Kleindienst had received only a thirty-day suspended sentence for lying to the Senate Judiciary Committee. That was good news in that his sentence could have been much worse (he'd worked out a plea bargain); the bad news was that the suspended sentence drew cries of outrage from the public. The heat was on to punish Washington's high-flying wrongdoers.

Bradford Morse, now a member of the United Nations delegation, wrote to the judge on UN letterhead, one of more than 150 letters that Judge Gesell received. Colson's father, recovering from a heart attack, wrote from his home in Massachusetts. Tom Phillips wrote too, with insights into Colson's spiritual awakening, as did Charlie Morin, who told the judge, "I have three sons of my own—all of college age. I can say with all sincerity that I would—I *have*, in fact—pointed to Chuck Colson as an example for them to follow in the conduct of their lives and in the pursuit of their professions or careers."

Pat Buchanan sent a letter on White House stationery, describing his former colleague's drive and dedication:

> He is a man with more than the average serving of talent, energy, drive and, candidly, political courage. Those attributes have been put to use in the White House, as I can testify, in many a good and honorable cause, when few others were willing to put their neck on the line . . .

True, Mr. Colson played politics rough; he almost invariably came into second base with his spikes high; but Charles Colson is not a criminal. He is an individual loyal to his family to a fault; and his loyalty to his country can only partly be measured by his volunteer service in the Marine Corps, and his giving up of hundreds of thousands in income from a lucrative law practice in exchange for a twelve-hour day in the White House with many headaches and few rewards.

At the probation officer's request, Colson wrote a letter of his own describing his recent religious awakening. Over eight single-spaced pages, he reviewed the night when Tom Phillips read aloud the chapter on pride from *Mere Christianity*: The message there "changed my life because it so completely described the great vice of my life—and Lewis made me face it . . . I felt like the typical movie version of a man about to die, when his whole life flashed before him. I recalled everything about the prior 42 years and realized that I had been driving, driving, driving, but I had never thought about why I was doing it or who I was or what I was . . . What really struck me most is that what was really driving me was the need to satisfy my own ego, to impress my friends and family and associates with really how good I was and how much I could accomplish."

He also tried to put into his own words what it meant to accept Christ, but admitted it was a hard task.

In a sense it is like trying to describe powerful emotions like love . . . It is not reducible to a mathematical formula or to carefully conceived rationales of logic. I can only say in my life it was, as I believe it has been in many other lives, an experience as real as anything that we can see, feel or hear with our physical senses.

Our society erects tremendous barriers against accepting anything on 'faith' . . . Almost everything in our technology-oriented society encourages skepticism and demands proof. Without attempting a lengthy, theological explanation here, I concluded that Christianity—the acceptance of Christ in

one's life—is either real or it is not; if it is not, then of
course it is the greatest hoax ever perpetrated on mankind
because so many wise and brilliant men over the years have
accepted Christ, followed Christ, and taught his Word. That
is perhaps the only rational way in which to explain one's
acceptance, although the real feelings and personal significance go far beyond this. One comes also to accept and to
believe, as I have, that Christ was the Son of God, that he
died on the cross to save each of us, that he rose again from
the dead and the Holy Spirit returned to earth after Christ
rejoined his father and that all three, the Father, Christ and
the Holy Spirit are one.

The family rallied to ease the burden of waiting for the sentence however they could. Wendell gave up a long-anticipated trip to Switzerland as a
member of the Princeton crew to spend the summer with Patty and keep up
with chores around the house. Chris and Emily came from their mother's in
Boston to visit with their father before the punishment was announced.

Friends and former colleagues pledged financial help if the Colsons
were to need it. Even columnist Jack Anderson, arguably Nixon's—and
Colson's—most relentless critic in the media, privately offered Patty
money to help get through whatever time Chuck would be
incarcerated.

In mid-June Bud Krogh was released from prison after serving four
months for the Ellsberg break-in. Soon afterward, Chuck and Patty joined
Bud and his wife Suzanne for dinner. After the meal, when the ladies
remained in the kitchen and the two men were alone in the living room,
Colson said in a low voice, "Okay, tell me what it was really like."

Krogh condensed his advice into a terse monologue that Colson jotted
down from memory later: "It's hell, Chuck. But you're tough; you'll do
okay. Be careful whom you associate with. You'll see a lot of ugly things
going on around you. A guy once had his skull crushed changing a TV
station in the middle of a program. Just stay out of it and keep to yourself.
The blacks will test you. Stand up to them if you're threatened. If they find
any weakness in you, your goose is cooked."

The day the Colson family thought would never arrive finally came at last. At the same time they dreaded the moment, they waited impatiently to have the veil of uncertainty lifted. June 21, 1974, Colson appeared in the courtroom of Judge Gerhard Gesell for his sentencing hearing. Coe and the other brothers were there with him, as were Patty and Wendell.

Colson and Shapiro came forward and stood before the bench, then Chuck cleared his throat and read his prepared statement.

> The president on numerous occasions urged me to dis-
> seminate damaging information about Daniel Ellsberg . . .
> I endeavored to do so, and willingly. I don't mean to shift
> my responsibility to the president . . . The president, I am
> convinced, believed he was acting in the national interest.
> I know I did . . .
>
> I watched the president agonize over casualty figures,
> wince in pain when the B-52s that he had had to order to
> bomb were shot down . . . I would have done almost any-
> thing I was asked to do without regard to the legal conse-
> quences if I believed it was justified as part of an effort to
> end the war in Vietnam . . .
>
> I had one rule: to get done that which the president
> wanted done. And while I thought I was serving him well
> and faithfully, I now recognize I was not—at least in the
> sense that I never really questioned whether what he wanted
> done was right or proper. He had a right to expect more
> from me. I had an obligation to do more for him.

Then David Shapiro spoke, beginning a lengthy statement he hoped would prove how unfairly his client had been painted in the press, therefore justifying a suspended sentence. He started softly, but gained both in passion and volume as he warmed to the topic. *Newsweek* described it as "a long, sweat-soaked plea."

Suddenly the judge interrupted him. "You are barking up the wrong tree, Mr. Shapiro. You are beating a dead horse."

The unmistakable note of finality in the judge's voice took all the wind out of Shapiro's sails. He finished his argument, but the fervor was gone. Colson looked around and saw the brothers in the courtroom, their heads bowed.

Colson and Shapiro stood together in front of the judge. Colson could feel Shapiro's hand on his shoulder. Judge Gesell lifted his gavel. "The court will impose a sentence of one to three years and fine of five thousand dollars." The gavel smacked down. A muffled scream welled up from the visitors gallery. It was Patty.

Colson gasped, pressed his lips together and shut his eyes. Patty ran into his arms with tears streaking her face. "Everything's going to be all right," she said, her words choked with emotion. Her voice was so husky that the *Newsweek* reporter attributed the statement to Chuck. The two of them, along with Wendell and the brothers, went into a small room to pray together. Few words were spoken; what they were thinking could scarcely be put into words.

Pressed for a statement by reporters as he left the building, Colson replied, "I can work for the Lord in prison or out of prison, and that's what I intend to do."

What does a man do with seventeen days between sentencing and sentence? Chuck got his financial matters in order, and at least in the short term there was no looming crisis. He had equity in his home on two acres in McLean, Virginia, and also owned the house in Massachusetts where his parents lived. He had an equity interest in his law firm as well—even though he was no longer a partner, he hadn't yet cashed out. There were also some savings and the money he had put aside for his sons. The real financial problem would come later if he were disbarred, which was likely now with a felony conviction and prison time.

He also spent many of those precious days testifying in Watergate and Ellsberg hearings, more than fifty hours of testimony in all. Those who thought Colson's religious conversion would prompt him to make a case against the president, or produce some shocking revelation, were disappointed. "Now that you're a Christian will you tell us the truth?" they kept asking in a hundred different ways. But Chuck Colson had been telling the truth all along; the biggest ticking time bomb yet to explode would be Nixon on tape driving the last nail into the coffin of his own presidency.

Most of all, Colson spent as many of those last days as he could with Patty and Wendell, and with the brothers, who prayed for him hour after hour. Physically they would soon be separated by concrete walls and concertina wire; but in spirit they could be as close then as they were now. They wasted no opportunity to fill Chuck's spiritual tank to the brim. He would need every drop of encouragement they could give him.

On July 8 the U.S. Supreme Court began hearing oral arguments on whether the president was required to turn over more Watergate tapes (as opposed to printed transcripts) in response to a subpoena from the special prosecutor, or if turning them over would be, as Nixon argued, a violation of executive privilege and the constitutional separation of powers.

But the more poignant story on the morning news shows that day was that Charles W. Colson, former special counsel to the president, was turning himself in to federal authorities to begin his prison sentence. Scarcely after daylight camera crews began setting up in front of the Colson house. Chuck told them he wasn't leaving until two in the afternoon. If they would let him alone these last few hours, he promised them a statement. To his relief, the reporters got back in their cars, and the broadcast trucks backed up and drove away.

At 2 P.M. Graham Purcell arrived to take Chuck and Patty to the transfer point, where the prisoner would be turned over to federal authorities. Judah Best went with them to manage the legal details. They dutifully stopped at the end of the driveway to answer reporters' questions. One of them wanted to know what books Colson was taking with him.

"Just two editions of the Bible," Chuck replied. The dark blue Buick pulled onto the road, and a flotilla of press vehicles followed. Purcell drove them to a hotel in downtown Baltimore, where they were met in the lobby by four federal marshals. After a too-hurried and awkward goodbye to Patty, Judah, and Graham in the glare of TV lights, Colson was hustled into an unmarked car and driven away, just another federal prisoner under armed guard headed for the slammer.

Holabird

CHAPTER 18

Chuck rode through a maze of dirty and deserted Baltimore backstreets to the edge of town and finally entered the gates of Holabird Army Base. The World War I vintage red brick buildings had been supplemented a generation later by green wooden barracks for World War II troops. Now the whole place was abandoned to weeds and decay except for one barracks building with its grass cut, its walls more or less painted, and its perimeter marked by a nine-foot fence topped with barbed wire.

The car carried Chuck through the gate in the fence; he got out and two armed guards approached the car door. When he stood up, they took up their positions flanking him and walked him through the door. The decor inside was authentic 1940s military issue with a heavy dose of neglect: steam pipes running along the hallway walls, single dim lightbulbs dangling from the ceiling at widely spaced intervals, paint flaked and peeling from every surface. A stale, greasy smell permeated the still air.

He was photographed, fingerprinted, searched for drugs and contraband, and given a stack of forms to fill out. After a warning from the deputy to "obey the rules and mind your own business," he picked up his luggage and followed another attendant to his assigned quarters, a nine-by-twelve room under the eaves where the temperature was at least a hundred degrees. There was a bed, a dresser, and a desk and chair—all of them small, dingy, and worn by years of hard use.

Holabird was a minimum-security federal prison where criminals stayed while waiting to testify in Washington courts. Less than an hour's drive from the District of Columbia, it was a convenient place for prosecutors to keep witnesses while hearings or trials involving them were going on. Colson's room had a door but no lock, and he and other inmates were allowed to move around inside the building freely. Colson was expected to testify at the Nixon impeachment hearings, and would stay at Holabird as long as the House Judiciary Committee might need his testimony.

In his first few hours as a prisoner, Colson met a number of the twenty or so other inmates and learned their stories. There were organized crime figures and ex-policemen, narcotics dealers, hit men, and former soldiers. Some of them were rough looking, with long hair, tattoos, and prickly dispositions, while others were friendly and soft-spoken.

One fellow inmate was an old acquaintance of Chuck's. Herb Kalmbach, Nixon's personal attorney and a key campaign fund-raiser, had been convicted of campaign financing violations for securing the hush money Howard Hunt had demanded, and, like Colson, was being held at Holabird waiting to testify in the impeachment proceedings.

Colson couldn't help noticing the difference between Kalmbach's reaction to prison and his own. As sad and depressing as it was to be there, Chuck knew without a doubt that God was with him and he had nothing to fear. But Herb was consumed with worry. He stayed alone in his room except for meals, and refused visitors because he didn't want his family to see him in prison.

Colson reached out to him, gave him a copy of *Mere Christianity*, and read the Bible with him every day, unfolding the gospel of Christ in small, simple steps. Chuck could see a gradual change in Herb's behavior, and the pace of change accelerated as Herb's vision of Christ's message became clearer. Kalmbach completed his testimony and was scheduled for transfer to Lampoc Prison in California. The night before he left, the two of them prayed in Chuck's small, stifling room for two hours. Fighting back tears, Herb told Chuck that he had accepted Christ and threw his arms around him. Over and over Herb kept thanking Chuck for leading him to the Lord; and over and over Chuck replied, "Don't thank me, thank the Lord."

Writing to Doug Coe and the other brothers about the events of that night, Chuck concluded, "If it takes Watergate and prison, it is a small price for any of us to pay for the greatest joy in life . . . I don't want to leave you with the impression that I like being in prison, but I have to say that God has made it a joyful time in my life."

Patty came to see him frequently, though their time together was strained. The marshals were never out of sight, and the end of visiting hours always came too soon. On his frequent trips to Washington to testify, he visited with Doug and the brothers whenever he could, and Patty accompanied him to the hearings because it gave them a few more cherished hours to be together.

As much as she loved and admired her husband, Patty struggled with his new spiritual point of view and what it meant to their relationship. They had gone to her Catholic church together on occasion, and everything had seemed fine. She considered herself a Christian and him one, too, even before all this evangelical fervor became such an important part of his life. He made no demands on her, but his new faith was pulling her out of her comfort zone.

Near the end of July, a few days after Erlichman and Liddy were convicted in the Ellsberg break-in, Patty made one of her regular visits to Holabird. She had been thinking about how important prayer had become in her husband's life, how it sustained him and seemed to keep him sane and even peaceful in a federal prison. Praying aloud was so foreign to her tradition—an old and respected tradition honored by tens of millions of Christians—yet she had begun to see prayer as a way to keep them close emotionally during what might be years of physical separation.

She wasn't ready to talk to him in person about the power of prayer, but she felt a new sense of its importance. So she wrote him a long letter asking him to pray with her. The next week Chuck and Patty missed visiting hours because Chuck was testifying. But later in the day, in Chuck's old Washington office, Patty came in, the ever-present federal marshal thoughtfully turned his back for a few minutes, and for the first time ever, Chuck and Patty Colson prayed aloud together. They thanked the Lord for the unity in their relationship. For Chuck, it was the most beautiful moment of their marriage.

Before the end of the month the judiciary committee had considered five articles of impeachment against Richard Nixon and adopted three. The first, adopted July 27, accused the president of obstruction of justice; the second, adopted two days later, charged the misuse of presidential powers; the final count, adopted on July 30, accused the president of refusing to comply with congressional subpoenas. Articles on the secret bombing of Cambodia, and on fraudulent use of government funds for home improvements combined with income tax evasion, were defeated in committee.

Chuck felt a profound sense of sorrow for his old friend, and even felt sorry for John Dean, who was sentenced on August 2 to one to four years in prison for his role in the Watergate affair. Dean was a duplicitous schemer who had betrayed many people, but he was still a human being with fears and feelings. Colson prayed for them both.

Also on August 2, unknown to Colson and to all but a select group of the president's advisors, Colson's old friend and former attorney James St. Clair listened privately to a particular White House tape demanded by the Watergate investigators. St. Clair had briefly taken over Colson's legal defense because Shapiro and Colson both thought, as law partners, a conflict of interest issue could arise if Shapiro continued with his representation. When Nixon found himself in need of criminal counsel, Colson recommended the best—his own attorney, St. Clair, who then resigned as Colson's head counsel in order to defend the president.

The tape St. Clair heard was recorded in the Oval Office more than two years before on June 23, 1972, six days after the Watergate break-in and months previous to the time Nixon insisted he knew of any connections between the burglary and the White House.

Nixon and Haldeman discussed a variety of mundane matters on the recording, including the timing for a meeting later in the day with Henry Kissinger. Then Haldeman changed the subject.

"Now on the investigation, you know the Democratic break-in thing, we're back in the problem area because the FBI is not under control . . . Mitchell came up with yesterday, and John Dean analyzed very carefully last night and concurs, . . . that the way to handle this now is for us to have [CIA Deputy Director Vernon] Walters call [acting FBI Director] Pat Gray and just say, 'Stay the hell out of this business here, we don't want you to go any further on it.'"

They talked back and forth for a while, then the president reached his conclusion. "When you get in touch with those people, say, 'Look the problem is that this will open the whole Bay of Pigs thing, and the president just feels that'—without going into the details: don't lie to them to the extent to say there is no involvement, but just say—'this is a comedy of errors. Without getting into it, the president believes that it is going to open the whole Bay of Pigs thing up again.'"

Under the ruse that the burglars were working on a secret national security assignment, the president had instructed his chief of staff to have the CIA order the FBI to stop investigating the Watergate break-in. When he heard the tape, St. Clair realized it so completely contradicted the defense he had been making on Nixon's behalf that unless the tape were released immediately, he would be guilty of a conspiracy to obstruct justice.

A transcript of the recording, known ever afterward as the "smoking gun tape" was released on August 5. Colson saw how badly and how completely even he had been deceived by Nixon. His two years of steadfastly defending the president had been based on lies. One spark of relief came at a point in the transcript when, after raising several questions about the cover-up plan Haldeman was presenting, Nixon said, "All right, fine, I understand it all. We won't second-guess Mitchell and the rest. Thank God it wasn't Colson."

The transcript wasn't released until 4 o'clock in the afternoon. At that moment Nixon and his family were cruising the Potomac aboard the presidential yacht, *Sequoia*. Nixon had planned the quiet evening by design. They were going to have a leisurely family dinner and talk about the future. His resignation was a foregone conclusion now; the only issue was when.

As rumors of resignation filled the airwaves in the week that followed, Colson stayed glued to the small, flickering, black-and-white television in the prison dayroom. More than once he had heard the president say privately, "The day will come when I will wipe the slate clean." This meant once the Watergate storm blew over that he would grant presidential pardons to those who had ended up in prison by doing his bidding. At a meeting with John Dean in 1972, Gordon Liddy was promised a pardon within two years, plus legal fees and $30,000 a year for his family. "Everyone's going to be taken care of, Gordon, everyone," Dean promised.

Now all bets were off. Nixon would be lucky to escape without being indicted and with his presidential pension intact. Pardons were the last thing on his mind. Still, every time Colson took a call from his attorneys he hoped that somehow Nixon had seen fit to end with a few pen strokes the misery of men who had served him so faithfully.

On August 8, 1974, the president announced his resignation, effective at noon the next day. Those intervening hours were intense ones for Chuck, Herb Kalmbach, and others with hopes of a presidential pardon as they waited through the night. Watching his small, dusty television screen the next day, Colson sat transfixed as Nixon and his wife walked from the White House to *Marine One*, the presidential helicopter. They climbed the stairs, then he turned to give the world one last victory salute and disappeared through the doorway. TV commentators made no mention of the earlier crowds around the White House that chanted "Jail to the Chief!"

Never in any of his remarks the week of his resignation did Richard Nixon mention the people who at that moment were in prison for protecting the president, following his orders, or trying to help him. Nevertheless, Chuck's heart went out to him, a proud man so publicly and completely disgraced. He remembered the passage in Isaiah 2:4 that the Nixon family Bible had been opened to when he took the oath of office in 1969: "They shall beat their swords into ploughshares." If only the president—and the too-loyal men who served him—had paid more attention to the admonition seven verses later: "The lofty looks of man shall be humbled, and the haughtiness of men shall be bowed down."

In spite of Nixon's resignation the impeachment hearings continued. On August 20, by a vote of 412 to 3, the full House voted to endorse the judiciary committee's articles of impeachment. Then, one month to the day after Nixon announced his resignation, President Gerald Ford, declaring that "Richard Nixon and his family have suffered enough," granted him "a full, free, and absolute pardon" for any offenses he committed or may have committed as president.

The news gave Colson new hope, even though there was no mention in President Ford's remarks of any other lawbreakers. There was more talk, both publicly and privately, of presidential pardons for Watergate and Ellsberg figures; the new president tested public reaction to the prospect of granting them with quick polls and a strategic press leak here and there. If the public response was politically manageable, Colson was certain further pardons would be granted—including his. Early polls opposed the Nixon pardon by two to one, a later one was almost 50–50, but then a third was strongly negative.

With the issue of pardons on every front page, Patty Colson gamely agreed to be interviewed on the *Today* show. It was a painful experience for her, and her lack of experience in the public eye showed, but her sincerity was unmistakable. Chuck watched the broadcast and felt a wonderful sense of peace and satisfaction about it. Sources in the press reported Colson would be released within hours; reporters camped out once again on their spacious lawn in Virginia in order to cover the joyous homecoming.

But it was not to be. Bowing to the forces of partisan politics and public opinion, President Ford finally announced that there would be no more Watergate pardons. Prisoners would continue with their terms, and defendants would continue with their trials.

It wasn't until the announcement that Chuck realized how sure he had been of a pardon or how desperately he longed for one. The disappointment was even greater for family members. Honestly assessing his feelings in a letter to Coe and the brothers, Chuck admitted, "The injustice (in human terms) of Mr. Nixon going free while those who followed his orders, and whom he betrayed by his lies, sit in jail is painful. I am not feeling sorry for myself—or at least if I am, I can confess it." But he remembered God's example to them all in the New Testament. "Paul found that God used jail to teach him lessons he needed to learn—humility in his case. I am learning patience, to trust each day in the Lord and not to the desires and expectations that may satisfy my own human wishes."

Word spread through Holabird that John Dean would be arriving. He came one night while Chuck was in the dining hall. Accompanied by five marshals, Dean was escorted to his room and placed under twenty-four-hour guard. He was the prosecution's star witness, and they wanted to be sure nothing happened to him. Remembering Christ's admonition to love his enemies, Chuck encountered John later that night eating dinner alone in the kitchen with an armed marshal standing beside him.

Colson thrust out his hand. "Whatever's happened in the past, John, let's forget it. If there's any way I can help you, let me know."

An astonished Dean could only stammer, "Chuck, I really appreciate that. Honest, I really do," before the marshal separated them. Later, in an occasional moment when the marshals looked the other way, Colson and Dean talked in cordial terms about their future and their faith. It was a reconciliation nothing short of miraculous: Nixon's most outspoken accuser now friendly with his most stalwart defender.

One Monday Patty appeared at Holabird in the morning, well before visiting hours began at 4 o'clock in the afternoon. One look at her eyes and Chuck knew the purpose of her errand. His father had died peacefully earlier that morning. He'd suffered a heart attack earlier in the year; the last time Chuck had seen him was afterward in the hospital, when he had gone to explain why he was pleading guilty. Wendell Colson had been so proud to stand by in the White House and listen to his son advising the president of the United States. Now he had died with him an inmate in the federal penitentiary.

Chuck's request for a furlough to attend the funeral was denied—there could be no whiff of favoritism for a Watergate prisoner—but he was granted permission to go in custody of two marshals whose expenses he had to pay.

Colson's stint as a witness was over, and so he was scarcely back at Holabird when he had to prepare for his transfer to the federal prison camp at Maxwell Air Base in Montgomery, Alabama. Whereas there had been a relative degree of freedom at Holabird—private rooms with doors, freedom of movement within the building, prisoners wearing their own clothes—Maxwell was another world: communal cells, prison uniforms, shotgun-wielding guards, a complete surrender of all physical freedom and privacy. His mail would be censored. Because of the distance from

Washington, Patty and the brothers would not be able to visit as often. In some ways the transition from Holabird to Maxwell would be as shocking and painful as the transition from freedom to imprisonment.

As he prepared for the move he wrote the brothers: "You are each in my prayers each day . . . Keep the president in your prayers as I will. If ever we needed God's guidance in our nation it is now. I fear that we have changed the people in high office but now the hearts of our countrymen are still filled with anger and despair. Without God's will new men will change nothing. The president needs to be held up in our prayers and we must look to God for His guidance every step of the way."

Chuck Colson would return to Holabird in only two months to testify at the Watergate trials of Haldeman, Erlichman, and Mitchell. But those two months would transform his life and career as completely as his screened porch discussion with Tom Phillips had transformed his faith.

Freedom

CHAPTER 19

On September 17, 1974, Colson, escorted by two federal marshals, was flown to Montgomery, Alabama, then driven from the airport to the federal prison at Maxwell Air Base on the edge of town. He knew that prisoners often traveled in handcuffs, and was relieved when he didn't have to wear them either on the plane or in the car. Friends of his who were Air Force veterans had spent time at Maxwell and tried to tell him what to expect. The prison camp was separated from the base by woods and surrounded by high fences and razor wire. Their memories would do him no good here.

Outside there were attractive flower beds and lawns, but the feeling of spaciousness vanished as soon as Chuck walked through the door. He was marched to a windowless reception room where he had to strip, shower, and put on prison clothes—even prison underwear. The only thing of his own that the clothing officer let him keep was a silver cross and dove on a chain around his neck; he had made Colson take off his socks and undershorts but never mentioned the necklace.

Then he was marched to the control room, a headquarters of sorts with big windows overlooking the whole compound. They gave him a new address: Dormitory G.

And they gave him a new identity: Prisoner 23226.

Through the windows he could see two rows of red-roofed stucco barracks buildings, home to 250 federal prisoners ranging from a few other white-collar criminals like Colson to rapists and murderers. Some prisoners were lounging around outside. Though it was a beautiful late summer afternoon, no one moved with any energy or sense of purpose and no one smiled. No sounds penetrated the double-layered bulletproof glass, giving the whole scene an eerie resemblance to a silent film of sleepwalkers.

Dormitory G was neat and fresh-looking on the outside, but when the guard opened the door Colson was knocked back by the stench of stale body odor and tobacco smoke. Peeling paint hung from the ceiling, wafting in the weak breeze stirred by the single large fan in the middle of the room. Dust was thick on the grimy yellow walls and every other surface.

Maxwell was a minimum security prison, which meant that instead of cells the men were housed in several big dormitories like this one. At one end were two dingy dayrooms, one for cards, reading, or writing letters and the other for watching television. At the other end was an open area with toilet fixtures and showers. The main living space in between held two rows of metal cots with a center aisle between them. Each cot had a metal nightstand beside it and was separated from the next by a four-foot partition. Each inmate also had a small locker near the entry.

He had scarcely gotten his bearings when he was summoned by the loudspeaker: "Colson, report to control."

Nervously he walked back to the control room where he was told to sit on a bench and wait to see the warden. After a moment Warden Robert Grunska came out of his office and introduced himself. A short, stilted conversation followed; Colson wasn't used to Maxwell, and Maxwell's warden wasn't used to having presidential advisors as inmates.

Finally the warden said, "I have an open-door policy. Anytime you need to see me, you just come right in."

"Does that apply to all prisoners?" Prisoner 23226 asked.

The warden was taken by surprise. Finally he stammered out that yes, it applied to all prisoners.

"I want to be treated like everybody else," 23226 explained. And this was true. There were two pieces of advice he'd received repeatedly: if you want to get out of prison alive and with your sanity, don't get involved with the problems and conflicts of other prisoners; and don't ask for special favors. The life of a warden's pet was sheer hell when the lights went out.

As the two men walked toward the office door, the warden asked the prisoner about the stories he'd heard of his Christian conversion.

"Yes, what you've heard is correct," the prisoner replied, and followed with a comment about the icthus tie clasp the warden was wearing; a simple two-line representation of a fish, universal symbol of Christianity and a reminder of Jesus' statement that his followers were "fishers of men." Warden Grunska thanked him for noticing it.

Again mindful of repeated warnings to mind his own business, Colson approached other prisoners warily his first day in Dormitory G. The range of characters was fascinating even in such depressing surroundings: a doctor and former official with the American Medical Association; a wizened old moonshiner; military veterans; drug dealers. All curious about this Washington big shot. But the more they got to know this Colson fellow, the more regular he seemed.

By the end of his second day at Maxwell, six inmates and a guard had asked him to share his testimony with them. He figured some of them were becoming friendly because they thought he would have the clout to help them somehow, but others were clearly open to the message of Christ. It reminded him of the apostle Paul, who claimed that if a seeker's heart is open the motive doesn't matter.

Colson also concluded within those first few days that the people around him were in desperate need of spiritual fulfillment and the restoration of their personal identity and dignity. Prison went out of its way to dehumanize inmates. It made his heart ache to see it, and it crystallized a line of thinking that had been lurking just below the level of consciousness for weeks now: when he got out of prison, he would do something about the concept of rehabilitation and punishment. He would work to bring Christian standards and goals to bear on what was largely a system of pointless retribution—not "deterrence" or "rehabilitation" or some other high-minded sociologically correct label. He was there as a part of it now, and he saw firsthand how prison needlessly turned men into empty, soulless shells.

There was no encouragement in the prison, no hope. Ruthless guards had complete power over prisoners, and could harass or cheat them any way they wanted to. They listened in on private telephone conversations and stole from the inmates' few meager possessions during locker inspections.

There was no recourse, no appeal; complaints jeopardized the prisoners' chances for parole or probation, or, even worse, got them condemned to "the hole," a solitary confinement cell where they might be locked away alone for months.

Chuck was convinced that the Lord had placed him at Maxwell to show him these things and use him somehow for His perfect purpose.

His first night Colson had slept little; the sounds of the other inmates and the smells of unwashed bodies and seldom cleaned toilet fixtures kept him awake, as did the guards coming through every two hours with flashlights for bed check. The second night he sat on the edge of his cot and wrote the brothers in care of Harold Hughes. Only by writing to a senator (or congressman, or his lawyers) could any prisoner get a letter out the door without it being censored. Colson didn't care who read his letter; he just wanted to establish contact with his Christian friends in Washington as soon as possible, and an uncensored letter went out a lot faster.

"I am glad for this experience," he reassured the brothers in a letter written the night of September 18, 1974. "I would never have understood before the things I understand now. I first had to learn who *I was* in relation to God and now I am learning who I am in relation to others and how the Lord works through us to reach others in need. One cannot come from the church downtown to visit the local prison and possibly know the frustration and hopelessness in their hearts. When this is all over I surely will—I'll never forget it."

Even before he left Holabird, Colson had started thinking about writing a book. He'd never written one before, and knew nothing about how the process worked. All he knew is that he was immersed in a world of hopelessness, hatred, and despair filled with men desperate for the assurance, peace, affirmation, and unconditional forgiveness that only Jesus Christ could bestow. There was a story here that Christians—and everybody else—needed to know. Perhaps the Lord had put Charles Colson here to tell it.

By early October he was keeping a daily diary, writing at night amongst the noise and stench of Dormitory G by the light of dim overhead bulbs. He perched himself on the side of his cot, filling yellow legal pads identical to the ones he had scribbled on during Oval Office meetings with the president of the United States, consulting with cabinet secretaries in his own magnificently paneled EOB office, or while sipping scotch from a glass etched with the presidential seal aboard *Air Force One.*

There was no shortage of material for his daily private summaries. The most basic routine of daily living was adventure enough. He noticed that a number of the inmates spent the whole day lying listlessly on their cots. Colson resolved early on to get up at a reasonable time, make his cot, and stay out of it until bedtime. He attacked his work assignments with the same single-minded resolve he had directed to solving a knotty legal issue for the New England Council or addressing a sensitive public relations matter for the president. Raking leaves and waxing floors replaced the great affairs of state in filling his days.

The other prisoners tested him. There was a rumor, ultimately proven groundless, that one of the inmates planned to kill him. Everyone viewed Colson with suspicion and waited to make him pay for the least sign of favoritism when his permanent job assignment was made. Prison brass asked him repeatedly whether there was a particular job he wanted, and he insisted every time that he would take whatever they gave him. Favoritism wasn't worth the grief it would get him back in Dormitory G.

An aggressive and widely feared black inmate began taunting Colson one day while Colson was mopping the floor.

"How do you like living with the scum after having servants waiting on you in the White House?" he sneered.

Colson answered evenly, "I was mopping floors for years before you were born, and I was in the Marine Corps when you were in diapers."

Not only did that prisoner respect Colson afterwards, but the clique of prisoners he led respected him too from then on. He was accepted by the unofficial but very real inmate leadership.

At last Chuck was assigned to the laundry, working in a warehouse-sized building sorting dirty underwear and prison uniforms, washing and drying them, and getting them issued to the prisoners. It was a hot job and a humbling one: there was something unavoidably humble about washing another man's socks and shorts. But the big advantage of it from a personal standpoint was that Prisoner 23226 could keep himself in the freshest and cleanest clothes available.

He made entries in his diary about the characters he met, including the other Christian prisoners who, one by one, identified themselves to him. A Bible outline he'd brought with him from Holabird was an instant hit with a small group of men interested in the gospel but in need of encouragement to start a study of it.

Paul Kramer was an athletic Marine Corps veteran from Atlanta who had made some unfortunate life decisions and was convicted of drug dealing. His first night at Maxwell, Colson noticed he had a big cross on a chain around his neck. Chuck learned that Paul accepted Christ in a Texarkana prison and was now devoted to his faith. Chuck suggested to Paul that the two of them might get a little prayer group together. Paul insisted the other inmates would make fun of them. "It's not the kind of thing you organize," he insisted, but agreed that the two of them could pray together for guidance.

Visiting hours were from 8 A.M. to 4 P.M. Saturday and Sunday. Patty had flown to Montgomery and planned to stay in a motel there during the week so she could spend all of every visiting hour with her husband. The first Saturday she was waiting for him when the visitors gate opened, and they both fought back tears as they embraced under the ever-present eyes of guards. According to the two-page list of regulations covering visitation, they could only embrace again when she left. He could tell she was surprised at the worn and tattered prison clothes he had on. At least, he could tell her, he knew for sure that they were clean.

Patty struggled to keep up a brave front, but at one point during their visit her pulse began to race and her face flushed. She was under incredible stress. Colson was heartbroken for her because she was so obviously suffering and there was nothing he could do to help her. They sat outside most of the day at picnic tables in the visitors area, talking freely with other inmates and their wives.

On Sunday they went to the prison chapel together, and read the Bible to each other later in the afternoon. Chuck realized it was the first time since he'd been at Maxwell that he had opened the Bible and determined to be more diligent in his reading. Doug Coe had sent him a "Design for Discipleship" Bible course from the Navigators.

The first reading was from the second chapter of Hebrews, verses 9–18, and the words spoke directly to Chuck Colson's heart: "But we do see Jesus—'made lower than the angels for a short time' so that by God's grace He might taste death for everyone—crowned with the glory and honor because of the suffering of death . . . For it was fitting, in bringing many sons to glory, that He, for whom and through whom all things exist, should make the source of their salvation perfect through sufferings . . . For since He himself was tested and has suffered, He is able to help those who are tested."

The next day Chuck wrote excitedly to the brothers to tell them he knew why he was at Maxwell.

> In Hebrews chapter 2 there is an eloquent statement of why God became mortal in the person and flesh of Christ so that he could experience the pain and suffering and feelings of other humans. He had to become one of them to truly love them and lead them to redemption. There is an analogy. No one can *observe* what it is like to be a prisoner. Most of them are not treated like human beings; there is the slow erosion of their souls. I doubt that any visitor could *feel* it— but I now can. I know the indignities and frustrations, the sense of loneliness and isolation, the loss of individual pride and self respect—the cumulative impact of a series of little and big things that are familiar to a prison. I have also felt the terrible spiritual longing of so many of these unfortunate souls. I know now that the Lord has a plan for me and that this experience will enable me to minister in a way I never could have otherwise—and a way that perhaps few others could. It wouldn't have been what I would have chosen—but then what I would choose is not what it is about.

Chuck thought it unwise to try and organize a Bible study or prayer group on his own; he didn't want to seem like he was trying to run the show or put himself in charge. But the inmates kept coming to him. Everybody knew his story before he set foot in the place, and they sensed he had a calm and assurance that most of them had never felt before behind prison walls.

Interest in Chuck's Christian message increased noticeably after he and a handful of others went to a room off the prison library to pray for inmates under consideration for parole. Parole hearings, as far as Colson could tell, were unpredictable and capricious, almost like a second sentencing hearing. The review board could free a man on the spot, or condemn him to months or years more behind bars. The randomness and inequity in the system was one of the most deeply resented aspects of prison life. The day before, only two of twelve men who appeared before the parole board were granted parole. The day after Chuck and the others prayed for the inmates and for the parole judges, five out of seven cases received parole.

Word spread about the prayer group and others joined in. Members of the group started saying grace at meals; they got some astonished stares but no taunting or wisecracks. That alone was a minor miracle.

Another answer to prayer was even more dramatic. Though Colson had been warned not to give legal advice to any of the prisoners, he found himself bending that rule to help barely literate prisoners who didn't even know what they had been convicted of or how to keep up with their case while they were imprisoned. One man Colson befriended was a white-haired, craggy-faced moonshiner named Cecil Barnes. When he figured out Cecil was completely illiterate but too ashamed to admit it, he "helped" him write a letter to his lawyer and earned the old man's everlasting appreciation.

One day Cecil fell ill. Though he was treated with antibiotics his fever rose and his white cell count skyrocketed—signs of life-threatening infection. When nothing the prison infirmary could do seemed to help, Colson suggested to three Christian friends that they pray for a miracle of healing. Gathered around Cecil's bed in the infirmary, the four prayed aloud for half an hour. The passion and fervor of their prayers inspired Chuck to leap up and shout "Hallelujah!"—a far cry from his usual reserved demeanor at prayer.

The next morning Chuck went in to check on the old man, opening the door slowly in case he was asleep. Cecil was sitting up in bed, and he greeted his visitor with a strong voice. His fever was entirely gone, white count and other tests perfectly normal. Chuck thanked the Lord for putting him there in Maxwell at that moment and allowing him to serve in such a special way.

Cecil's recovery came at the end of a tense week of fighting, special punishment, bad news from home for a number of inmates, and heightened bitterness between prisoners and guards. Chuck had no doubt it had been a week of spiritual warfare; and no doubt that the angels of the Lord had triumphed.

On October 14, 1974, Chuck Colson celebrated his forty-third birthday in prison two days early so Patty could share it with him. She brought him all his favorites: trout, shrimp, and gumbo, plus a birthday cake. She also gave him a wedding ring—he'd never had one from her before—engraved on the inside with "April 4, 1964—forever."

During a meeting with Charlie Morin on the sixteenth, Colson realized their conversation was being secretly taped by the prison guards. It reminded him of his trip to the Soviet Union early the year before as envoy for the president. Charlie had hoped to bring Chuck some good news for his birthday, but all he could report was that they were making little headway arguing for his release.

A few days later he received a letter dated October 16 from his old boss. Former president Nixon wrote that his thoughts and prayers had been with his old counsel "through this difficult time."

Nixon continued, "When I think of the enormous service you rendered to the Administration, your loyalty to me personally, and your friendship, my heart really goes out to you in what I know must be a terribly trying time for you." It was the closest thing to thanks and an apology that the ex-president, at his seaside estate at San Clemente, could bring himself to write.

"In the end this will pass," Nixon concluded, "and we will all live to fight another day."

By the end of October Chuck was still uncomfortable in prison but he was no longer afraid. He had claimed the power of prayer, nurtured the small Christian community among the inmates, and had received absolute assurance about why he was there. In fact, on the same day Colson wrote his brothers to tell them about reading Hebrews 2, they wrote him to say they were reading Hebrews 2 and it would do him good to read it too. Some might call it a coincidence, but Chuck called it the workings of the Lord to achieve His perfect will.

His only real worry was for Patty. Until his imprisonment they had never been apart for more than a couple of days. When he was out of town longer she always went with him. Being separated from her made him appreciate his relationship with her all the more. Patty was so wonderful, so precious to him, and yet this ordeal was trying her to the utmost. She had been ill; that combined with the stress of her husband's imprisonment had caused her to gain weight. The roller coaster of possible pardons had exhausted her.

But as concerned as he was, Chuck could tell that Patty's faith was growing stronger by the day. They prayed aloud whenever they were together, and Patty prayed for Chuck when she was alone. As evidence of her growing Christian maturity, she prayed not for her husband to be released, but that the Lord would reunite them in His time according to His perfect will. Chuck unburdened himself in a letter to Doug Coe: "I can entrust my problems to the Lord, and I do, but it is hard to see my problems causing so much anguish for someone I love so much. I can only entrust that to the Lord's care but it is much, much harder."

Unexpectedly, Charles Colson was ordered back to Holabird prison in mid-November to testify in the Watergate break-in trials of Erlichman, Haldeman, and Mitchell. As miserable as the place had been, Colson knew he would miss Maxwell for the Christian fellowship that was there. In the same way Al, Graham, Doug, and Harold were his brothers in Christ, so would Paul Kramer, Cecil Barnes, and a small circle of other believers at Maxwell be with him always in spirit.

Holabird meant that Patty wouldn't have to choose between flying to Alabama—she was a very nervous flyer—or spending the week between weekend visits in a Montgomery motel. It also meant that Doug Coe and his other faithful brothers could see him often. Not least of all, a certain measure of personal freedom and identity would be restored.

The place felt almost deserted after two months in Dormitory G with its forty men as part of a prison population of 250. Herb Kalmbach was still there among the two dozen or so inmates, as was John Dean. Jeb Magruder, Mitchell's deputy during the 1972 campaign, had arrived as well.

Every few days Chuck would be driven to Washington to testify, and there were times when it seemed his answers pleased nobody. Colson's responses didn't ingratiate him with the prosecution because they didn't fit neatly into their strategy. His comments didn't please the defense, who were on the lookout for any signs of burnishing the truth to please the government. They didn't please the columnists and pundits. The fact was that the truth seemed to please nobody except Charles Colson, who was deeply relieved to be telling it. On New Year's Day 1975, all but one of the Watergate defendants, including Erlichman, Haldeman, and Mitchell, were found guilty.

On January 8, Colson was in his lawyer's office in Washington between court sessions on other related cases when he got an urgent call from John Dean's lawyer. Dean, the caller explained, couldn't use the phone at Holabird, but he wanted Colson to know right away that Judge Sirica had ordered him released. The judge had also released Kalmbach and Magruder. But Colson's case, which was Ellsberg-related and had nothing legally to do with Watergate, had been handled by a different judge, Gerhard Gesell.

There was no clemency for Prisoner 23226. When he arrived back at Holabird from Washington that night, the three of them were already gone. Chuck watched them return to their homes on the network news. He thought of Patty watching the other women welcoming their husbands. It was almost more than he could bear.

But the tribulations continued. On January 20 Charles W. Colson was disbarred in Virginia. Shapiro and Morin had argued valiantly to prevent it, even getting a sworn statement from Leon Jaworski about his implying a year before that Colson could plead guilty to a misdemeanor, thus keeping his law license secure. However, with the public eye on them judging every aspect of a "Watergate criminal's" treatment, the review board voted for disbarment.

Two days later Chuck was summoned to the telephone at the prison office. It was one of his lawyers. Chuck's heart pounded as he took the receiver. Shapiro had warned him that Judge Gesell was not likely to do anything that could be interpreted as following Judge Sirica's lead, so not to expect a pardon any time soon; even so, the urgent call filled him with hope.

Ken Adams was on the line. "Chuck, are you ready for a tough one?"

Colson wondered in the Lord's name how many tough ones could be left.

"Your son Christian has been arrested for narcotics possession." Chris, a freshman at the University of South Carolina, had invested $150 in a stash of marijuana with the hopes of turning enough profit to buy a car. His comment to the arresting officer, quoted on front pages across the country, cut Colson to the heart: "Now you've got both of us."

It was a time of fearful testing. His father had died with Chuck a federal prisoner. His livelihood had been taken from him by disbarment. All the others who were convicted with him had been pardoned. His son had been arrested for drug possession. His wife was near nervous collapse out of physical and emotional strain.

Then word came that Holabird prison would be closed and Colson would be transferred back to Maxwell: back to the fetid dormitory, the dreary monotony of the laundry, prison uniforms and the control room loudspeaker and the anonymity of being Prisoner 23226.

Doug Coe and the brothers redoubled their efforts, filing motions, writing to President Ford, praying, and writing and visiting the prison almost constantly. Chuck wondered how Charlie Morin could keep his practice open as much as he visited. And he was astonished almost beyond words when Al Quie, the sixth-ranking Republican in the House, offered to petition the president to allow Quie to serve the rest of Colson's sentence.

Only Christian love was a powerful enough force to sustain Chuck during those dim winter days, days he later affirmed were the most difficult of his life. They were also days that transformed his life. On January 29, alone in his small, plain room at Holabird, he totally surrendered his life to Christ, completing the process that had begun that muggy August night in Tom Phillips's driveway. He prayed, "Lord, if this is what it is all about, then I thank You. I praise You for leaving me in prison, for letting them take away my license to practice law, yes—even for my son being arrested. I praise You for giving me your love through these men, for being God, for just letting me walk with Jesus."

And with that final release came the greatest joy imaginable—a "real mountaintop experience" he called it later—where in that dark prison room he felt his whole being surging with more strength and flowing with more contentment than he had ever dreamed of while sitting in the White House. For the first time in his life, he felt truly free.

On January 31, 1975, Judge Gesell issued an order terminating Colson's sentence on account of "serious family difficulties," though Chuck would always insist he received his freedom two days before in a mountaintop experience he would never forget.

Shapiro phoned Holabird to deliver the news a little after 5 P.M. By 9 the release papers were signed, Patty was waiting at the gate, and Chuck Colson walked through the door a free man. Their eyes red from crying separately and then together, Patty climbed behind the wheel while Chuck sat beside her in the front seat. She would have to drive them home; his driver's license had expired.

Back Inside

CHAPTER 20

Chuck Colson was the last of the inner White House circle to be released. Any hope of a quiet return to his Virginia home was dashed when he and Patty pulled into the driveway about 10 P.M. and found the front lawn packed with generators, equipment trucks, news reporters, and lights, with black cables of various sorts snaking across the grass in every direction. Still adjusting to his new freedom—six hours earlier he was a federal prisoner with no idea when he would see his house again—Colson was surrounded by reporters and pelted with questions. Most of them wanted to know what he thought about Nixon and when he would see him next.

At last Chuck and Patty made their way to the front porch, walked inside, and shut the door behind them. They were safe in their own front hall; and there with his arms outstretched was Doug Coe.

"Hi ya, Brother," he said with a wide grin. Doug, his wife, and their daughter had arranged fresh flowers throughout the house, prepared a late-night snack, and stoked the fireplace to a cheerful blaze. They were indeed his brothers and sisters in Christ.

That night, lying on crisp, clean sheets in his own bed, free of the stench and constant apprehension of Maxwell, Colson began thinking about what he would do now. *I've paid my debt; now I'm free, ready to build a new life.* His felony conviction notwithstanding, Colson would be a valuable catch for a Washington lobbying group or another business whose ties to government were essential to success. Nobody had been closer to the center of power than the special counsel to the president.

Yet as he waited for the sleep that eluded him, Chuck remembered a rough-looking fellow prisoner named Archie who asked him what he was going to do for the rest of them when he got out.

"I'll help in some way," Colson answered sincerely. "I'll never forget this stinking place or you guys."

But Archie heard it all before. "They all say that," he shot back derisively. "Then they get out and forget us fast."

"I'll remember, Archie."

"Bull—!"

Whatever he did to help his fellow inmates at Maxwell, his first task as a free man had to be to bring Christian discipleship and fatherly counsel to his son Christian. And so a week after Chuck's release, he and Patty flew to Charleston, South Carolina, to visit him. The best news they learned on their trip was that Chris might qualify for a counseling program that would lead to his record being cleared.

Since they were so close to Alabama, Chuck decided to travel on to Montgomery and check on the Bible study group he had helped start at Maxwell, especially Paul Kramer, the cofounder of the group. If Chuck never expected to be released from prison the Friday before, he certainly never expected to be back in prison seven days later as a visitor. Yet here he was, returning to the too-familiar dirt and stench and darkness voluntarily in order to give encouragement to his new Christian brothers.

Once again the reporters were out in full force, and their presence was an irritation. Though the visit was a great time of fellowship, Chuck knew the prisoners could scarcely be themselves with TV cameras in their faces. But it was soon evident that, like it or not, Chuck Colson was still a story wherever he went.

Barbara Walters invited him for an hour-long interview on the *Today* show. His first instinct was to turn her down. If the questions the reporters had asked the night he returned home were any indication, the only things people seemed interested in were whether he was mad at Nixon for neither defending nor pardoning him, and whether this religious conversion thing was real or bogus. Many people thought then—and continued thinking—that Chuck had had a jailhouse conversion, not knowing that his commitment to Christ had come first, and had in fact led him to plead guilty to a crime he hadn't even been charged with. He wasn't a Christian because he had been in prison; he had been in prison because he was a Christian.

But Barbara Walters was a special case. She had encouraged him and Patty over the months of his ordeal, and had wished him well on the air at the beginning of his sentence when life seemed so dark. And so Chuck agreed to appear on the program. During the live broadcast, Walters brought up the rumors of conflict between Colson and Henry Kissinger, prompting Chuck to criticize Kissinger even though he had actually admired him for the most part when they served in the administration together. However, as he wrote later, criticism "was not a comfortable position for an ex-con to take about the Secretary of State."

The old Chuck—scrappy, opinionated, ruthless, determined to have the upper hand—was still at war with the new Chuck, follower of Jesus Christ. After his halting testimony beneath the relentless gaze of Mike Wallace for *60 Minutes* a year before, he had felt uneasy about sharing his faith under the gun of skeptical questioning on network television. Here again he felt he had failed to show Christian behavior; the feeling was reinforced a few days later when Richard Nixon called from San Clemente to say Colson had done a good job overall in the interview, but needed to remember that Kissinger was a government leader and as such deserved every citizen's respect and support.

Colson's Christian testimony was incomprehensible to many reporters and commentators, and they made little effort to understand or interpret it. Nor did they seem clear on the basic facts of his imprisonment. It was widely assumed that Colson went to prison on a Watergate-related offense, when the fact was that his violation of Daniel Ellsberg's rights took place long before the Democratic National Committee break-in. Shortly after his release, *Newsweek* reported that Colson had "copped a plea" and was sentenced to serve his time in "various minimum-security, minimum-discomfort lockups," a description very much at odds with the facts (one wonders whether the reporter had been to Maxwell), and one that would continue to gall Colson down through the years.

Another example of misinformation came in a CBS television interview with H. R. Haldeman broadcast on March 30, two months after

Colson's release. Correspondent Mike Wallace took a moment to summarize what had happened to some of the other Watergate figures: "Dean confessed; Krogh confessed; Colson made a bargain with the prosecutor . . ." In Colson's case, this was exactly the opposite of the facts; his declining to make a bargain had been a shock both to his lawyers and to the prosecutor.

No doubt Colson agreed with Haldeman's characterization of him in the same interview, even if he didn't agree with the opinion that he had gone too far: "There was some concern about what Colson was doing in some areas, because he tended to function in a way that I don't believe a presidential aide should function, which is to automatically carry out, literally, all of the president's orders . . . It wasn't a matter of disloyalty [in ignoring orders that might have negative consequences]. It was a matter of loyalty in not carrying them out."

Colson had certainly protected the president from himself by not executing certain orders, but he had been willing to go further to please his chief than anybody else. That was what had made him so valuable to Nixon; now he was being condemned for it by Nixon's chief of staff.

One of the few who made an effort to understand the new Chuck Colson was conservative commentator William F. Buckley, Jr., who observed "the leers that greet the news of Charles Colson's conversion to Christianity." The public, he wrote in his syndicated column, seemed to "treat the whole thing as a huge joke, as if W. C. Fields had come out for the Temperance Union. They are waiting for the second act, when the resolution comes, and W. C. Fields is toasting his rediscovery of booze, and Colson is back practicing calisthenics on his grandmother's grave." It appeared to Buckley "less implausible than it apparently does to others that he should have found Christ."

Well-meaning friends, including Nixon, advised Colson to give up his position as a public figure and go quietly into business, rebuild his personal fortune, and leave the stress of explaining and defending his Christian conversion to a hostile press behind for good. He could still serve Christ without enduring the barbs of the media and the sacrifices in time and money public life demanded.

Through the winter and into the spring of 1975, Chuck and Patty talked almost daily about what he should do. His closest friends at Fellowship House—Doug Coe, Al Quie, Harold Hughes, and Graham Purcell—encouraged him to spend more time getting involved in their outreach in the name of Jesus. Lucrative consulting contracts were his for the asking, and he could eventually go back to law; though disbarred in Virginia, he was only suspended in Massachusetts.

One concrete goal he could focus on was finishing the book he had started writing in prison. His early notes referred to it as his "religious book." He wanted to write it in part as a memoir of his days in the Nixon White House, which would give him the platform to explain why he never lost his respect and admiration for his old boss. More important, it would allow him to explain fully his journey from White House hatchet man—willingly doing whatever that required—to servant of Jesus Christ, willingly doing whatever that required.

He had turned down big advances from major New York publishers to work with a smaller Christian company, Chosen Books, whose publisher was Leonard LeSourd. Leonard's wife, Catherine Marshall LeSourd, was herself a distinguished writer, author of the best-selling novel *Christy* and of *A Man Called Peter*, an acclaimed book about her late first husband, Peter Marshall.

Chuck, Patty, and their friends at Chosen Books had struggled over what to title Chuck's work. Attending Catholic mass with Patty one day, Chuck felt her nudge him. He looked over and saw her pointing to the title of a hymn, "Born Again."

"That's you!" Patty whispered. "That's your book!" The name struck him forcefully as the perfect description of the way he felt after dedicating his life to Christ. Others later explained to him that "born again" was a cliché in evangelistic circles, but he had never seen it in that context and after extended discussion, the title stuck.

One Saturday morning in April, after indulging in the customary weekend luxury of an extra half hour's sleep, Chuck got up and walked into the bathroom to shave. Suddenly and without warning, as he looked into the mirror, he had a vision (though he would always hesitate to call it that): a vivid image of a process for taking selected prisoners out of their prisons, training them to lead Bible studies, then returning them to teach and encourage fellow prisoners, establishing a core of Christian fellowship behind bars where his own experience proved it was so desperately needed.

The whole progression of images and ideas took only a few seconds, but Chuck had no doubt this was a supernatural inspiration. A few minutes later he was on the phone to Harold Hughes; within an hour Harold was in Chuck's basement office helping devise a plan of action. Their friends at Fellowship House were enthusiastically behind the concept, unanimous in their belief that Chuck had received divine direction and was called by God to initiate a prison ministry.

Praying and planning together, the Fellowship House team went down several dead ends before contacting Norman Carlson, head of the Bureau of Prisons in the Justice Department. Hughes and Colson went to see him and explain their idea. Colson reviewed his own experience in prison and how it was a place that crushed men's spirits and destroyed their dignity. Christian teaching, Chuck explained, could help prisoners learn from their mistakes, endure the disgrace and loneliness of prison, and come out ready to make their way in the world as responsible citizens. As it was, prison often did inmates more harm than good.

Chuck was keenly aware as he talked that his words were a scathing criticism of the system Carlson ran, and fully expected the prison chief to be defensive at best, totally against his plan at worst. But to his surprise, Carlson replied with the story of a visit he and his wife had made to a prison in California. On Sunday they had gone to chapel, and the chaplain asked any prisoners who wanted to pray to do so.

Carlson was astounded to hear one of the prisoners pray for him and his wife.

"Well, Mr. Carlson," Colson explained, "he's a Christian. We're taught to pray for those in authority. I did for the wardens at Maxwell."

"I know that." Carlson maintained his military bearing, jaw set, his face framed by close-cropped blond hair, as tears welled up in his eyes. "But I'm the one keeping him in prison."

Colson later described it as "an electric moment." Meeting the prison chief's gaze, the ex-con replied, "Mr. Carlson, that man prayed for you because he loves you."

Before the meeting was over, Colson and Hughes had permission to take any inmate out of any federal prison in the country for a pilot program to train inmate Bible teachers.

The Southern Baptist Convention, representing the largest Protestant denomination in America, was convening in Miami Beach at the end of June, and had invited Colson to speak there while he was still in prison. Though he had accepted, he hadn't expected to be released in time to appear before the twenty thousand delegates—known in the denomination as "messengers"—as a free man, having faith that somehow he would be allowed to go.

It turned out that he was free by then after all, and that he had an idea for ministry to prisoners he was eager to tell them about. The meeting was at the same Miami Convention Center where Colson had watched Richard Nixon accept the nomination to run for reelection in the summer of 1972. That seemed like a distant dream now, a memory from another world. Chuck Colson's new reality was a life of service to Jesus.

The sight inside the hall was intimidating. What could an ex-lawyer and ex-con have to say about evangelism to twenty thousand Baptist pastors and lay leaders? As the speaker ahead of Colson strained to be heard, members of the audience walked around the hall and talked in small groups that formed, broke up, and reformed, completely ignoring the man on the rostrum. If one of their own couldn't keep their attention, how could he? Colson was pleased to see an old friend from Maxwell, Reverend Edmond Blow, there to introduce him. It was Brother Blow's visit to preach to the inmates that gave Chuck one of his first experiences hearing the gospel proclaimed behind bars.

When Brother Blow introduced him, Chuck was surprised to hear the roar of conversation fade to a whisper and then to nothing at all. House lights dimmed, television lights blazed, and he was on. Colson's assistant Fred Rhodes, former deputy chief of the Veterans Administration, was in the front row ready to signal if his speech was too long or the delivery too fast, but Chuck couldn't see him through the lights. He could feel the sweat trickling down his neck and back.

He began with a quotation of 1 John 1:3: "What we have seen and heard we also declare to you." It was the Christian's job, he said, to take the message of Jesus the Savior into prisons. He recounted his first meeting with Brother Blow at Maxwell and how he set such an example.

"Before going to Maxwell I felt awkward and uneasy about speaking of Christ. But as I saw and heard Brother E. W. Blow preach Christ boldly, all of those awkward reservations passed from my life. It was yet another step in my journey . . .

"While despairing my fate, I heard an announcement that prisoners could attend services in the auditorium. The country preacher was so overflowing with Christ's love and the Holy Spirit that tears rolled down his cheeks. They began to roll down mine as I felt that night a tremendous surge of strength and the thrill of Christ's presence."

Blow's sermon was one of the experiences that gave him a "new freedom" in prison he had never known on the outside, and helped make his time behind bars "one of the richest experiences of my life." He shared his hope that Christ could be brought to prisoners by prisoners themselves, and told of his encouraging meeting with Norman Carlson.

As he finished his remarks and turned to leave the podium, he heard a strange loud clattering sound. It was thousands of seats springing up against the seat backs as the audience stood as one, applauding heartily and punctuating the air with heartfelt amens. The response was so phenomenal that as soon as they got back to their hotel, Fred insisted the two of them pray for protection against pridefulness.

Chuck had made the conscious decision not to go on the lecture circuit because he thought it took time away from more important work, and because public appearances held him up to continuing criticism about Nixon, Watergate, and Vietnam that could compromise his effectiveness at prison reform. (Also, he had been frustrated more than once at finding himself used as bait to improve the response at an altar call.) But occasionally, circumstances conspired to convince him to speak.

Near the end of the year, he agreed to address the students at George Washington University, his law school alma mater, where the student body was half Jewish and leaned heavily toward liberal views. The scene could scarcely have been more different from the Baptists in Miami. Originally he was scheduled to speak to the small group of committed Christians on campus, but as word spread about his appearance the demand for admission tickets soared. And so instead of an informal gathering of believers, he found himself facing a rude and hostile crowd of nearly a thousand.

Standing at the lectern after his introduction, it looked at first as if he would not be allowed to speak on account of hecklers. But then he grabbed the microphone in his hands and offered a prayer in the name of Jesus Christ. The hall grew still and Chuck had the chance to share his testimony and his dream of a ministry for prisoners. The speech ended without incident, but during the question and answer period the audience grew restless again.

Then someone asked what Colson thought about Richard Nixon after what Colson had been through on account of the disgraced president. "I could tell you his good points," Colson answered, "but I don't believe I could persuade you to accept them. What it comes down to is . . . Mr. Nixon is my friend. And I don't turn my back on my friends."

The room erupted with applause, and hundreds of belligerent adversaries were won over on the spot by his loyalty and sincerity.

Training for the first group of prisoners as Bible teachers was scheduled to begin in November of 1975. Though Chuck and his friends at Fellowship House were optimistic, and though Norman Carlson was supporting them fully, there were plenty of challenges and distractions to deal with. The Watergate affair was essentially over, but leftover bits and pieces of it still roiled to the surface once in a while. In September the news media reported that Watergate burglar Howard Hunt claimed he was once ordered to kill anti-Nixon columnist Jack Anderson. Since Hunt had been hired originally by Colson, the story brought Chuck back into the news, and back on the defensive. The story soon died away, but not before raising the question whether Colson had a would-be murderer on the White House payroll.

Another challenge to moving ahead with the first class of prisoners was placating the neighbors around Fellowship House when the news broke that twelve felons would be spending two weeks there for Bible training. The building, formerly the Danish embassy, was in one of the most exclusive parts of Washington; the neighbors threatened a lawsuit.

Then there was resistance from prison chaplains. Chuck had been adamant from the beginning that he and others at Fellowship House be the ones to choose the inmates who would take part. Prison chaplains, Chuck knew from experience, were viewed as part of "the system" and if they chose the participants there would be charges of favoritism. That would make life miserable or even dangerous for those selected once they returned to prison. The chaplains countered that they knew their prisoners best, and that turning the process over to Colson and his team compromised their official authority. In the end, Norman Carlson's support allowed Colson to develop the pilot program exactly as he had planned.

The inaugural group of prisoners—ten men and two women, two people each from six different federal prisons—arrived in Washington on November 2. Hours of prayer and weeks of planning paid off: the training went smoothly. Dressed in street clothes, the prisoners were indistinguishable from many of the other visitors at Fellowship House. Even skeptical neighbors invited over for lunch to meet the "criminals" had to admit they couldn't tell the teachers from the taught.

The secret fear among the Fellowship House sponsors was that a taste of freedom would be more of a temptation than some of the prisoners could bear, and that some would escape during their training. There were no bars on the doors, no locks, no federal marshals, and nothing to keep them from walking away. The entire program, and the future of hundreds of thousands of other inmates, depended on the behavior of this dozen trailblazers. But their commitment to the program was stronger than their instincts. There were no incidents, and at the end of the training the twelve went back to bring Christ into prisons, working two by two the way Jesus' disciples evangelized in the Bible.

By the time *Born Again* was published on February 18, 1976, the first printing of 40,000 copies was already sold out. Colson appeared that day on the *Today* show and on *The Mike Douglas Show*. Both hosts were more interested in Washington and Watergate than in Chuck's Christian journey, and both cautioned him in advance about discussing Christianity on the air. Yet in both cases, when the subject came up, the shows abandoned their standard format—Mike Douglas ignored his usually indispensable cue cards—for a penetrating and thought-provoking discussion on living a life in service to Jesus Christ.

Within a few weeks, the discussion of Jesus and being born again went from television taboo to a central topic in public discussion. It even became an issue in the 1976 presidential election, which was won by former Georgia governor Jimmy Carter, who unashamedly answered reporters' inquiries by saying he was indeed born again.

Born Again was a runaway best-seller. Chuck spent two months traveling from coast to coast giving interviews and speeches about the book and his story, then in June went to Europe at the invitation of his European publisher. Colson was joyous that his heartfelt account of giving his life to Jesus was touching so many lives. Still, there were occasional disappointments and distractions.

The media lost no opportunity to knock the polish off of the old hatchet man's new image whenever they could. *Time* reported there was evidence that Colson had accepted a $500,000 payment from Teamsters Union thugs in Las Vegas on behalf of the Nixon campaign. The FBI came calling and all of Colson's personal financial records were subpoenaed, despite the fact that Colson had never set foot in Las Vegas. *Parade*, the Sunday newspaper insert with a circulation of 27,000,000, published a story claiming Colson had gotten drunk at dinner with John Dean. The story was fabricated by a ghostwriter on Dean's book *Blind Ambition* who was looking for more attention and recognition than the book had given him.

Colson also found himself with important misconceptions to straighten out. His conversion experience in Tom Phillips's driveway had been so emotional, dramatic, and sudden that some of his readers feared they couldn't be born again without something similar happening to them. Colson did his best to explain that God's personal redemption came to different people in different ways. He reminded worried readers that neither D. L. Moody nor Billy Graham experienced any great cataclysmic moment of conversion. The only important thing was that Jesus was their Savior. The terminology didn't matter; the nature of the experience was secondary. What mattered was that Jesus was theirs and they were Jesus.'

While sales of *Born Again* continued strong, the Fellowship House prisoner training program was struggling. The second group of inmates was a disappointment compared with the first, and nagging points of discord continued between Colson's prison outreach and other prison programs. All the while Charles Colson was trying to figure out what to do with the rest of his life. As much as he had hated being in prison, he could scarcely imagine making prison outreach his career. Anything but that.

On the other hand, that was where the opportunities kept falling and where his heart led him. The old Chuck was still resisting; the new Chuck was being drawn steadily toward prison ministry.

The question came to a head in a rare moment of calm. Chuck and Patty had accepted an invitation from Senator Mark Hatfield to borrow his vacation home on the coast of Oregon, high on a bluff overlooking the Pacific. Since Chuck had started speaking publicly about his faith, Patty had resisted being wedged into a mold other people expected her to fit. Her faith was her own, and she had felt assailed over the past year and more by reporters and others eager for tidbits about her conversion. Was she born again? Did she have a profession of faith? The questions troubled her, as did the thought of her husband going into prison work when she knew how desperately he hated being behind bars under any circumstances. With his track record in Washington, his connections, and his intellect, there were many, many good opportunities ahead.

But Patty had watched Chuck over the spring and summer of 1976 and knew now that prison ministry was his calling. Her calling was to be his partner.

Sitting in front of the fireplace at Senator Hatfield's with the Pacific crashing far below, the moment reminded her of the night that Chuck had resolved to plead guilty in the Ellsberg case. As they talked, she felt this would be another life-changing night.

"Prison work is your life, isn't it?" she asked. Haltingly, not knowing how she would react, Chuck admitted that it was.

"I see now that God wants you to be in a full-time ministry . . . I just want you to know that if that's what you want, I'm with you all the way." Just as he felt the calling to embrace the prison environment he despised, she felt called in that moment to give up her cherished privacy and a secure future to support him in his ministry. As they embraced warmly, both felt a unity and sense of purpose that had been missing from their relationship since Chuck's Christianity became a public issue.

Two days later, when Fred Rhodes and his wife arrived for a previously arranged visit, Chuck and Patty told them excitedly about their decision to enter prison ministry full time. Chuck's immediate concern, he admitted, was getting all the paperwork done for incorporating, establishing non-profit status, and all the rest. It could take a year.

Fred replied that he had all the forms in his briefcase in the next room. The process was a matter of days.

"Wait a minute, Fred," Chuck said. "I just made my decision. How could you have those papers with you already?"

"I knew this day was coming," Fred answered happily. "I thought I'd be ready."

To the Least of These

======== CHAPTER 21 ========

By midsummer Colson and his nucleus of Christian brothers had formed a nonprofit corporation to bring the good news of Jesus Christ to men and women in prison. Because it was closely allied with Fellowship House and focused on prisoners, the founders decided to call it Prison Fellowship. Fred Rhodes was installed as president, presiding over a grand total of six other employees. They found a three-room office suite in Arlington just across the Potomac from Washington for $350 a month, and bought some used typewriters and office furniture. Chuck's oldest son, Wendell, a recent Princeton graduate, made desks for the company out of inexpensive doors. Operating funds came almost exclusively from royalties from *Born Again*, which continued as an international best-seller, generating hundreds of thousands of dollars in income.

Prison Fellowship was incorporated on August 9, 1977, almost exactly four years after Chuck's life-changing evening with Tom Phillips and three years to the day after Richard Nixon became the only president in U.S. history to resign from office. The selfish excesses of the Watergate era had brought heartache and hardship to many people: twenty-seven men eventually went to jail for their part in the scheme; careers were ruined; families were devastated. A president was publicly disgraced, and his government faced a constitutional crisis of unprecedented proportions.

In less than six months Chuck Colson had gone from presidential special counsel and hatchet man to prisoner 23226. But with the incorporation of Prison Fellowship, Colson could see what a miracle God had worked in his life. Out of his selfishness, mistakes, and brokenness, God had fashioned a ministry unlike any other and given him the passion to carry it

223

forward. Now all the energy and intellect once devoted to dirty tricks and winning at all costs would be redirected to taking the message of Jesus to society's most despised people and places. He would serve some of society's most hopeless outcasts—those Jesus had called "the least of these"— where the need was the greatest. And where he himself had been.

An early challenge that seemed like a major setback at first came from the isolated federal penitentiary in Oxford, Wisconsin. The warden refused to allow any of the prisoners selected by Prison Fellowship to attend the Washington training program because their remaining sentences were too long. When Colson and Fred Rhodes tried to persuade him, he said, "If you guys are so good why don't you bring your teaching team into our prison and run your course from here?"

The warden meant it as a bluff, and the Prison Fellowship staff countered with a bluff of their own: Fred called Oxford to say they would accept the offer, expecting the warden to back off from his position. Then the warden raised the stakes: he told them to be there in three weeks.

Of all the places to begin an in-prison program, Oxford was one of the least promising. Most of the inmates were hardened offenders with long sentences. The prison compound was hours by car from any metropolitan area, meaning there were few local volunteers available to mentor and follow-up with the inmates.

Against all odds, the program was a success. Nearly a hundred of the five hundred inmates participated in the prison chapel Bible study, including ten Muslims. Even the hard-boiled warden realized there was something at work in the hearts of the men unlike anything he had seen before.

This inworking of the heart by the Holy Spirit was the key to Prison Fellowship's success. As Chuck Colson would tell thousands of audiences over the next quarter century, no amount of punishment can ever rehabilitate a criminal. Fear and threats are meaningless because as soon as the fear and threats are gone, the criminal resumes his life of crime. Only the love of Jesus can change a criminal's behavior, and that happens through changing a criminal's heart.

As he would explain bluntly in his second book, *Life Sentence*, "Prisons do not reform individuals; people rot and decay inside, often learning techniques for more violent and serious crimes later. Consumed by bitterness, many vow to get even once they get out. Yet, I saw personally how God's power, transforming lives, could truly rehabilitate."

While supporting rehabilitation for inmates, Prison Fellowship never attempted to excuse illegal behavior, and never opposed appropriate prison time for those convicted of wrongdoing. What they continued to oppose was prison time for nonviolent offenders, and inhumane living conditions for any prisoner.

Colson and the Prison Fellowship argued that nonviolent offenders should perform public service work rather than waste away behind bars; that in fact being housed with violent criminals made it more likely they would come out of prison worse than they went in. Furthermore, nonviolent criminals were at risk for their very lives when they were locked up with killers—hardly a fair punishment for embezzlement or tax evasion.

As the philosophy of Prison Fellowship took shape, its programs grew. Two other milestones took place in 1977. One was Norman Carlson's invitation to run the entire chaplain program at a new federal prison in Memphis. The Bureau of Prisons was short of funds, and some of the chaplain programs were slated for curtailment. Colson jumped at the chance to have Prison Fellowship fund and direct the entire prison chaplain operation there.

As he rounded up volunteers in Memphis—counselors, fellowship and discipling participants, church supporters, and local financial contributors—Chuck eagerly shared his vision for prison ministry with the city's pastors and civic groups. He explained how government-paid chaplains were seen as part of the system, meaning inmates refused to trust them or confide in them.

State chaplains, some of whom attended one of the luncheons where Colson spoke, were livid at the implication they were doing a poor job with the prison population. The archbishop of Memphis wrote to Norman Carlson that unless government-paid chaplains served in the new prison he might not allow the Catholic sacraments to be administered. One Protestant church official complained, "We've got a lot of jobs at stake, you know!"

The previous head of the prison chaplains unit, Reverend Richard Summer, had tried to squelch the Memphis program, but Carlson overruled him. In time Summer saw the advantages of the new approach. "Nobody gets a hearing like Mr. Colson does," he later told the press. "The benefits outweigh the problems."

Others saw Colson's clout as a threat to their influence, and soon the story became national news. On September 23, the *New York Times* carried the Section B banner headline, "Colson's Prison Evangelizing Proves Irksome to Chaplains."

While most prison officials "applaud Mr. Colson's ability to cast the spotlight on conditions of prison life," the article reported, the program "has also aroused a number of complaints.

"For example, some regular prison chaplains, employed by the Bureau of Prisons, resent the fellowship's ardently evangelical approach and its apparent ability to circumvent regular prison practices."

Reverend Richard Houlihan, Reverend Summer's successor, said, "It's very frustrating for some chaplains. The world goes around on political clout. Mr. Colson comes along and can accomplish instantly what they have been refused permission to do in the past. Institutional regulations get stretched for him."

Chuck Colson had been one of Nixon's favorites because he could cut through the red tape and get things done. Now he was using the same bureaucracy-fighting skills in the service of Jesus Christ.

It was during the middle of that same summer, speaking to hundreds of inmates in the Atlanta Penitentiary, that Chuck Colson first articulated the goal of Prison Fellowship in its simplest and most complete form. Previous speeches had various elements of this one; all that followed would use it as a model.

Ten of Atlanta's 2,000 inmates had been killed by fellow prisoners in sixteen months. Visitors were banned. Even armed guards were afraid to walk through the cell blocks. The temperature inside was over 100 degrees in the summer, and it was during the dangerous dog days of August, when most prison riots take place, that Colson and a small group of Prison Fellowship leaders and community volunteers came with the idea of sharing the good news of Christ. "No religious talk," the warden warned him. "The prisoners won't stand for it."

A short time later, facing nine hundred surly prisoners in hundred-degree heat, his clothes completely soaked through with sweat, Chuck Colson prepared to give a talk on prison reform. But something—he would say later it could only have been the Holy Spirit—compelled him to put his notes aside and speak from the heart.

"Let me tell you why I'm here," he began. He and the other outside participants had come "because we have committed our lives to Jesus Christ and this is where He calls us to be." He talked about the formation of Prison Fellowship and about the prisoner training sessions in Washington, when neighbors couldn't tell prisoners from counselors. He talked about his decision to spend his life bringing Jesus into prisons.

> Jesus Christ came into this world for the poor, the sick, the hungry, the homeless, the imprisoned. He is the Prophet of the loser. And all of us assembled here are losers. I'm a loser just like every one of you. The miracle is that God's message is specifically for those of us who have failed . . .
>
> Christ reached out for you who are in prison because He came to take those chains off, to take you out of bondage. He can make you the freest person in the entire world, right here in this lousy place . . .
>
> This is the Jesus Christ to whom I have committed my life. This is the Jesus Christ to whom I have offered up my dream and said, 'Lord, I want to help these men because I have lived among them. I came to know them. I love them. There is injustice in our society, but we can change it. Yes, God, we can change it. I give my life to it.'

The instant he finished, the prison audience roared its approval, clapping, shouting, and standing on chairs. Many had tears in their eyes. Chuck's words were an individual message of hope for each of them like they had never heard before. It was a triumph of the spirit in the face of terrible odds, one that Chuck and his staff would see repeated again and again in the years that followed.

In 1978 a movie version of *Born Again* brought Prison Fellowship a new level of public awareness and a new wave of volunteers. That same year, Colson was baptized by Pastor Neal Jones at Columbia Baptist Church, Falls Church, Virginia. He wanted to be immersed as "an outward sign in affirmation of what had happened inwardly." The next year Colson's second book, *Life Sentence*, was released, further enhancing the ministry's profile. As the staff and ministry grew, so did expenses, now going beyond $750,000 annually despite the work of many hundreds of volunteers and a modestly paid staff. Colson's book royalties continued to pay the majority of the bills, though private support was increasing. One of the earliest supporters was Arthur DeMoss, a wealthy Philadelphia insurance executive whose foundation made generous gifts to Prison Fellowship. Moss died in 1979, but his widow continued to support PF, including help with the purchase of a beautiful home in Virginia in 1983 that became PF headquarters. It was christened DeMoss House.

As the Fellowship grew, attracting more volunteers, donors, and publicity, it expanded on several fronts. First it grew geographically with the establishment of Prison Fellowship International. The seed was planted in the fall of 1978 at a meeting with prison workers, ministers, and others in London to explore the possibility of bringing Prison Fellowship programs to the primitive and squalid prisons of Great Britain. The next year PFI was inaugurated to work with local authorities, church leaders, and volunteers to bring Jesus into prisons around the world. Word of the program's success spread to Australia, and a PFI program was launched there. Two decades later there were PFI ministries in more than ninety-five countries around the world.

Prison Fellowship also broadened its focus to include people other than inmates who were affected by crime and imprisonment. In 1982, Mary Kay Beard, a former prisoner working for PF in Alabama, began encouraging volunteers to send Christmas presents to children whose mothers were behind bars. She got the idea after seeing fellow inmates saving soap and other small gifts they received from visitors, then wrapping them and giving them to their own children when they came to visit at Christmas.

Mary Kay set up two Christmas trees in a shopping mall and decorated them with cutout paper angels listing a child's name and age. Shoppers were encouraged to take an angel and buy a present for that child. From that humble beginning the Angel Tree program developed into a network of church-based volunteers that provides Christmas presents for more than half a million children every year.

Prison Fellowship also established local outreach programs for victims of crime, developing what PF leaders described as "training and resources to offer victims compassionate care, encouragement, and practical assistance in the name of Christ."

Another way Prison Fellowship expanded was by taking a stand on various issues that went beyond direct involvement in prison ministry. In his earliest interviews following his conversion, Chuck Colson had found himself blindsided and rhetorically cornered by the likes of Mike Wallace and others angling for a story. Later, as Prison Fellowship matured in its calling to reform prisons, Chuck Colson matured as a Christian, clarifying his own understanding of faith and the interwoven issues that dealt with Christianity as a force for positive change in the face of a skeptical culture.

In June 1982, the tenth anniversary of the Watergate burglary, Colson gave a number of interviews looking back over his life. Questions generally covered well-worn ground about the hatchet man years, as well as the story of his personal conversion and the history of Prison Fellowship. But perhaps the most thought-provoking statement was one he made to *Christianity Today* magazine: that one of the most important lessons of Watergate was it reinforced the truth of the resurrection of Jesus.

A little-known Watergate fact, Colson explained, was that "the serious cover-up—the part everyone knew or should have known was criminal—lasted successfully only weeks, perhaps a month or two by the most generous interpretation. With the presidency of the United States at stake, a small band of hand-picked loyalists, numbering no more than ten, could not contain a lie."

However, in order to deny the historical accuracy of the Resurrection, "one ultimately has to conclude . . . that there was a conspiracy of silence perpetrated by . . . maybe up to 500 men [the groups and crowds who saw the resurrected Jesus according to the Bible], and that each "was willing to be ostracized by friends and family, live day by day under fear of death . . . then ultimately to die without once renouncing that Jesus was Lord and had risen from the dead . . . Is it not likely that just one of the apostles would have renounced Christ before being beheaded or stoned?"

Ten people with everything to lose couldn't keep the fundamental deceit of Watergate to themselves. By contrast, those hundreds who saw the resurrected Christ couldn't deny the truth, even when it meant their own agonizing death.

Colson also underscored the importance of the organized church in Christian worship and outreach. From the earliest days of Prison Fellowship he had rejected suggestions that he transform the organization into a parachurch ministry. His aim was to work with churches, he explained, and to have church volunteers shoulder most of the responsibility for PF programs. The Bible described a body of believers as the model for preaching the gospel of Jesus and doing works in his name. Colson's calling as a Christian was to work within the body of the church universal, not to compete with it.

He explored the issue in detail in his 1992 book, *The Body*. The organized church, he wrote, had become weak and unfocused, and too consumer oriented. It was time to reinfuse formal denominations with the fire of the Holy Spirit. There was, he believed, no such thing as true Christianity apart from the church.

This stance led to an exploration of denominational differences Colson saw as impediments to the work of Prison Fellowship and to Christian ministry in general. He emphasized his belief that people of all denominations should concentrate on the characteristics and goals they have in common, not on their differences—the "mere Christianity" of C. S. Lewis that had brought him to Christ in the first place.

A series of meetings at the Fellowship's DeMoss House headquarters in Virginia produced a document, released on March 29, 1994, titled

"Evangelicals and Catholics Together." It recognized the commitment these two groups had to evangelism, and established a framework for cooperation within the biblical worldview. A book containing the ECT document and a collection of essays about it was published the next year.

While many Christians saw this joint effort at evangelism as a welcome and long overdue step, there were those who strongly opposed it. Among others, R. C. Sproul, who had tutored Colson in theology and was an early supporter of the Fellowship, considered the Catholic-Protestant gulf too wide to bridge without unacceptable compromise. Many felt the evangelical and Catholic views of salvation are just not compatible. As in any matter challenging fundamental and long-held beliefs, it was an issue upon which reasonable and dedicated Christians could, and did, disagree.

As Prison Fellowship grew, it adopted new methods of communicating with prisons and the community. In 1998 the Wilberforce Forum was established to sponsor conferences, publish Christian literature, award scholarships to former prisoners, and serve as a place to develop and promote a Christian worldview on questions of public policy. In 1990 PF launched *Inside Journal*, a newspaper for inmates that is now distributed to every prison in the United States.

In 1991 Chuck began a daily radio commentary called *BreakPoint*, sponsored by the Wilberforce Forum and syndicated in one hundred markets. Little more than a decade later the program reached five million listeners a day on a thousand stations.

To those who wondered what a radio show or a Christian think tank like the Wilberforce Forum had to do with prison reform, Chuck's response was simple: that to do anything in the name of Christ, including reforming prisons, people had to have an accurate biblical worldview.

At the same time Prison Fellowship has grown larger, it has penetrated deeper into the prison system. Beginning with training sessions outside the prisons, PF conducted its first in-prison training in 1977. Later the same year, in Memphis, PF had its first chance to assume responsibility for the entire prison chaplain program. In 1991, North Carolina's director of prisons, recognizing the power of spiritual transformation to change lives in a way nothing else could, invited PF into every prison in the state. That eventually fostered the development of Operation Starting Line, a joint effort with other Christian organizations to reach out to the entire population of a prison with music, comedians, pro athletes, and dynamic speakers, leading up to a presentation of the gospel.

In 1997, at the invitation of then Texas Governor George W. Bush, PF started a pilot program in Houston where volunteer prisoners spent their entire day with PF volunteers studying the Bible, taking vocational training, attending counseling, and preparing for life on the outside. Prisoners in the program weren't required to be Christian, but there was no mistaking the Christian bent of the teaching.

Colson modeled the operation, called the InnerChange Freedom Initiative, after one he saw in Brazil, where the recidivism rate (percentage of ex-prisoners who end up back in prison) was dramatically lower than the national average on account of the Christian training—training the heart, not merely punishing the body.

In the United States, about 75 percent of released prisoners are convicted again. For participants in the Houston IFI pilot program, the rate was less than 15 percent. This outreach has spread since then to several other states, and the list continues to grow.

Early in 1993 Charles Colson was awarded the Templeton Prize for Progress in Religion. Sponsored by multimillionaire investor and financier John Templeton, the prize is given annually to the person whose religiously inspired work makes a signal contribution to humanity. It is one of the richest prizes of any kind in the world: a million dollars, entirely exempt from IRS taxation. In the same way he has turned over millions in book royalties to Prison Fellowship, Colson endorsed the Templeton check over as well.

Charles Colson diligently and consistently said throughout his ministry that his only aim is to serve Christ. Though he admits that celebrity has its advantages in giving him a forum for his message, he has no more desire for publicity as the Templeton Prize honoree than he did when he so skillfully avoided the White House photographer during the Nixon years. (Nixon sent Colson a handwritten letter of congratulation for the

Templeton honor, dated on Colson's birthday 1993, only months before the former president's death; the letter hangs today in Chuck's Virginia office.)

His Templeton Prize address, given at the University of Chicago in September 1993, afforded a worldwide forum for Colson's view of contemporary civilization. The award, he reminded his international, interfaith audience, was for progress in religion. "But progress does not always mean discovering something new. Sometimes it means discovering wisdom that is ancient and eternal . . . The greatest progress in religion today is to meet every nation's most urgent need: a revolution that begins in the human heart. It is the Enduring Revolution . . . [which] teaches that freedom is found in submission to moral law. It says that duty is our sharpest weapon against fear and tyranny. This revolution raises an unchanging and eternal moral standard . . . This fire will not be quenched: The Enduring Revolution of the Cross of Christ."

Charles Colson gave up his position as CEO of Prison Fellowship in 1990 but remains its heart and conscience, speaking, writing, and hosting his daily *BreakPoint* radio show. More than 250,000 financial donors and tens of thousands of volunteers support a worldwide ministry with an annual budget of over $40,000,000. Though PF today has a presence and momentum unimaginable in 1976, size and visibility bring their own challenges.

The economic downturn of 2000–2001 led to a reduction in donations, triggering painful cuts: 20 offices and 100 staff positions. Difficult as the times were, the experience had two providential benefits. First, it showed the ministry ways to work more efficiently that they would never have discovered otherwise; they learned to do more with less. And second, it prompted Chuck and Fellowship CEO Tom Pratt to revisit the organization's role as an adjunct to the church, not a replacement for it. More operational aspects of the programs were turned over to the local churches and volunteers.

Heading into his middle seventies, Charles Colson has lost none of the energy and passion that drove him to begin his prison ministry more than twenty-five years ago. The former Marine Corps captain and White House counselor still pushes his people hard; the burnout factor at Prison

Fellowship is relatively high. (When he sold a million copies of *Born Again*, he wanted an explanation why it wasn't two million—though the second million came in time.)

It's the same insatiable drive that sustained Charles Wendell Colson through his years in the military; an ivy league education and law school at night; a failed first marriage. The same intellect and competitive spirit that made him the youngest administrative assistant on Capitol Hill and ushered him into the Nixon White House at thirty-eight. Then into a prison cell at forty-two.

Beginning one August night in the driveway of a Christian friend, he redirected all that power he had used serving his president, his party, and himself, to serving his Savior. And the lives and hearts of prisoners around the world have never been the same. The hope of Christ the Creator is proclaimed at last to the most hopeless of his creation.

During a 2001 interview marking the twenty-fifth anniversary of Prison Fellowship, Colson said, "I always felt politics was a strenuous business, because you had to put everything into it to win an election. But there was an election, then it was over.

"There's no election day on this. There's only Judgment Day."

Chuck's Message to Us

EPILOGUE

Though this is not an "authorized" biography, Chuck Colson was gracious enough to be interviewed for it. Near the end of our time together, I asked him what the book could do to help him in his ministry today. His reply was so deeply felt and so comprehensive that I saw no benefit in paraphrasing or interpreting it. And so I am privileged to pass it along in his own words.

Mr. Colson:

I think the way a book like this could help the most is to challenge people to pick up the vision of reaching out to "the least of these," to people in need, and sharing the gospel.

It's a double-edged sword. Number one, we take the Gospel to people who need it; we're evangelizing, we're fulfilling the Great Commission in the prisons. It is an important mission field if you get to these men and women in prison. It has an effect on the future crime rate in this country. And so for many, many reasons, it's a great place for us to take the gospel.

But the great blessing comes to those of us who do it. Because when you go into the prisons you feel closer to God. People come away blessed. Men and women inside witness to us. Often times you find the prison church much more on fire than the church in your neighborhood. So we get a blessing going into prisons, and I want Christian volunteers to get a blessing. I want them to be the salt and light, I want them to share the gospel, but I also want them to get blessed.

So the biggest thing your book could do is encourage more volunteers.

The ministry will get its financial support, as it does, through its mailing lists and that sort of thing. But the lifeline of the ministry is people who decide that just going to church on Sunday morning, singing our praise hymns and listening to a good message, and then maybe going to a prayer meeting on Wednesday night, or to a Bible study—maybe all that isn't enough.

We're looking for people who want more out of the Christian life than that, and who recognize that God wants more from us. He wants us to live the gospel in every walk of life and to do the gospel every day of the week, not just make it a Sunday morning experience. That's why He's raised us up.

The '90s were the most self-obsessed period in American history, yet here we are challenging people to think about Christianity in a much more muscular way, about its affecting art and science and literature, politics, and every area of life, which is crucially important as people get more obsessed with their own selves; or as they turn inward and begin to look for the answers to life within themselves, and begin to think in terms of this radical individualism that is so prevalent in the American culture today.

People care only about themselves. We're saying you've got to forget about yourself, surrender yourself, die to yourself, and live for Christ. That's a very radical message.

But I can see the pattern that God has used in my life and the things he's led me into. And the one thing I can tell you that may be helpful to you in the biography is that I never planned any of this out. I didn't plan to start a resurgence of the born again movement. I didn't plan to try and be the driving force in getting people to take up the gospel, salt and light, in the form of prison ministry.

I wasn't the guy who sat down and thought, "You know maybe some time we should start talking about Christian worldview because we live in an era of radical individualism and people need to be thinking about these things." I didn't strategize that, I just felt a real hunger for it, and studied it, greatly influenced by Francis Schaeffer. And I started to pick that up after Schaeffer died; it was just a natural thing.

It was a kind of outgrowth of what I was doing, and an outlet for my own intellectual pursuits. And yet it's turned out to be extremely timely, certainly after the terrorist attacks of September 11 [2001]: this is a worldview clash that we're in the middle of, the battle of worldviews between Islam and Christianity.

So I look at my ministry and my life and I realize first of all I didn't figure it out. I didn't sit there and decide I'm going to do this thing or that or the other thing. I didn't have a long-range plan, didn't have a short-range plan, didn't have a business plan, just went out and did what I believed God was calling me to do. And now I look back on it and see God's sovereign hand. He obviously had a reason for each of the things that happened.

And the lesson one draws from that, and the lesson I hope one draws from my life, is that what matters is not so much what we do, or our great plans, but whether we're available to simply be obedient to Christ and let Him work through us.

Chapter Notes

Chapter 1, Two of a Kind

1–5. Most of the details here on the 1960 campaign are from contemporary newspaper accounts; however, Colson's quotation about distracting the campaign worker (5) is from his book *Born Again* (see bibliography for details on all sources).

6–11. Information on the 1950 campaign comes from contemporary accounts and *Tricky Dick and the Pink Lady*.

Chapter 2, A Very Fortunate Young Man

12–22. Details about Colson's early life come from an interview with the author, from *Born Again*, and from a variety of press information issued over the years. Reconstructed conversations are from *Born Again*.

Chapter 3, Big Ambitions

25. In a recent interview with the author, Colson did not remember the speech he delivered to Vice President Nixon as being the renomination speech Governor Herter would give. However, when told the information came from newspaper archives, he agreed that it was possible, and that he simply didn't remember that particular detail. The story of Nixon's mental agility is from an interview with the author.

25–26. Bradford Morse's comments are from the letter written years later to Colson's parole officer in hopes of getting him a reduced or suspended sentence.

26. This and subsequent information about club memberships, home addresses, and other personal details are from an application Colson filled

out when applying for his White House security clearance. A copy of the application is in Colson's papers at Wheaton.

27. This comment from an unnamed staffer was quoted in a *Boston Globe* story about Colson during the White House staff shakeup after the 1972 election.

27–32. Information about Colson's early law career comes from various contemporary newspaper accounts.

28–29. Colson's comment on the reason stories like the McNamara confrontation are written is from an interview with the author. References to this story came up repeatedly for years afterward.

30–31. This description of a typical speech is taken from speaking notes in the Wheaton collection and from an interview with the author.

33–34. Information about Colson's divorce is from the security clearance application at Wheaton. Details about meeting Patty are from an interview with the author and from *Born Again*.

Chapter 4, The Job of a Lifetime

38. Colson's changing views on the Great Society come from speaking notes at Wheaton.

38. This account of Colson's first meeting with Tom Phillips comes from the letter Phillips wrote years later to Colson's parole officer. A copy is at Wheaton.

39–40. Quotations from speeches come from speaking notes at Wheaton.

40–41. The episode about adoption is from *Born Again*.

46. This November 3 date is taken from Colson's White House calendar. The calendar was photocopied during the Watergate hearings, and there is a copy at Wheaton.

Chapter 5, Into the Deep End

47–48. These details of Colson's first week are from the copy of his White House calendar at Wheaton.

47. The exchange between newsmen and Ziegler are from a copy of the official White House transcript of the press conference at Wheaton.

48. Copies of these letters are in the Wheaton collection.

48–51. Quotations are from a handwritten memorandum at Wheaton.

50. There may be two Perot stories here, or only one. The ten-million-dollar version came from published accounts; the thirty-million-dollar version came from an interview Colson gave to the National Archives in 1988. It is unclear whether these are two interpretations of the same story, or two separate events.

51. Colson's birthday greeting to his father is in the Wheaton collection.

52. This memo to Haldeman is in the Wheaton papers.

53–54. Colson's comments on riding out the election are from the 1988 National Archives interview. His comments on the Supreme Court nominations are from newspaper archives and *Born Again*.

54–57. Details on post office reform are from Colson's notes in the Wheaton collection, and from newspaper archives.

57. This memo is in the Wheaton papers.

Chapter 6, The Levers of Power

58. The account of Colson helping President Nixon honor his promise to Catholic schools was widely reported in the press, and the story often retold in subsequent stories about Colson's work in the White House. It is also discussed in detail in *Born Again*.

60. This description of a typical day is from an interview with the author.

61. The account of the White House summons in the movie theater is from an interview with the author.

64. This speech introduced the "Silent Majority," a term used afterwards to describe the satisfied, loyal, law-abiding Americans who silently and dutifully supported administration policies, as opposed to the headline-grabbing protesters, who commanded media attention all out of proportion to their numbers.

65. Quotations about Colson's reaction to the Kent State killings are from *Born Again*.

68–70. The memos to and from Haldeman are in the Wheaton papers.

Chapter 7, Lightning Rod

71. This and other memos to Haldeman are in the Wheaton collection.

73. This quotation is from a White House memo to the president from Colson; from the Wheaton collection.

73–76. This analysis is taken from a long report from Colson on a range of strategic issues found in the Wheaton collection.

77–78. The background on Dean is from information in *Watergate: The Downfall of Richard Nixon* by Fred Emery.

Chapter 8, Hatchet Man

80–81. This account of Kissinger's reaction to the release of the Pentagon Papers is from an interview with the author and from *Born Again*.

82–83. This conversation is taken from transcripts of the White House tapes at the National Archives.

85. Of the many accounts of the Ellsberg break-in, perhaps the most complete is in Emery's book. Liddy's memoir *Will* is also useful. Colson's account in *Born Again* has only limited information, as Colson was not aware of the operation until long afterwards. Other memoirs and the historical newspaper accounts are only intermittently reliable.

86. The author listened to a portion of the White House tapes at the National Archives, and has everlasting respect for the unsung archivists who endured thousands of hours of listening to, indexing, and transcribing them. They are extremely hard to understand at times, which no doubt accounts for the variations in wording among the transcriptions.

88–89. These details about Colson's care in avoiding conflict of interest or other questionable activities come from various interoffice memos among the Wheaton papers.

Chapter 9, "Let's Get on It"

90–91. A copy of Colson's letter to his son Wendell is at Wheaton, as are notes about Colson's investments on behalf of his children.

92. The memo on Mrs. Nixon's trip to Africa is at Wheaton.

92–94. Background on the ITT matter, and the quotations, are from confidential memos in the file at Wheaton and at the National Archives.

94–95. The attempt to get Reverend Graham's mailing list is detailed in Colson's 1988 interview with the National Archives. Portions of the interview, including part of the discussion involving Graham, have been blanked out and stamped "Sanitized Version." This is done, according to the Archives, in order to keep libelous or irrelevant information confidential.

95. Hunt's office being used to store copies of *The News Twisters* is from the 1988 Archives interview.

96. The account of Nixon's call from Moscow is from an interview with the author.

96–97. This memo is among the Wheaton papers.

97. A photocopy of this flyer is in the Wheaton collection.

100. This account of Colson's part in approving money for Liddy and Hunt is consistent in both Fred Emery's and Liddy's versions.

Chapter 10, No Air of Triumph

102. A typewritten copy of this speech corrected by hand is in the Wheaton papers.

105–107. This account of election eve and the following day's meeting is based on information from *Born Again*.

107–108. The list of jobs Colson would have accepted for the second term are from his 1988 Archives interview, as is the story that follows of surprising Haldeman and Erlichman in the president's office aboard *Air Force One*.

108–109. Colson's letter of resignation, and his letters of farewell to various members of the administration, are in the Wheaton archives.

110. Time and again from the moment John Dean arrived at the White House, Colson asked him for legal advice on a wide range of matters, many of them involving minor issues of propriety.

110. The comments about Nixon's distractedness are from the 1988 Archives interview.

112. This comment captured on tape is the most compelling of numerous pieces of evidence that Colson had no advance knowledge of Watergate, and, eight months after the fact, still believed Nixon was innocent of any cover-up attempt.

Chapter 11, A Sinking Ship

115–116. This conversation, which has been transcribed, was recorded on a Dictabelt.

117–118. Information about Colson's lie detector tests is taken from *Born Again*.

119–123. Quotations here and following from Watergate related phone calls or office meetings are from transcripts of the White House tapes.

121–122. This memo is in the Wheaton archive.

124. Information and direct quotations about the resignations of Haldeman and Erlichman are from Fred Emery's book *Watergate*.

Chapter 12, In the Crosshairs

126–127. Colson seems to have spent more time with Smith than any other correspondent. Even before Watergate, Colson's calendar shows they met numerous times both on official business, and socially with their wives.

127. Letters and telegrams from viewers are among the papers at Wheaton.

127–128. Transcripts of this and following television broadcasts are at Wheaton.

129. Nixon's comment is from his memoir, *RN*.

129. These words would come back to haunt Colson once the transcript of the "smoking gun" tape of June 23, 1972, revealed that his old boss had been misleading him at this point for almost exactly a year.

131–132. This transcript is at the Wheaton archive; as of this writing, Irv Kupcinet, or "Kup," is still on the air (and now on the Web as well) in Chicago.

133–134. In an interview with the author, Colson recalled watching Butterfield's testimony with Shapiro, but wasn't certain if he had been watching it first and called Shapiro into his office, or Shapiro had been watching and called Colson.

Chapter 13, The Great Sin

144–145. Colson first described his conversion experience in *Born Again*, and various versions have appeared in other books and speeches ever since.

Chapter 14, A New Perspective

150. Doug Coe remains the head of the Washington fellowship organization. Their annual Prayer Breakfast is one of the most widely publicized and widely attended religious events in the capital.

151–154. Information on the Watergate investigation under Archibald Cox is derived from the Wheaton archives, Colson's writings and speeches about the events, and newspaper archives.

Chapter 15, If Christianity Is True . . .

157. The issue of Nixon's use of government money to pay for improvements flared up from this point until President Ford pardoned him; it was the basis for one of the two articles of impeachment that failed in the judiciary committee (three others passed).

158. The spirit of Fellowship House is still very much alive, though now in a different location. The elegant old mansion on Embassy Row eventually became too famous for its own good, threatening to compromise its effectiveness as a place where political leaders could meet, in the name of Jesus and in a spirit of friendship and reconciliation, completely off the record.

160. Conversational quotes are from *Born Again*.

161–162. The exchange between Jerry Warren and Dan Rather is from a transcript of the press briefing.

163. This was one of the nightly television commentaries Eric Sevareid delivered from Washington. It was quoted repeatedly in newspapers and magazines over the following week.

163–164. This letter is in the Wheaton archives.

165. A transcript of the meeting between Colson and Jaworski is among the Watergate papers. There is also, at Wheaton, a sworn statement by Jaworski saying he never offered Colson a deal. Clearly Jaworski was offering to trade a misdemeanor plea for a suspended sentence, but said it in such a way that he could deny it under oath later on.

Chapter 16, Innocence and Guilt

166–167. A draft of Colson's letter to his children is in the Wheaton archive.

170–171. In an interview with the author, Colson said that the prosecutors' threat against Dick Howard was "the last straw" in his decision to plead guilty.

171–173. Quoted conversation is from *Born Again*.

Chapter 16, The Gavel Falls

180–182. These letters written on Colson's behalf by his friends, and Colson's own letter to the probation officer, are at Wheaton.

183. Colson remembered Patty saying these words, while *Newsweek* attributed them to him.

Chapter 18, Holabird

187–188. A copy of Colson's letter to Coe is in the Wheaton papers.

Chapter 19, Freedom

198–199. Colson's prison diaries are among the Wheaton papers.

198–204. Copies of these and following letters to and from Colson in prison are at Wheaton.

Chapter 20, Back Inside

212–213. For more on the period immediately following Colson's release from prison and his decision to go into prison ministry, see his book *Life Sentence*.

Chapter 21, To the Least of These

221–232. Information in this chapter comes chiefly from Prison Fellowship Ministries publications, especially *To God Be the Glory*, a twenty-year retrospective.

Bibliography

The most complete sources of documents by and about Charles Colson are in the archives of the Billy Graham Center at Wheaton College, Wheaton, Illinois, and in the Nixon Presidential Papers at the annex to the National Archives in College Park, Maryland. In both cases, there are a significant number of documents that are sealed or censored, some at Mr. Colson's request and others on account of government policy. New material will be incorporated into later editions of this book as opportunity permits.

Other important information comes from correspondence and telephone conversations between Mr. Colson and the author, which the author gratefully acknowledges.

Barnes, Dick. "Teamsters Switch Law Firms: Union severs ties with lawyers investigating Watergate bugging." *Newsday*.

Bernstein, Carl and Bob Woodward. "Aides Say Colson Approved Bugging." *The Washington Post*, 27 April 1973.

Bernstein, Carl and Bob Woodward. "Break-In Memo Sent to Erlichman." *The Washington Post*, 13 June 1973, A1.

Bernstein, Carl and Bob Woodward. "Bug Suspect Got Campaign Funds." *The Washington Post*, 1 August 1972, A1.

Bernstein, Carl and Bob Woodward. "Dean Alleges Nixon Knew of Cover-up Plan." *Washington Post*, 3 June 1973, A1.

Bernstein, Carl and Bob Woodward. "FBI Finds Nixon Aides Sabotaged Democrats." *Washington Post*, 10 October 1972, A1.

Bernstein, Carl and Bob Woodward. "GOP Security Aide among Five Arrested in Bugging Affair." *Washington Post*, 19 June 1972, A1.

Bernstein, Carl and Bob Woodward. "Mitchell Controlled Secret GOP Fund." *Washington Post*, 29 September 1972, A1.

Bernstein, Carl and Bob Woodward. "White House Aide Tied to Smear Try." *Washington Post*, 30 June 1973.

Bernstein, Carl and Bob Woodward. *All the President's Men*. New York: Simon & Schuster, 1974.

Bonafede, Dom. "Men Behind Nixon/Charles W. Colson, President's 'Liaison with the Outside World'." *National Journal* (8 August 1970): 1689f.

Briggs, Kenneth A. "Colson's Prison Evangelizing Proves Irksome to Chaplains." *New York Times*, 23 September 1977, B1-B2.

Buckley, William F., Jr. "Breaching Church-State at Taconic." *National Review* 36 (19 October 1984): 63.

Buckley, William F., Jr. "Colson and Christianity." *National Review* 26 (19 July 1974): 833.

Buckley, William F., Jr. "Prison Reform." *National Review* 34 (14 May 1982): 585.

Cannon, Lou. "Colson May Leave White House Post." *Washington Post*, 25 November 1972, A1, A6.

"Charles Colson's Conversion." *60 Minutes* (CBS), 26 May 1974.

Chomsky, Noam. "The Pentagon Papers and U.S. Imperialism is South East Asia." *The Spokesman* (Winter 1972/3).

"Chuck Colson: Founder of Prison Fellowship Ministries." *www.christianity.com/partner/Article_Display_Page/*, 15 June 2001.

Clawson, Ken W. "Colson: Nixon's Go-Between." *Washington Post*, 28 February 1971, A1, A14.

"Colson: Beat the Devil." *Newsweek* 83 (17 June 1974): 19f.

Colson, Charles and Nancy Pearcey. *How Now Shall We Live?* Wheaton, IL: Tyndale House Publishers, 1999.

Colson, Charles and Richard John Neuhaus, ed. *Evangelicals & Catholics Together: Toward a Common Mission*. Dallas: Word Publishing, 1995

Colson, Charles with Ellen Santilli Vaughn. *Kingdoms in Conflict: An Insider's Challenging View of Politics, Power, and the Pulpit*. A Judith Markham Book: William Morrow/Zondervan Publishing House, 1987.

Colson, Charles with Ellen Santilli Vaughn. *The Body*. Dallas: Word Publishers, 1992.

Colson, Charles. "'Watergate' Ten Years After: Tapping It for the Truth." *Christianity Today* 26 (18 June 1982): 36–38.

Colson, Charles. "A New Awakening." *Newsweek* 88 (9 August 1976): 11.

Colson, Charles. "A Worldview that Restores." *Jubilee Magazine* (Winter 2000).

Colson, Charles. "America's Way Is to Help Thy Neighbor." *www.christianity.com/partner/Article_Display_Page/*.

Colson, Charles. "C.S. Lewis: Prophet of the Twentieth Century." *www.christianity.com/partner/Article_Display_Page/*.

Colson, Charles. "Capital Punishment: A Personal Statement." *www.christianity.com/partner/Article_Display_Page/*.

Colson, Charles. "Engaging the Culture." *http://news.crosswalk.com/articles/*.

Colson, Charles. "Foundering Feminism: What Do Women Really Want?" *http://news.crosswalk.com/articles/*.

Colson, Charles. "God and Caesar." *www.christianity.com/partner/Article_Display_Page/*.

Colson, Charles. "God's Surprises: The Influence of C.S. Lewis." *www.christianity.com/CC/article/*.

Colson, Charles. "Life and Death." *The Saturday Evening Post* 256 (Jan./Feb. 1984): 24f.

Colson, Charles. "Light in the Darkness: Abortions Decline." *www.connectionmagazine.org/archives/1999/may/chuck_colson.htm*.

Colson, Charles. "Mr. President, Don't Copy My Boss, Nixon." *USA Today*, 3 September 1998.

Colson, Charles. "Neighborhood Outpost." *Christianity Today* (13 November 2000).

Colson, Charles. "New Light on an Old Phrase." *Jubilee Extra* (June 2000).

Colson, Charles. "Nixon's Surprising Flaw: The President I Knew." *www.christianity.com/CC/article/*.

Colson, Charles. "Our Nine Robed Masters." *Dallas Morning News*, 8 July 2000.

Colson, Charles. "Personal Integrity and Public Service." *www.christianity.com/partner/Article_Display_Page/*.

Colson, Charles. "Religion Up, Morality Down." *Christianity Today* 22 (21 July 1978): 26–28.

Colson, Charles. "Remove the Blinders." *www.christianity.com/partner/Article_Display_Page/*.

Colson, Charles. "Salad-Bar Christianity." *Christianity Today* (7 August 2000).

Colson, Charles. "The Court's in Session." *Christianity Today* (24 April 2000).

Colson, Charles. "The Cultivation of Conscience." *www.christianity.com/partner/Article_Display_Page/*.

Colson, Charles. "The Difference Jesus Makes." *http://news.crosswalk.com/articles/*.

Colson, Charles. "The Problem of Same-Sex 'Marriage.'" *Jubilee Magazine* (Spring 2000).

Colson, Charles. "The Ugly Side of Tolerance." *Christianity Today* (6 March 2000).

Colson, Charles. "Tornado-Designed 747s: The Irrationality of Atheism." *www.christianity.com/CC/article/*.

Colson, Charles. *Born Again*. Old Tappan, NJ: Chosen Books, 1976.

Colson, Charles. *Chuck Colson Speaks: Key Messages from Today's Leading Defender of the Christian Faith*. Urichsville, Ohio: Promise Press, 2000.

Colson, Charles. *Life Sentence*. Lincoln, VA: Chosen Books, 1979.

Colson, Charles. *Loving God*. Grand Rapids, MI: Zondervan Publishing House, 1983.

"Colson Connection, The." *Newsweek* (25 June 1973): 24–25.

"Colson: From Tough Politics to Religion?" *U.S. News & World Report* 76 (17 June 1974): 27.

"Colson's Motivation." *National Review* (21 June 1974): 686–7.

"Colson's Triumph: A notorious Watergate figure wins $1 million for his religious work.." *Time* 141 (1 March 1993): 16.

"The Dark Hour of Our Nation's Soul." *www.breakpoint.org/partner/Article_Display_Page/*, 17 September 2001.

Documents from the National Archives: Watergate. Dubuque, IA: Kendall/Hunt Publishing Company.

Doyle, James. "The Two Charles Colsons: A White House Aide on the Rise." *Washington Evening Star*, 14 June 1971, A7.

Emery, Fred. *Watergate: The Corruption of American Politics and the Fall of Richard Nixon*. New York: Touchstone, 1995.

Evans, Rowland and Robert Novak. "Mutuals Tied with Nixon Via Lobbyist." *Washington Post*, 20 October 1968.

Evans, Rowland and Robert Novak. "Nixon and the Funds." *Washington Post*, 20 October 1968.

Face the Nation (CBS), 1 July 1973.

Farley, Christopher. "The Pentagon Papers." *www2.prestel.co.uk/Littleton/br7109cf.htm*.

"Fast Bounce." *New York Times*, 12 December 1972.

Fenton, John H. "Kennedy's Magic Aids Saltonstall." *New York Times*, 30 October 1960, p.48.

Fenton, John H. "Race Seems Safe For Saltonstall." *New York Times*, 23 October 1960, 56.

Fitch, Bob. "Nixon: With a Little Help for His Friends." *Ramparts* (February 1970): 58f.

Glasser, Vera and Malvina Stephenson. "Presidential Aides on Thin Ice." *San Francisco Chronicle*, 4 February 1971, 21.

Haldeman, H.R. (w/ Joseph DiMona). *The Ends of Power*. New York: Times Books, 1978.

"Haldeman: The Nixon Years" (CBS), 30 March 1975.

Hefley, James C. "Colson, Cons, and Christ." *Christianity Today* 19 (4 July 1975): 57.

"Humbled Hatchet Man." *Time* 107 (2 February 1976): 20.

"Inside Watergate." *Newsweek* 81 (25 June 1973): 19f.

"An Interview with Charles Colson." *The Today Show* (NBC), 2 June 1973.

"Interview with Chuck Colson/Houston Christian Worldview Conference/ September 23, 2000." *www.worldview.org/colsonint.htm.*

Jones, Timothy. "A Church Against the World, for the World." *Christianity Today* 36 (23 November 1992): 30–31.

Kelly, Harry. "Colson's Plea is a Shocker." *Chicago Tribune,* 4 June 1974.

Knap, Ted. "Chotiner, Old Ally, Named Nixon Aide." *The Washington Daily News,* 14 January 1970.

Kutler, Stanley I., ed. *Watergate: The Fall of Richard M. Nixon.* Brandywine Press, 1996

Lardner, George, Jr. "Bittman Tells Of Actions on Hunt's Memo." *Washington Post,* 20 November 1974, A10-A11.

Lardner, George, Jr. "Hunt Clemency Plan Revealed." *Washington Post.*

Lasky, Victor. *It Didn't Start with Watergate.* New York: The Dial Press, 1977.

Lewis, Alfred E. "5 Held in Plot to Bug Democrats' Office Here." *Washington Post,* 18 June 1972, A1.

Lewis, C. S. *Mere Christianity.* New York: Macmillan Publishing Co., 1952.

Liddy, G. Gordon. *Will.* New York: St. Martins Press, 1980.

"The Man Who Converted to Softball." *Time* 103 (17 June 1974): 15–16.

Meyer, Lawrence. "Last Two Guilty in Watergate Plot." *Washington Post,* 31 January 1973, A1.

Meyer, Lawrence. "Nixon Lawyer, Full Tape Text Differ on Hunt." *Washington Post,* 20 November 1974, A11.

Mitchell, Greg. *Tricky Dick and the Pink Lady: Richard Nixon vs. Helen Gahagan Douglas."* New York: Random House, 1997.

New York Times staff. *The Watergate Hearings: Break-in and Cover-up.* New York: Viking Press, 1973.

Nolan, Martin F. "Chuck Colson—A Star Still Rising." *Boston Globe,* 5 September 1972.

"Nixon 1: Major Reshuffle at White House." *New York Times,* 14 June 1970.

"Nixon: Fly Now—Pay Later?" *Newsweek* 84 (1 July 1974): 16–18.

"One Lord, One Faith, One Voice?" *Christianity Today* 40 (7 October 1996): 34f.

Osborne, John. "The Nixon Watch: Kicking Sand." *The New Republic* (16 December 1972): 9–10.

"The Pentagon Papers: Gravel Edition—Summary." *www.mtholyoke.edu/acad/intrel/pentagon/pent1.html.*

"The Pentagon Papers: Secrets, Lies and Audiotapes." *www.gwu.edu/nsarchiv/NSAEBB/NSAEB48/supreme.html.*

Pierson, John. "Nixon Hatchet Man: Call It What You Will, Chuck Colson Handles President's Dirty Work." *Wall Street Journal* 178, no. 75 (15 October 1971).

Plotz, David. "Charles Colson: How a Watergate Crook Became America's Greatest Christian Conservative." *http://slate.msn.com/Assessment/00–03–10/Assessment.asp*

Plowman, Edward E. "Religion in Washington: An Act of God." *Christianity Today* 18 (4 January 1974): 48–49.

"Question of Nixon." *New York Times*, 4 March 1956.

Rangell, Leo, M.D. *The Mind of Watergate: An Exploration of the Compromise of Integrity*. New York: W.W. Norton & Co., 1980.

Sheils, Merrill. "Chuck Colson's Leveler." *Newsweek* (9 September 1974): 72–73.

"A Short, Partly Sunny Wait Between Planes." *Time* 104 (1 July 1974): 8f.

Sidey, Hugh. "The Presidency: Of Reconciliation and Detachment." *Time* 102 (24 September 1973): 24–25.

Storin, Matthew V. "Colson Shepherds Special Interests through Nixon's Office." *Boston Globe*, 23 March 1970.

Storin, Matthew V. "Nixon's Staff: Nary an Argument Can Be Heard." *Boston Sunday Globe*, 7 June 1970.

Storin, Matthew V. "White House rise of 'Chuck' Colson: He's Found Where the Action Is." *Boston Sunday Globe*, 6 June 1971, A3.

The Kup Show. 6 July 1973.

To God Be the Glory: Celebrating Twenty Years of Prison Fellowship Ministries. Wheaton, Illinois: Tyndale House Publishers, Inc., 1996.

Toth, Robert C. "Controversial Aide to Nixon May Resign." *Los Angeles Times*, 19 October 1972.

"25th Anniversary: The Conversion of Charles W. Colson." *www.christianity.com/CC/article/*, 1998.

" 'Watergate or Something Like It Was Inevitable': An Interview With Charles Colson." *Christianity Today* 20 (12 March 1976): 4f.

"Watergate: The Last Prisoner." *Newsweek* 85 (10 February 1975): 19.

Weintraub, Richard. " 'Fix-it' Man Colson Has Zest for Intrigue." *Boston Sunday Globe*, 3 December 1972, 8.

"Whispers About Colson." *Newsweek* 81 (5 March 1973): 21.

"White House Intrigue: Colson v. Dean." *Time* 102 (2 July 1973): 14.

"White House: The Man Who Is In." *Newsweek*, 6 September 1971.

White, Theodore H. *Breach of Faith: The Fall of Richard Nixon*. New York: Atheneum Publishers/Reader's Digest Press, 1975.

"Why Charles Colson's Heart Is Still in Prison." *Christianity Today* 27, (16 September 1983): p.12f.

Wooten, James T. "Ex-Counsel to Nixon Is Sought as Lawyer." *New York Times*, 29 March 1973, 22.

"Zero Defect White House." *The New Republic* 169, no. 9, (1 September 1973): 7–9.

Zoba, Wendy Murray. "The Legacy of Prisoner 23226." *Christianity Today* 45 (9 July 2001): 28f.

Index